EAST SUSSEX CHURCH WALKS

30 Walks to 70 Churches

Diana Pé

Published by ***PP (Pé Publishing)***
Email: Tonype@onetel.com

ISBN 0-9543690-3-3

Cover: Audrey Stevens

Maps: Stephen Good

Photographs: Diana Pé

Printed by: Downland Print Services Ltd, 2009

Disclaimer: the information in this book is given in good faith and is believed to be correct at the time of publication. No responsibility is accepted by the author and publisher for errors or omissions, or for any loss or injury howsoever caused. Only you can judge your own fitness, competence and experience.

Preface

This is the last of three books of 'Walks to Churches' in Sussex. Each venture has brought its own delight. Whilst walking in East Sussex, I was conscious of the underlying importance of rivers to the life and history of this part of the county.

Streams and rivers flow through all the walks. In the dense forest of the Weald, myriad streams have arisen and sustained human and animal life from Mesolithic times onwards. Shy forest folk could stay remote from the battles and struggles for power that were waged on the southern shores. They were also the last Sussex people to convert to Christianity. Forestry, farming and iron smelting became the main wealden activities. Woodland was cleared and rivers were dammed and manipulated. Successive waves of immigrants from Europe were attracted to the iron in the forest.

The streams gathered strength and headed for the sea. The Cuckmere and the Ouse pushed through the Downs to the South Coast. The Rother and its tributaries headed eastwards and now enter the sea south of Rye. One river, the Medway took a different course northeast to Kent.

All rivers have supplied water and transport for the settlers in Sussex. Until recent times, roads were impassable through the Weald and rivers carried the produce to the southern ports.

Communities have grown at river crossings. People have settled in the forest or on the Downs or above the marshland at the eastern end of the county. A river is always nearby. In the Middle Ages it was a religious duty to maintain the bridges across the rivers. The village church rising above the banks of a gently flowing river is a feature of the landscape in East Sussex. The churches are built of stone with wooden rafters to support the roof. Timber from the forest of the Weald has been used for these rooves. It has also been the material for the timber framed houses of East Sussex.

Acknowledgments

My thanks for their help in the preparation of this book go to John Avenell, Stephen and Christiane Good, Windy Leung, Alan Loweth of RSPB, Gabrielle and Robert Pé, Tony Pé, David Perks, Doreen Peskett, Daphne Reeve, Karen Standing, Audrey Stevens and Peggy Synge.

I dedicate this book to my erstwhile walking companions and nature lovers, Doreen Peskett and Kathleen Ramsay.

SURREY
ROYAL
TONBRID
WELLS
River Medway
Hartfield
14
Withyham
Frant
20
Wad
WEST SUSSEX
Crowborough
Tidebrook
Rotherfield
15
May
11
Maresfield
Fletching
12
Buxted
UCKFIELD
Hea
Newick
Framfield
EAST SUSSEX
Isfield
13
Chiddingly
8
Ouse
Hellingly
Ripe
Arlington Reservoir
Chalvington
Cuckmere
LEWES
7
Arlington
3
Firle
Selmeston
Beddingham
Alciston
Wilmington
River
4
Berwick
NEWHAVEN
Bishopstone
Alfriston
6
Folkin
Lullington
5
Litlington
Jeving
BRIGHTON
1
West Dean
2
Friston
East Dean
SEAFORD
0
5
10
Miles

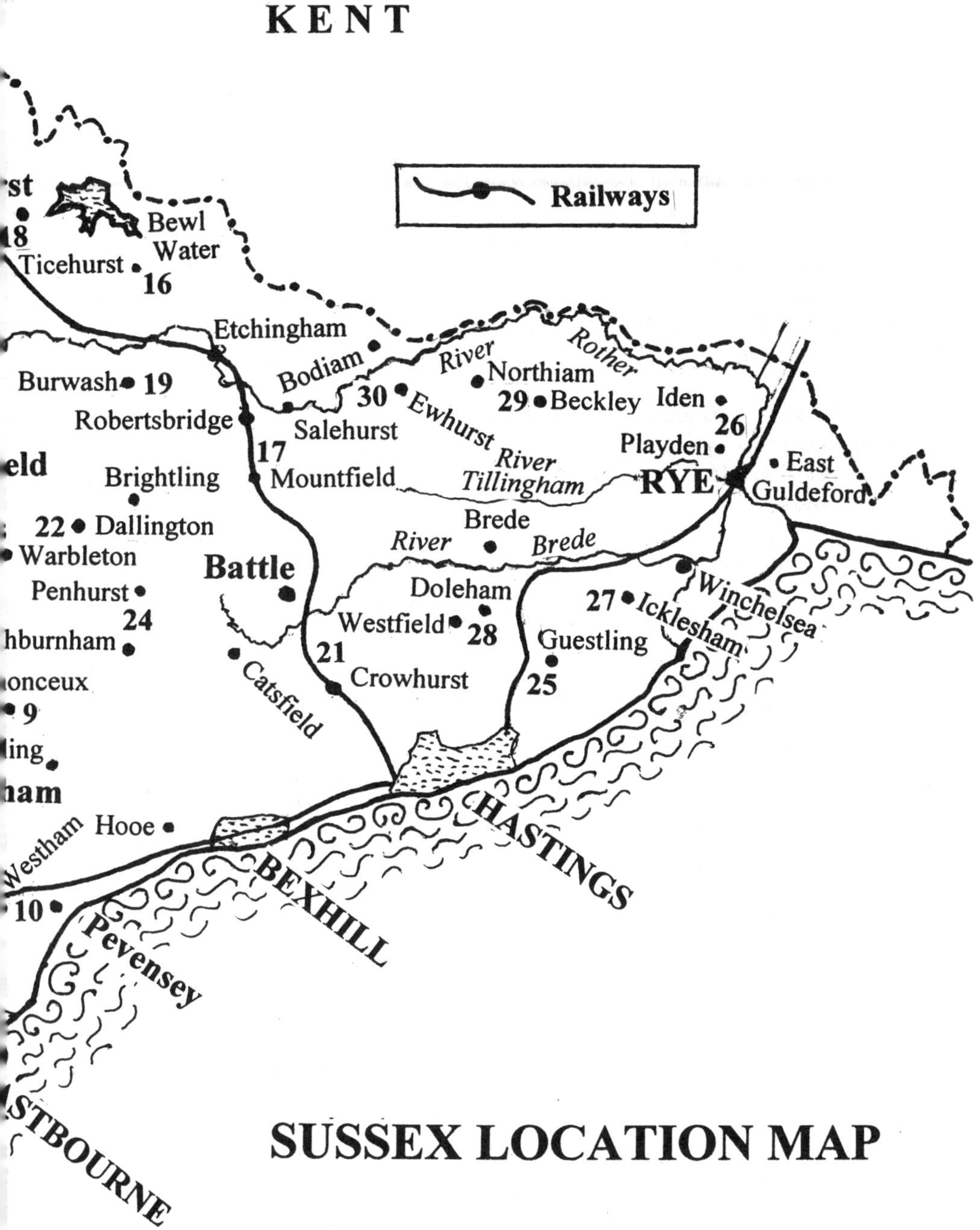

SUSSEX LOCATION MAP

Contents

*Walks that start at railway stations or can be adapted to start at railway stations **

INTRODUCTION

'...tucked away in corners, hardly on the map at all are little hamlets and secret farmsteads that in some marvellous way seem completely outside this desperate century. But to find such places it is well to keep to the northern side of the Downs – there is very little on the seaward side'.

'Sussex' by Esther Maynell.

In these walks I have sought out some of the secret places, mentioned in the quotation above. Esther Maynell was writing in the 20th century. The hamlets north of the Downs still hold their charm in this even more 'desperate' 21st century and many are included in this book. I have not totally avoided the coast. After all we expect to visit 'Sussex by the Sea'. A bracing walk along the sea front in Hastings or Seaford should not be missed. Several walks lead up into the Downs and give a prospect of both sea in the south and forest or grazing land in the north.

In our trek through the Weald, the great forest that once covered the land below the Downs on the north side, we are close to the source of several rivers. We follow and cross many little feeder streams and rivers. In other walks we pursue these rivers through the Downs to the sea.

Rivers flow gently in and out of our walks. Streams or tributaries meander through meadowland, then shady woods and pass by a quiet hamlet with its church on a rise. It is a delight to walk beside these rivers and cross them on wooden footbridges, sometimes on stone bridges and occasionally on stepping stones.

The Ouse rises west of Slaugham, trickles east then south past Lindfield and is a gentle stream at Isfield where **the Uck** joins it. (Walks 13 and 12). The Victorians tried to harness the river with locks and weirs and mills. These were soon made redundant when railways became the main means of transport. The Ouse flows on freely now through woods and meadows. It has widened to pass through Lewes. The river first headed for Seaford (Walk 1), then changed its course 600 years ago to enter the sea at Newhaven.

The Cuckmere rises near Heathfield (Walk 23) where many feeder streams head south. It makes its way as a stream over the Weald (Walks 8 and 7). The river forms a wide valley through the Downs (Walk 5) and takes such a sinuous route it seems reluctant to reach the sea at Cuckmere Haven. We can imagine King Alfred`s fleet on the river near Westdean (Walk 2).

Christians River also rises near Heathfield. Three Cups Corner on B2096 is so named as three rivers have their sources hereabouts. We cross the little Christians River on Walk 22. It joins the Ash Bourne (Walk 24)

The eastern Rother or **'Limen'**, as the Romans called this river, starts near Rotherfield (Walk 15). One tributary, the **River Limden** comes from the hamlet of Lymden near Ticehurst and joins the Rother from the north at Etchingham (Walk 16). Another tributary, the **River Dudwell** rises near Broad Oak, passes Batemans (Walk 19) and also joins the Rother at Etchingham (Walk 16). Swollen with its tributaries, the river proceeds past Robertsbridge (Walk 17) and through the wide valley it has made through Bodiam and Ewhurst (Walk 30). In the Middle Ages the river, tidal from Bodiam, carried iron from foundries at Robertsbridge, Brightling Warbleton, Burwash and Ticehurst. It also carried timber from the Weald. The river banks, once thick with trees, were now bare. Clearance caused top soil to wash away and over centuries the river silted. It glances at Kent as it glides over the lonely Rother levels. The river finally heads south to Rye and the sea (Walk 26). Rye was a ship building port, one of the defences of the south coast, known as the 'Cinque Ports' in medieval times. By 17th century silt from three rivers clogged Rye Port and the sea retreated. When Rye was left stranded on a rock, men continued to sail on the Rother to reach the sea that had receded. Today the river is tidal only as far as one mile north of Rye. Water companies keep a check on the river. Flood water is penned in the valley below Bodiam and released when conditions are suitable. Ten miles of river are dredged every year. Sea walls are repaired at the estuary and there are pumping stations to deal with floods. Wildlife conservation is important and should be given priority.

The River Brede rises in the Weald and has formed a wide valley below the village of Brede (Walk 28). As with the Rother, this river was also manipulated for the iron industry. Some of the leats bringing water to the dam were a mile long. In medieval times the river was a major waterway carrying cannon balls to Winchelsea. (Walk 27). It flowed past the inner harbour below Strand Hill to the main anchorage at the Camber. The sea has receded and the river has silted up. It now heads for Rye where it joins the **River Tillingham**, also a stream from the Weald, and enters the Rother southeast of Rye (Walk 26).

The Medway has four headwaters in Sussex. The source headstream rises south of Miswell Wood near Turners Green. The other streams join the Medway before it reaches Forest Row. The Medway flows through the Weald clay valley between Ashdown Forest and the greensand hills. A tributary, Kid Brook enters from the north. We walk beside the Medway on the cycle track 'Forest Way' at the section near Hartfield (Walk 14). Another tributary Steel Forge River flows under Pooh Sticks Bridge and joins the Medway from the south near Withyham (Walk 14). The river makes it way north to Ashurst and deserts Sussex to flow through Kent to Sheerness and the North Sea. In the past it was the major means of transport carrying timber, iron and agricultural products. The upper Medway is now a source of peaceful walks beneath willows and alders.

Before Christianity

The first people to plough the Downs were the New Stone Age or Neolithic people (3000 – 1500 BC). They made and enclosed clearings, there is one at Combe Hill above Jevington. Ploughing continued in the Bronze Age (1500 –500 BC). In order to get a depth of soil they kept digging into the same strip and left a permanent mark on the ground in the form of 'Lynchets'. Celts came from Europe to Sussex around 500 AD and improved the ploughing by fitting iron tips to wooden ploughs and making bigger lynchets. They also started to work the iron in the Weald.

When the Romans came in 40 AD, they overcame all resistance, including the defence of Mount Caburn by the Celts. The Romans were attracted to East Sussex by the prospect of iron. They increased iron working in the Weald and improved the agriculture on the Downs. They introduced new trees, including walnut and sweet chestnut. They built straight roads and their most impressive and lasting structure, Pevensey Castle (250 –300 AD). Roman walls enclose 10 acres, built on an island in the marsh. The walls are 12 feet wide and 28 feet high. There were greensand blocks, rubble and flat red tiles set on a bed of clay and oak stakes. Originally there were 12 towers.

When the Romans left in 410 AD, people from north Europe invaded. They gave Sussex its name, 'Suth-Seaxe', 'South Saxon'. The Saxons preferred to live in clearings in the Weald or villages on the coast and manor houses at the north base of the Downs. They were nervous of the upland tumuli and barrows where the Devil might lurk. The Saxons built in wood. The Roman skill in brick and tile making was lost. Consequently, few Saxon buildings have survived. Instead they left their mark on the names of places and people: the endings 'ING' and 'TON' are Saxon, also 'INGHAM', 'INGTON', 'HAM', 'FIELD' and 'FOLD'. Forest settlements have Saxon names: 'HURST', 'DEN', 'LYE', 'WORTH'.

The fierce Saxons pillaged and rampaged, massacring the inhabitants and destroying the Roman villas and temples. Eventually they settled into a quiet life of toil.

Christian Sussex

Saxon Kings were converted to Christianity. King Ethelwatch gave land in West Sussex to St Wilfrid in 7th century. From there he converted the whole of Sussex. See West Sussex Church Walks and Mid Sussex Church Walks. Saxon features can be seen in Bosham, Sompting, Clayton and Worth Churches. In this book, East Sussex Church Walks, we visit the Saxon Church of Bishopstone. We also go to Mayfield where St Dunstan is fabled to have recognised the Devil hiding in the form of a damsel. Dunstan seized his red hot tongs and fastened them on the Devil`s nose. This made the Devil resume his true shape and run howling to cool his nose in a spring at Tunbridge Wells. The Convent at Mayfield was a Palace of the Archbishop of Canterbury from Saxon to medieval times (Walk 15).

The eastern Downs stretch from the River Cuckmere to Pevensey. Names, such as Wilmington and Lullington show that Saxons settled here. Hellingly has a round churchyard, an indication of pre-Saxon building. Arlington Church, south of Hellingly has traces of Saxon work. Winton Street on the north side of Alfriston has a Saxon burial ground where jewellery, weapons, pots and glass of the period have been found.

The secretive forest folk of the Weald clung to their Pagan practices and were the last to convert to Christianity.

In the extreme east of Sussex, the Weald gives way to marshland criss-crossed with waterways. Here, Saxons settled mainly on the coast. One inland place is Hooe, from the Saxon 'hoh' meaning raised land above the marshes. The church at Hooe is dedicated to Oswald, a contemporary of Wilfrid. A Saxon chest has been found in this church.

A later Saxon saint, King Alfred (871 – 899) had a palace in East Sussex, probably on the site of the ruined manor house at West Dean near Cuckmere Haven. Asser, the biographer of Alfred was summoned to meet the king there. The manor later passed to Edward the Confessor (1042 –1066).

The Norman Invasion (1066) took place in East Sussex. William, Duke of Normandy landed his fleet at Pevensey. The Battle of Hastings was actually fought six miles away on Senlac Hill near Battle. The gentler Saxon way of life was gone forever. The Saxons had even devised a primitive sort of democracy allowing lords to question the king and thanes to question their lords. The 'Witan' was a council of wise men, mainly nobles and clerics.

All such ideas were alien to William who exerted the power of a dictator. He did learn something from the Saxons. William kept the old Saxon divisions of 6 'Rapes' and gave them to his followers to rule. Rapes were administrative regions. Each rape had a town, a castle, a river and a forest. Their name, a 'rap' was originally a roped area for an open air court.

The rape of Hastings was bounded by the sea in the south, Kent in the north and east, the parishes of Wadhurst and Mayfield in the northwest and Dill and Pevensey in the west. It had its own sheriff. Powerful men vied for control of the rape. In 1591 Sir Thomas Pelham gained control and through him it went to the earls of Chichester. The Pelham buckle is a feature of many properties on the Laughton estate. The honour of displaying the buckle was probably first granted to John de Pelham after the battle of Poitiers in 1356. Sir John Pelham was appointed Constable of Pevensey Castle in 1401. He settled in the Manor of Laughton. In 1955 the last links with the Pelham family were severed when the Earl of Chichester had to sell the estate. On our walks, we find the Pelham buckle on several church towers.

Under William, the Conqueror

Hastings was given to the Count of Eu

Pevensey to Robert de Mortain, William`s brother

Lewes to William de Warenne

Bramber to William de Braose

Chichester and

Arundel to Roger de Montgomery, William`s cousin.

The Earl of Eu erected a chapel in his castle at Hastings and established a college of Prebendaries. They were resident clergymen who received a 'prebend', a share in the revenue of the college. It was dissolved in 1547.

Under the Normans, the Downs suffered further clearance and the Weald was exploited for iron. Castles were built at Arundel, Bramber, Lewes, Pevensey (inside the Roman fort) and Hastings. The Norman barons then had control of river and sea crossings.

The Normans built churches to impress and to endure. Wooden buildings were replaced with sturdy stone structures. Cathedrals and churches were rebuilt.

Timber Roofs

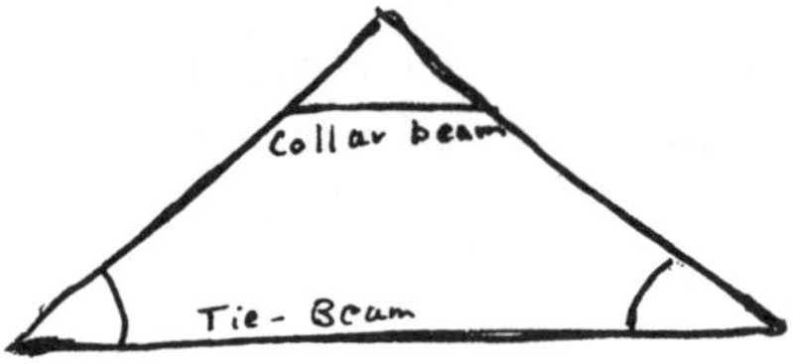

Tie-Beam Truss

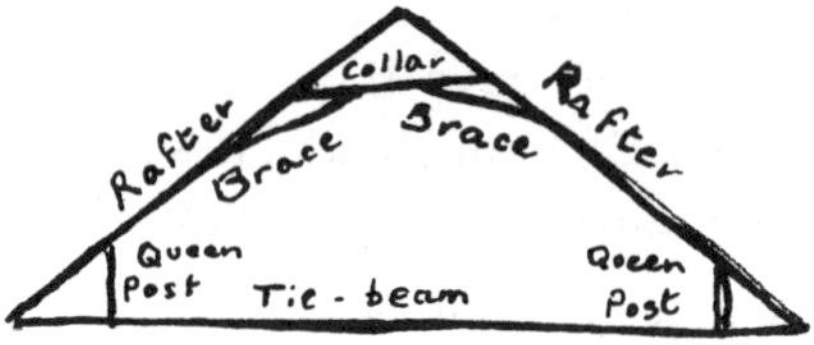

Collar-Beam Truss

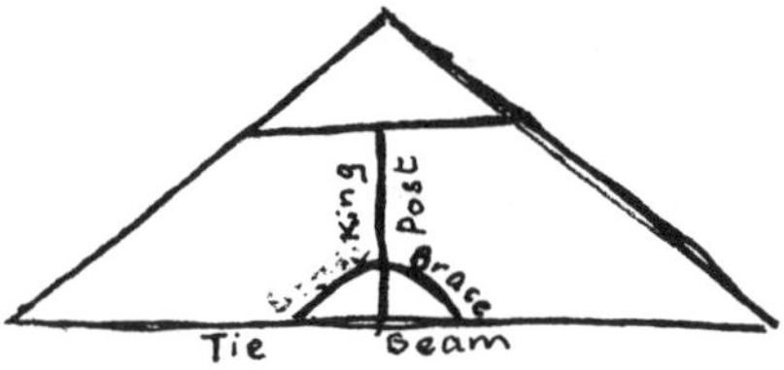

King-Post Truss

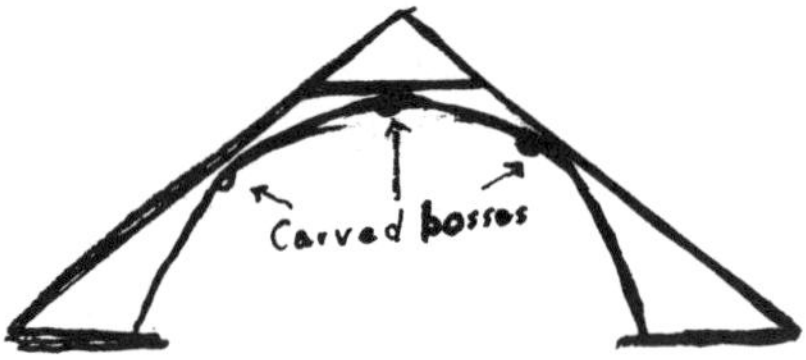

Wagon Roof

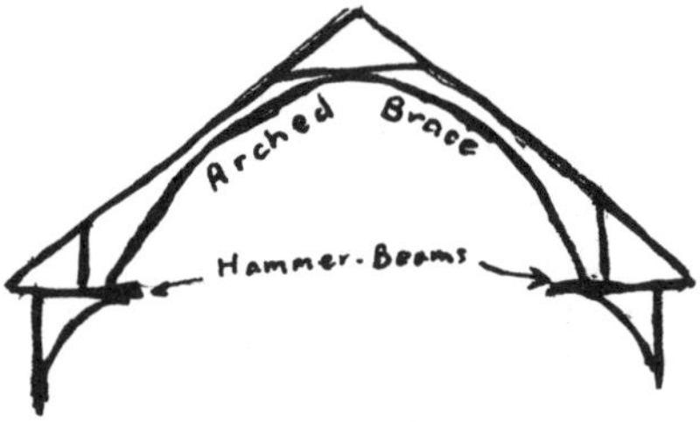

Hammer-Beam Truss

Hammer-Beam Truss

Abbeys and monasteries were established. The Benedictine Abbey of St Martin was built with a high altar over the site where Harold fell and died. Salehurst Cistercian Abbey was founded in 1175, Wilmington Priory in 1100. William de Warenne and his wife Gundrada founded a magnificent Priory of St Pancras at Lewes.

Fine Norman churches have survived throughout Sussex. See also West Sussex Church Walks and Mid Sussex Church Walks. In East Sussex we visit basically Norman churches found in Rye, Westfield, Beckley, Icklesham, Playden, Battle, Guestling and Wilmington, to name a few. Sadly, abbeys and priories are in ruins, mainly thanks to Henry V111 in the Dissolution of the Monasteries1536.

Fortunately, the fearsome Normans were absorbed into the life here in Sussex as were the Celts, Romans and Saxons before them. Styles of architecture developed and emerged to form the Gothic arches of the light and elegant Early English period. In East Sussex Pevensey has an Early English church. Other churches with Early English details (Mid Sussex Church Walks) include West Hoathly, Horsted Keynes, Fletching with chancel and transept in that style, the lancet windows of Salehurst and parts of Playden and Iden.

The next stage in Gothic architecture is the Decorated (1260 – 1360). Churches in this style are rare as it demands fine stone suitable for the intricate tracery. East Sussex has two very fine Decorated churches; Etchingham and Winchelsea. These magnificent buildings flourished under the feudal system in Medieval Sussex. Farming was the main activity then. People grew grain and vegetables below the Downs and watched over their sheep on the Downs.

The Perpendicular Period (1360 – 1485) is known for its towers, tall, strong and castellated. Hastings is fortunate to have two Perpendicular churches. Despite being contemporaneous they are quite unlike each other. Mayfield is unusual in having an Early English tower on a Perpendicular church. Brede is an Early English church with a Perpendicular tower, a more usual combination. Ticehurst has a fine Perpendicular tower. Northiam has an Early English nave, Perpendicular aisles and windows and a Norman tower.

Whilst the sheep nibbled the grassland and crops grew below the Downs, the iron industry was flourishing in the Weald. Frant was the centre of this industry and Wadhurst and Ashburnham were the last places in Sussex devoted to iron. Timber was also used to build wood framed houses, ships and the roofs of churches. Different types of roofs can be seen opposite.

5 Walks Near Seaford

Bishopstone

Walk 1: Seaford to Bishopstone

This walk has a bit of everything: seaside, tide mills, downland, suburbia, parks and sea views. We visit a Saxon village church, a modern suburban church and a medieval church in a former harbour town.

Starting Point: Buckle Car Park with toilets faces the sea. **GR**469997.
(This car park is just south of Bishopstone Station). **Map:** OS Explorer 123
Terrain: Mainly flat with no too demanding hills. **Distance:** 5 Miles

The Churches

Note: Bishopstone Church is open Wednesdays and Saturdays until 4 p.m. and Seaford Church is open every day until 12 noon at the time of writing. You may prefer to rearrange the walk to fit in with these times and start from Seaford town. See the end of the Walk below: 'From Seaford Parish Church….'

Bishopstone Parish Church, St Andrew, between the conurbations of Denton and Seaford, still dominates a remote downland hamlet. As the name suggests, there was a Saxon 'tun' or farmstead belonging to a bishop here. The south wall of the nave and south porch are Saxon. The porch was once used as a side chapel. Outside, the Saxon sundial has the name 'Eadric' on it – who was he? The tower in four stages is early Norman. Inside the tower are lofty round 12th century arches. Normans added the north aisle with round windows. A restoration in 2006 uncovered the remains of a medieval wall painting on the west wall. The chancel, now the choir is Transition Norman. It has a high arch with deep cut mouldings and leaves on the capitals. A small sanctuary was added in 12th century. The east window depicts the Ascension of Christ.

Seaford Baptist Church is an impressive modern (1973) circular building at a fork of roads in the suburbs of Seaford. In 1987 the hurricane ruined the glass fibre roof. It has been replaced with a wood frame roof. Under the main church a maze of offices and meeting rooms are in constant use.

Seaford Parish Church, St Leonard is a large medieval church, built when the town was a busy harbour near a ford of the River Ouse. In 1597, a storm changed the course of the river so that the Ouse now enters the sea at Newhaven. Despite a Victorian restoration, the west end retains its Norman character. The arcades are 12th century. As you enter the church from the south porch, note the circular pier nearest to you; it has worn carvings on the capital showing scenes from the Bible. In the centre front of the nave a fine carving of St Michael slaying the Dragon has been rescued and displayed. The tower in four sections, starting at the bottom, is Norman, Transition Norman, Perpendicular and modern. It was originally built inside the Norman nave. There are handsome clocks on two sides.

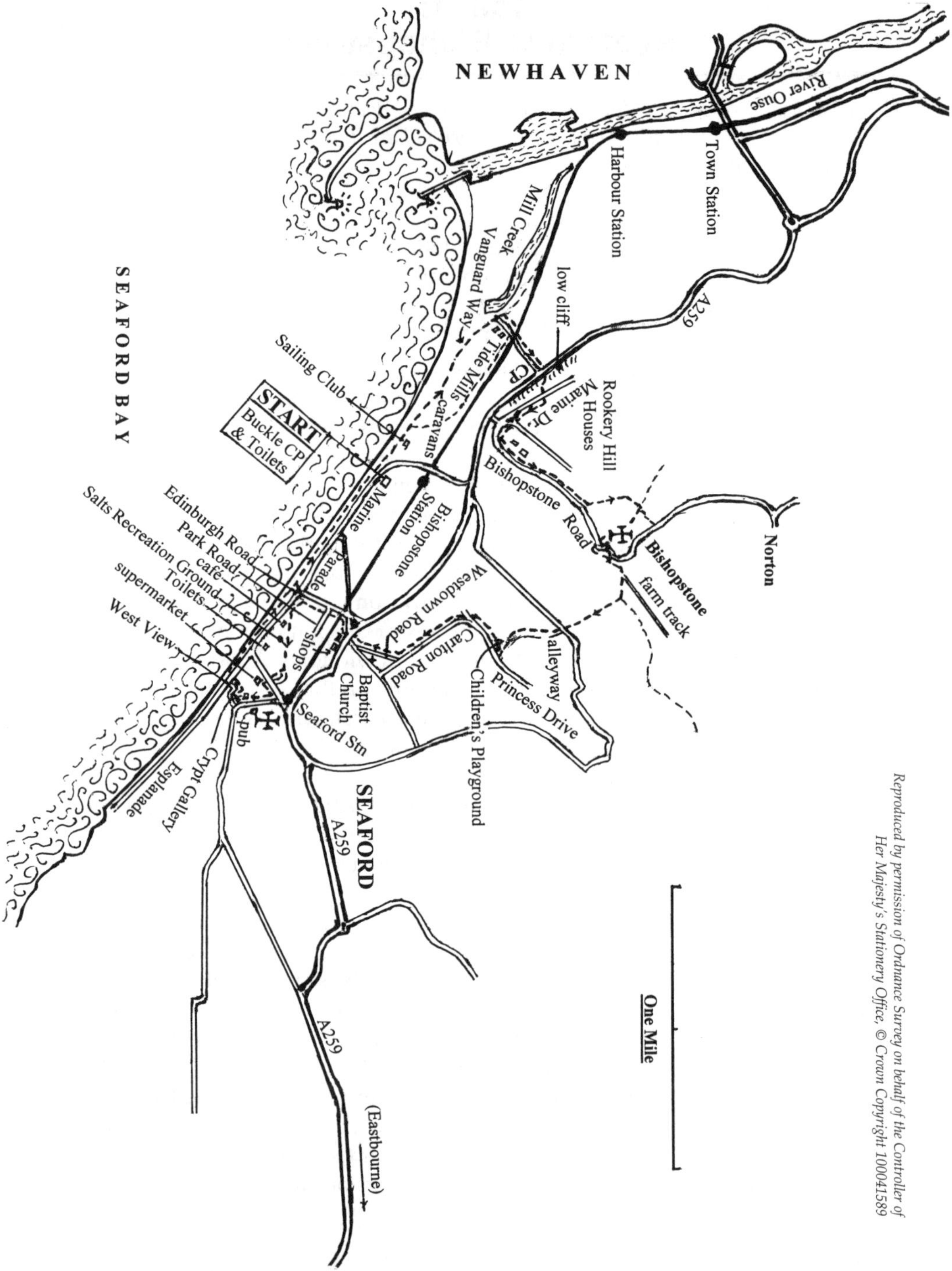
NEWHAVEN
River Ouse
Harbour Station
Town Station
Mill Creek
Vanguard Way
low cliff
A259
Tide Mills
caravans
CP
Rookery Hill
Marine Dr.
Houses
Sailing Club
START
Buckle CP
& Toilets
SEAFORD BAY
Bishopstone Road
Bishopstone
Norton
farm track
Marine
Bishopstone
Station
Parade
Edinburgh Road
Park Road
café
Salts Recreation Ground
Toilets
supermarket
West View
shops
Westdown Road
Carlton Road
alleyway
Princess Drive
Children's Playground
Baptist
Church
Seaford Stn
pub
Crypt Gallery
Esplanade
SEAFORD
A259
A259
(Eastbourne)
One Mile

The Walk

Cross the road, Marine Parade with care and step over the low wall onto a cycle way. Turn right towards Newhaven. Keep to the coastal way and you come to signs: Sussex Ouse Valley Way and Vanguard Way. Walk on the concrete cycle track, passing the sailing club building on the right. Veer to the right on a raised bank. A small caravan site is on your right. Avoid an unofficial path along another raised bank on the right. It goes to the railway line. You are heading for the tide mills. Several placards at intervals explain their history.

In one kilometre at cross paths, you leave the Vanguard Way and turn right onto the 'exercise path'. A concrete path leads between flint walls, all that remain of a village that grew up around the tide mills. Explanatory placards help us to imagine the lively activities here. Cross the railway line via the pedestrian gates and continue along the concrete path as far as the main road, A259. There is a car park on the right.

Cross with care to the low cliff opposite. A path on the right climbs the cliff to back gardens. Turn right at the top and you have a view over the way you came and the sea beyond. Follow the path as it turns left through an alley to Marine Drive on Rookery Hill. There are more bungalows than rooks here now! Turn right to walk along the drive on the edge of this housing estate. Avoid a turning to the left and continue on Marine Drive as it descends to the main road.

You avoid the main road by turning left into Bishopstone Road. Walk on the grass verge below bungalows on the left. When the bungalows end, there is a short raised path to keep you off the road. Bishopstone Church can be seen ahead. Avoid footpaths to the left until you come to a wide field entrance on the right, blocked with concrete slabs. Our path is opposite.

Either *turn left on this path and head towards some old brick walls beyond a clump of trees. In 300 metres, at crosspaths turn right for the church.*

Or continue up the road to the church on the left.

Bishopstone

From Bishopstone Church go through the lychgate to the small car park. Go to the road and turn left. Follow the road for another 50 metres. Here on the right is a track between cottages. Turn right and walk uphill on the track, a bridleway.

In 250 metres fork right to stay on the bridleway and head southeast. Peer over the wall on your right for a view across fields to the sea and look behind for the church. In 300 metres you come to the lone heights of Grand Avenue on the edge of Seaford. Keep on course and cross the field to the housing estate.

An alleyway leads for 250 metres down to a children`s play area. Go through to the road at the bottom, Princess Drive and turn right. This quiet suburban road is on a bus route.

In 350 metres fork left into Carlton Road. Follow the road as it climbs and veers southeast. Take the third turning to the right, Westdown Road. It actually heads southwest downhill. On the corner at the bottom is the round Baptist Church.

Seaford Baptist Church

Carry on down to the main road. There is a pub on the corner on the left. Turn right on the pavement and cross to the Claremont Road shops. Turn right, pass the shops then turn immediately left into a pedestrian way over a railway bridge. Go down the wide straight Edinborough Road towards the sea below.

***Either** turn left at Park Road to enter Salts Recreation Ground*

Or go to the seafront, turn left then left again to descend into the recreation ground.

The tower of Seaford Parish Church can be seen across this field. Follow the path to pass a café then toilets. Turn left and leave the recreation ground on a wide sloping way up to a supermarket across the road.

Turn left and pass a Health Centre on the left. At a roundabout, turn right for the church.

From Seaford Parish Church go through the lychgate to the neighbouring pub then cross the road to the signpost to the Crypt Gallery. Go through the short alley to the crypt car park and come out to cross to West View, a road leading to the sea.

Turn right and walk along the Esplanade to return to Buckle Car Park.

Walk 2: Exeat to Westdean Friston Forest, Friston and East Dean Friston to East Dean, South Downs Way, Seven Sisters, Exeat

People come from all over the world to see our famous cliffs. Enjoy an air of holiday on this walk through forest and over downs - some quiet paths too.

Starting Point: Car Park for the Visitor Centre, Seven Sisters Country Park, Exeat. Enter from the road to Litlington. Café, shop and toilets are available.
GR518996 **Map:** OS Explorer 123 **Terrain:** Hilly **Distance:** 10 Miles
A frequent bus service on A259 enables you to do this walk in two sections:
From the Visitor Centre through Friston Forest to East Dean, 4 miles ***Or***
Bus to Friston, walk to East Dean then over coastal downland, 6 miles

Local Information:

1. Friston Forest was planted after the First World War. Beeches were grown to provide planking for trenches. Then in 1926 Eastbourne Water Company planted woodland to preserve the land surface over the water catchment area.
2. Birling Gap is a cleft in the South Downs, home of a Saxon tribe, 'Berlingas'. In 18th century a gate failed to keep out smugglers.
3. 'The Seven Sisters' (there are in fact eight) are the chalk cliffs where the Downs meet the sea.
4. Cuckmere Haven. The River Cuckmere winds over a flat plain to enter the sea here. The straight section is man made.

The Churches

Friston and East Dean churches have rare tapsell gates. These have a central spindle enabling people to enter and leave the churchyard at the same time.

Westdean Church, All Saints stands in the Saxon village of Dene. Alfred the Great used a palace here. In 885 he came to visit the monk Asser. He kept a fleet on the river. Apart from sailing and agriculture, the villagers also made a living on the saltpans. Fragments of the Saxon palace may still lie in the ruins of the Elizabethan Manor House behind the walls. The church also has vestiges of its Saxon past: a tiny narrow window northwest in the nave. Otherwise, the church dates from 1200. The round tower arch set on short pillars is Norman. The wide oblong tower is Norman in the lower part and 14th century above. The chancel is Early English as is the Parsonage next door, built in 1280. The porch is Victorian. In the 20th century the Victorian tiles were removed and replaced with York stone. The church had a new roof. Woodpeckers had attacked the wooden shingles on the spire. In 2000 clay tiles replaced them.

Friston Parish Church, St Mary the Virgin. A Saxon church stood here on the South Downs a mile from the coast. The companion 'dewpond' was already here. In 1974 it was the first pond to be scheduled an Ancient Monument. Little remains

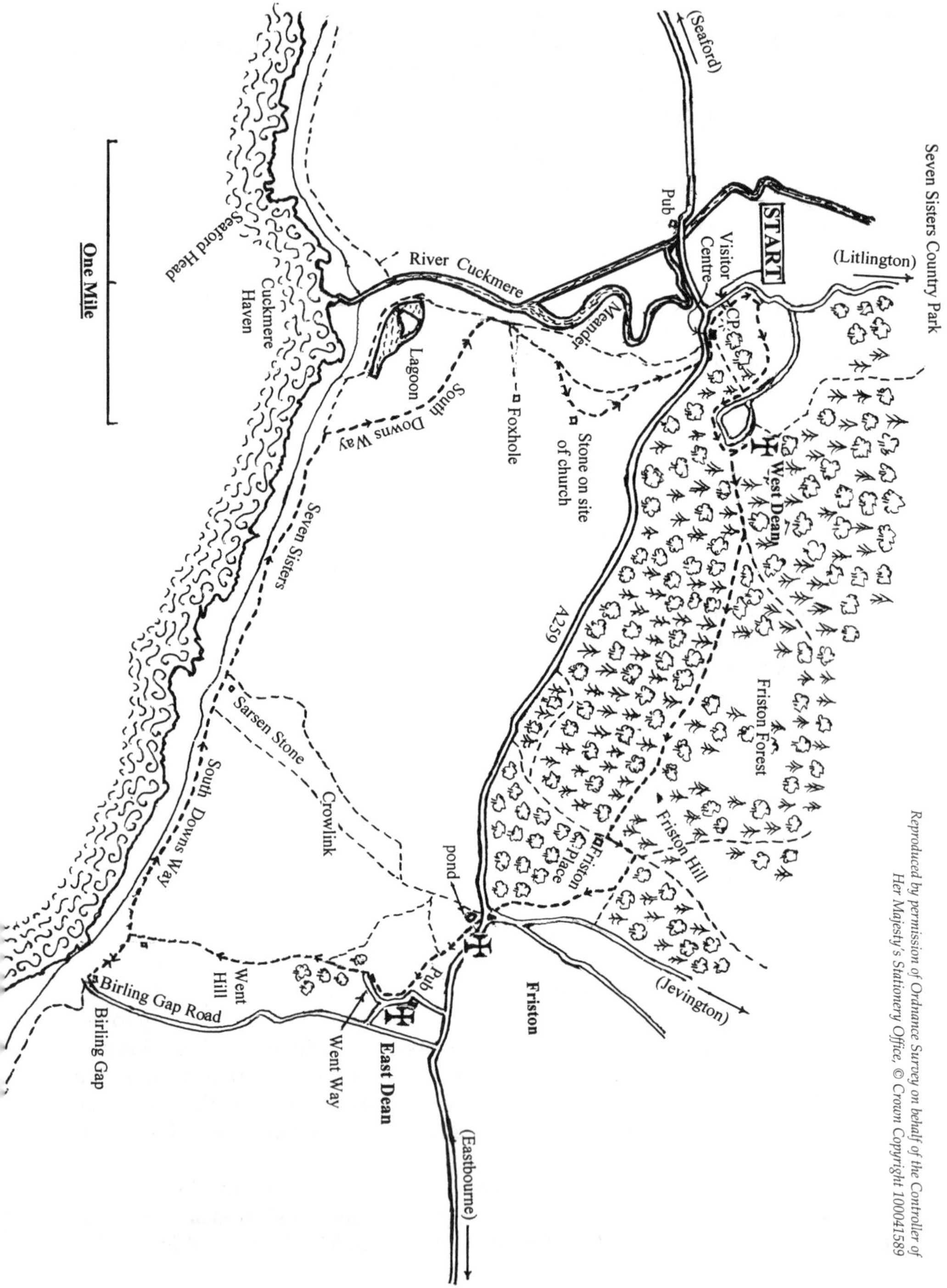
(Seaford)
Seven Sisters Country Park
(Litlington)
START
Visitor Centre
CP
Pub
River Cuckmere
Meander
Seaford Head
Cuckmere Haven
Lagoon
South Downs Way
Foxhole
Stone on site of church
West Dean
A259
Seven Sisters
Friston Forest
Sarsen Stone
Crowlink
Friston Hill
Friston Place
pond
Friston
(Jevington)
South Downs Way
Went Hill
Pub
Birling Gap Road
Birling Gap
Went Way
East Dean
(Eastbourne)
One Mile

of the Saxon church. The blocked window and door just visible from the outside, to the right of the porch are probably Saxon. The nave was extended westwards in 12th century and has round-headed Norman windows. The little 14th century chancel has blank arches on the sides. The chancel arch is wide and low. The new glass in the east window is by Jane Patterson (2002). The Annunciation window in the north transept is by Marguerite Douglas Thompson (1960). The 19th century north transept contains Selwyn memorials. Thomas Selwyn came to Friston Place in 1500. A later Thomas died in 1613 and has an alabaster monument of himself, his wife Elizabeth and their six daughters. The 15th century roof still has some original timber from the Weald.

Parish Church of St Simon and St Jude, East Dean is in a sheltered valley near Birling Gap. The Saxon tower was then the nave and there would have been an apsidal chancel. The tower is now the north transept. The present nave is 12th century with an extension in 1885 and a further extension in 1961. The chancel is 13th century and is built at a noticeable angle to the nave. The lancet windows have been filled in, possibly to strengthen the walls. The east window, originally three lancets was later transformed to Perpendicular and then restored with modern glass by the Victorians. The oak timbers in the roof are 15th century. The pulpit is dated 1623. The organ is built on a bridge over the nave. The finely carved Norman font is probably the work of a Saxon sculptor.

Exceat Church once served a wealthy parish, linked with Westdean. It is recorded as 'Essete' in Domesday. The Black Death (1348-9) and later attacks from French raiders probably destroyed the village. Now there is just a memorial stone on the ground. Today Exceat is a small area where A259 crosses the River Cuckmere.

The Walk

Once you have parked in the leafy Car Park, return towards the entrance and turn right on a bridleway signposted to Westdean. This is also a cycle way and has a smooth firm surface. You are in Friston Forest. Keep to the main track heading first north. The track curves to the right and northeast for ¼ mile. It then makes another curve southeast to arrive in Westdean near a green phone box.

Westdean

Turn right and walk along the village lane with the tall flint wall on your left. This encloses the ruins of an Elizabethan Manor House, possibly the site of Alfred`s Palace. The lane bends left and you pass the round medieval dovecote on the left.

At the end of the lane, **stop** before the private drive straight on and turn left to visit the church and parsonage.

After visiting Westdean Church, return to the private drive now on your left and walk uphill heading east and passing an occasional house. The drive becomes a bridleway through **Friston Forest**. Avoid a left fork in ¼ mile.

You now maintain a steady course southeast for 1 mile with only trees for company. This is an elevated route along a wide track with forest views. Do not be tempted down any side tracks. Your bridleway is only rarely signposted with blue arrows. In ½ mile look for an arrow on the right. The main track veers left here but you go downhill on a rougher narrow path to cross ways at the bottom. Cross the cycle track here to your own modest path and climb to the edge of **Friston Hill**. Pass high meadowland on the left and forest on the right. Re-enter the forest to come down to the road at **Friston Place**. This gabled house stands on the ancient site of Bechington.

Friston

Turn left and walk along the tree-lined drive for 200 metres. At cross paths turn right onto a bridleway that runs parallel to the drive. In 250 metres turn right again to cross the drive to a footpath heading south. It is good to be out in the open fields. Pass the buildings of Friston Place away to the right. Cross another private drive to the footpath opposite and veer left uphill to the far corner of the field. Turn to admire the view before entering the strait- jacket of an enclosed path up to a triangle of roads at **Friston**.

Go across this triangle then cross the A259 to the pond and church opposite.

Go through Friston churchyard to a footpath that takes you southeast down through meadows with a view to the coast and Belle Tout lighthouse.

East Dean

In ¼ mile you reach East Dean. Keep straight on along the lane, Lower Street. Pass a village green complete with 11th century pub on the far side. On your side of the green, pass a restaurant and café with delicatessen. Continue down Lower Street to East Dean Church at the bottom. On your way down, note a fork to the right, Went Way.

From East Dean Church return to Went Way and turn left. The village school here has a commemorative plaque to war time evacuee children who were here. Pass houses overlooking the tennis courts in the valley on the left. Keep on to the end of Went Way then take the downland bridleway ahead.

The bridleway curves left and uphill to go through elevated woodland. We are in National Trust land known as Crowlink. The Saxon 'Hling' means wooded hill. Not all is wooded as we soon emerge to open downland.

Continue south on a wide grassy track to the glistening sea below. You are on Went Hill and pass a barn on the left. Birling Gap comes into view with beach, pub and toilets.

Seven Sisters

Enter enclosed land at a cottage and continue down for 75 metres. Turn right to follow South Downs Way northwest on the cliffs known as the Seven Sisters. This is a stimulating switchback route with the sea below and glimpses of sparkling white cliff. The Downs in all their glory unfold for miles.

In 2 miles you are over the last summit and see the distinctive sinuous River Cuckmere below with cliffs of Seaford Head across the estuary. Continue on South Downs Way as it turns right above the river, now on your left.

Descend gently for ½ mile to the river where a wide, flat path heads north. At crosspaths there is a sign to Foxhole Camping Barn on the right. Avoid this and take the path half-right uphill, still the South Downs Way as it rises away from the flat easy path. As you climb, veer to the right to visit the stone that marks the site of Exceat Church on a remote mound above the river.

From Exceat Church veer left to find a path back to the South Downs Way and continue north down to the A259. Cross with care to the Visitor Centre and car park. **Note:** for buses to Friston, turn left and go right round bend.

Walk 3: Beddingham to Firle and along the South Downs Way

Two churches, with similar ancient roots, are now very different. We climb from the plain to enjoy views to the coast from the South Downs Way.

Starting Point: The lay-by at Beddingham Church **GR**445078
Map: OS Explorer 123 **Distance:** 7 Miles (can be shortened)
Terrain: Flat fields followed by a climb up into the Downs and back.
Local Interest: 1 A Roman villa has been discovered at Preston Court Farm.
2 Firle Place was built in Tudor times for Sir John Gage and remains in the family who open it to the public occasionally.

Note: *The fields may be wet sometimes but it is possible to follow lanes all the way if you study the attached map.*

The Churches

Both churches were acquired by Robert, Earl of Mortain, half-brother of William the Conqueror who tended to reward his supporters with gifts of lands and churches.

Beddingham, St Andrew. There was a 'monasterium' here in 801. It was probably a church with more than one priest. A Norman church replaced it and Matilda, wife of Robert of Mortain gave the advowsen to the Abbey of Grestain in Normandy. The only remnant of the Norman church is the blocked window over the north arcade of the nave. The south arcade is Transition Norman; the north aisle Early English, the chancel is Decorated and the tower and font Perpendicular.

The Parish Church of St Peter, Firle was also given to the Abbey of Grestain and became known as 'Grissens Minster'. The north door is all that remains of the Norman church. The rest is mainly Decorated. Tower, nave and chancel are early 13th century. Note the fine tower arch. Aisle arcades were added in 14th century. The Gage Chapel is late Perpendicular. It contains the altar tombs of the Gage family. Note the beautiful, colourful John Piper window, depicting the Tree of Life in the heavenly Jerusalem.

The Walk

Just opposite Beddingham Church go through a field gate and head east. There is no signpost, but the footpath leads over a small patch of rough grassland to the A26. Cross with care to the footpath opposite. Here is a finger post. Follow it to continue eastwards over a field towards farm buildings. Pass these on your left.

Leave this first field over a double stile with a footbridge in the middle. In the next small field go straight on then veer right to a stone stile. Pass stables here on your left then continue southeast with a field boundary on your right. Below left is the A27 and beyond that the buildings of Glynde. You are in the lea of the Downs on your right. Ahead are the buildings of Little Dene. In ½ mile you go down some steps to the access lane through **Little Dene**.

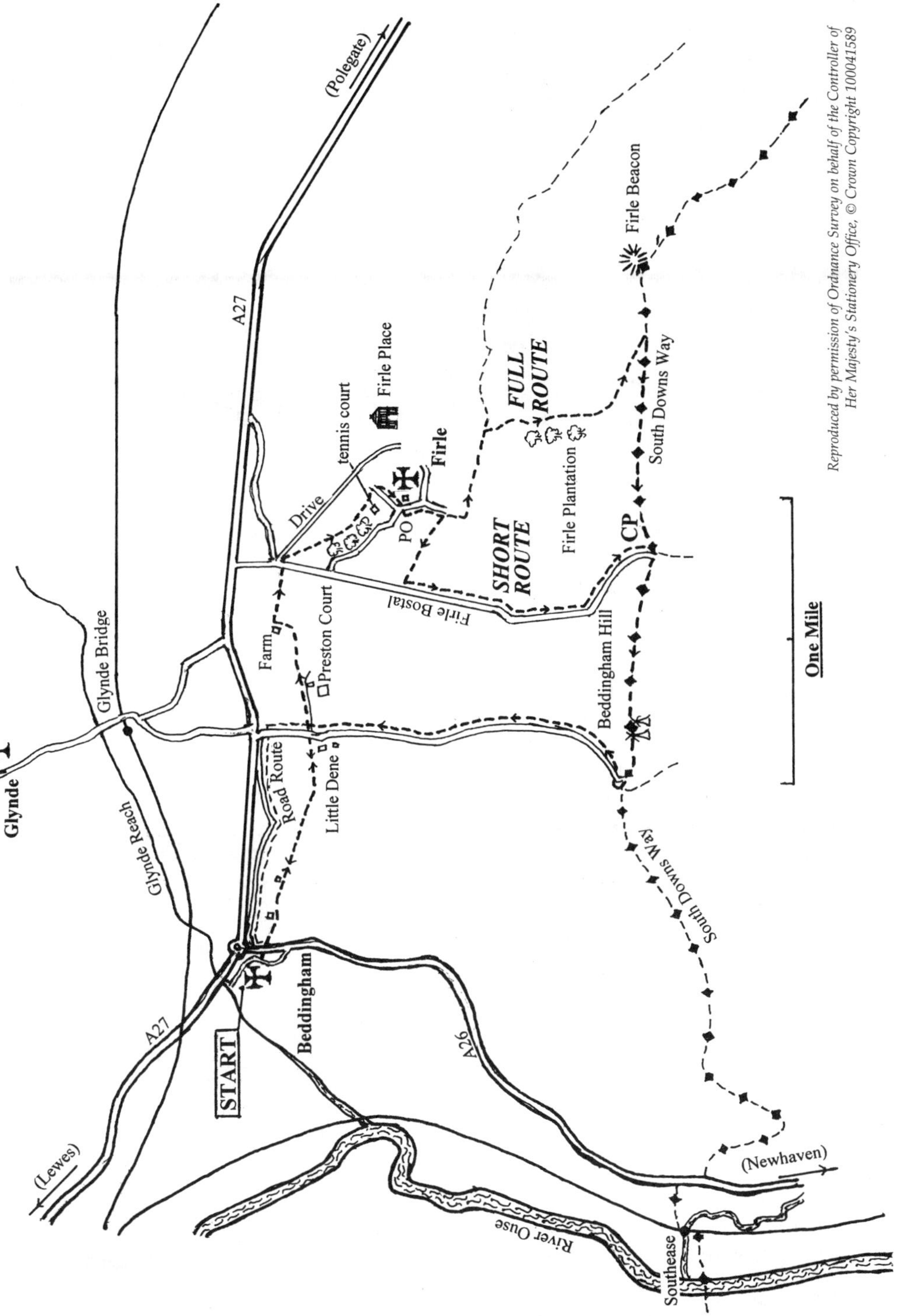

Reproduced by permission of Ordnance Survey on behalf of the Controller of Her Majesty's Stationery Office, © Crown Copyright 100041589

Cross the lane to a drive opposite. Pass Preston Court on your right then leave the drive by turning left into a field at a footpath sign. Pass a little cottage on your right. You are now heading northeast. In 400 metres you reach farm buildings on your left and join the rough track. Turn left then right on this track which brings you to crossroads at the entrance to Firle Place.

Enter the grounds of Firle Place on the driveway. Do not linger but turn right to walk over parkland. There are no signposts. Head for a pedestrian gate into the next field, ignoring the farm gate into woodland on the right. Keep the fringe of woodland on your right and head southeast over the field. (Fear not the ponies who ignored us!). You should reach a tennis court on the other side of the field. Pass this on your right and find a little lane leading out of the estate into the village of Firle.

Turn left at the village road in Firle. Go up past the post office and shop to the church on your left.

From Firle Church return to the village road and turn left. You are heading south on a byway that becomes a farm track and stays a right of way.

For the slightly shorter route *(with a tarmac road up to the Downs).*

In 50 metres turn right into a flat track heading west with the Downs on your left and views over the plain on your right. In 400 metres you reach a tarmac road, Firle Bostal. Turn left and follow this road for 1 mile up to the car park at the top of the Downs. Turn right and walk along South Downs Way.

For the full walk (with paths up to give a good stretch on South Downs Way).

Continue south on the byway, now a farm track heading for the Downs. The track curves to the left so that you have the estate wall on your left and the Downs on your right. In 500 metres you reach a strip of woodland. Turn right onto a track following the woodland on

Downs above Firle

the right. As you climb, you can look back to Firle Tower. The wood thickens and is known as Firle Plantation. You leave the wood after 500 metres and begin the downland climb. There are deep folds in the Downs on your left. Here masses of cowslips thrive in the spring. The path curves left and takes you steeply up to South Downs Way at the top. Turn right, heading west for ½ mile to the car park where you veer slightly right to continue on South Downs Way.

Both routes: Enjoy the soft turf on the top of the Downs with magnificent views to the coast on the left. Even the River Ouse can be seen making its way to the sea at Newhaven. On your right you look down to the plain you crossed earlier. Ahead are the radio masts on the top of Beddingham Hill. Pass these on your left. In another 200 metres, at cross paths, turn right away from the sea and northwards back down to the plain.

In a mile of descent on the flinty track you come down to join the access lane through **Little Dene**. Continue through this hamlet to the familiar cross path. Turn left to go up the steps. Retrace your steps to Beddingham.

Or, if you prefer a hard surface, continue northwards along the access lane for another ¼ mile, almost to the A27. Find the lane on the left that runs parallel to the main road. You are heading westwards on this lane for nearly 1 mile. You pass Comps Farm then, at the end of the lane a row of houses. Turn left at the A26 and cross to Beddingham Church.

View to Newhaven near Firle Beacon

Walk 4: Selmeston to Berwick and Alciston

Three ancient churches lie under the Downs where the ground is fertile and the going is easy. The old coach road took this favoured route.

Starting Point 1: Selmeston Church **GR**509069
Starting Point 2: Berwick Station **GR**526068
Map: OS Explorer 123
Distance: 4 ½ - 5 Miles **Terrain:** Gently undulating
Local Information: Nearby is Charleston Farmhouse, once the home of the artists Duncan Grant and Vanessa and Clive Bell. House and gardens are open to the public in spring and summer. On this walk we see some murals by the artists, mainly Duncan Grant in Berwick Church.

The Churches

Selmeston Church stands in a circular churchyard close to an important Stone Age centre. In 1930s Archaeologists uncovered axes, tools and pottery in a sandpit southeast of the church. In 1086 William de Cahanges was patron of 'Sielmestone'. In 12th century the Bishop of Chichester was the patron. By 1242 the name 'Selmeston' was established. There is no known dedication. In 1867 the church was virtually rebuilt in flint copying the existing Perpendicular style. The east window is in Decorated style. The south arcade has two handsome octagonal oak columns on stone bases. The altar has the original marble slab. A medieval water stoup is in the modern porch. The bell tower caps a neat building.

Berwick Church, St Michael and All Angels makes a strong visual impact both inside and outside. It has a commanding view of the Downs from its lone position on top of a sloping field, a prehistoric site. In Domesday 1086 it is recorded as 'Berewice' or 'barley farm'. Inside, many walls are covered in striking 20th century murals by Duncan Grant, Vanessa Bell and Duncan Bell. They are beautifully offset by the clear glass windows in the north and south aisles. The church has a Saxon font set in the wall by the tower arch. The tower was built in 1603. The spire was struck by lightning in 1773 and has been replaced. The chancel retains some 13th century features despite the Victorian rebuilding of the east end. The north aisle was also rebuilt in 1856. The south aisle is 14th century. There is a memorial to Parson Nutt on the north wall of the tower. He was Rector here 1613 – 1645 and wrote 'Remembrances of the Parsons of Berwick'. When Cromwell replaced him, he went to live in his private house, 'Mays' in Selmeston. Another parson, Revd. E. Boys-Ellman, who was here for 66 years, 1837 – 1906 with a gap of 3 years, also wrote a book: 'Recollections of a Sussex Parson'. He is also responsible for the 1856 restoration of the 'rabbit warren' as he first described the old church.

Alciston Church (dedication unknown) stands on a small hillock, well above local floods. The name 'Alciston' means 'tun' or farm of Aelfsige, a Saxon resident. In 1984 the remains of a Saxon apse were found under the East window. The present

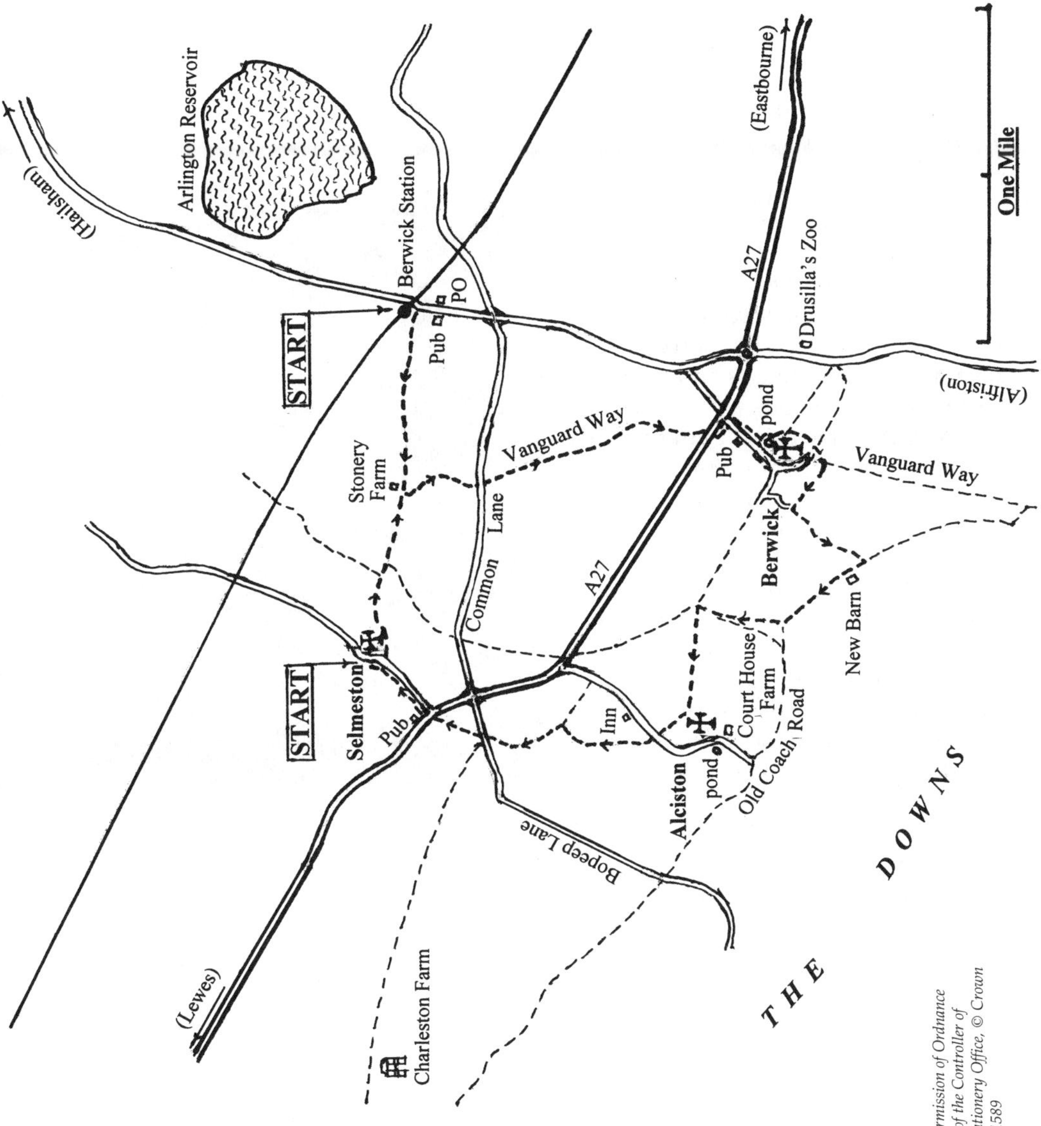
Arlington Reservoir
(Hailsham)
Berwick Station
START
Pub
PO
(Eastbourne)
A27
Drusilla's Zoo
One Mile
(Alfriston)
pond
Pub
Vanguard Way
Vanguard Way
Stonery Farm
Common Lane
A27
Berwick
New Barn
START
Selmeston
Pub
Inn
Court House Farm
Old Coach Road
pond
Alciston
Bopeep Lane
THE DOWNS
(Lewes)
Charleston Farm

building dates from 13th and 14th centuries. A Norman window is in the north wall of the chancel. To the right of this are two Early English windows. Further to the right the remains of a blocked Early English window indicate that the chancel was longer then. In 1853 most of the building underwent Victorian restoration. In 1951 the porch was rebuilt. The door is 15th century. East of the door a scratch dial marks where arrows have been sharpened. Before the Reformation the Manor and lands of Alciston belonged to Battle Abbey. Monks came to Alciston on retreat. Part of nearby Court House Farm is 14th century. The old tithe barn is 170 feet long. There is also a dovecote and fishpond.

The Walk

1. From Selmeston Church head south along the village lane in the direction of A27. Do not go far! You turn left immediately so that you pass close to the church. The footpath starts on a driveway to houses and takes you eastwards. In ¼ mile you come to a junction of paths. Avoid both the paths to the left and the more intrusive path to the right. Instead take the narrow path straight ahead. The ground is now soft but not too muddy. Views open to the Weald in the north and the Downs in the south. Stonery Farm is ahead.

At Stonery Farm you join Vanguard Way and the route of walkers from the station. Turn right on the farm track following Vanguard Way south.

Selmeston

From Berwick Station *head south towards the Downs. Do not go as far as the pub and post office. Instead turn right on the Vanguard Way. This takes you westwards. In ½ mile you reach Stonery Farm and follow the track as it bends to the left, still Vanguard Way.*

Both routes enjoy a gentle descent on this firm track. The spire of Berwick Church is ahead and the Downs behind. You come down to a byway, Common Lane and a house on the right. Cross diagonally left to the footpath opposite.

Continue diagonally left across fields for ½ mile. This is still Vanguard Way and well marked. You then come to adjoining field corners. Ahead to the left is a hedge. Go through the gap in the hedge and veer right. You now hug the hedge on your right and soon come to the A27.

Cross with care to the lane on the left opposite. This is in the village of Berwick. Follow the lane past a pub on the right. In 150 metres turn left into an unmade road. Go round the village pond on the right and enter a short narrow alley

Berwick

leading to a field with many footpaths. Go straight on up the grassy slope to the church ahead. There is a kissing gate into the churchyard.

To continue the walk, go behind Berwick Church where you find further views over downland. Walk past the chancel and down into a field with more footpaths. Turn sharp right then immediately right again so that you have circumnavigated the churchyard. You have now left Vanguard Way. You are on a farm track and bridleway heading west. You can peer through the hedge on your right to a little avenue where snowdrops adorn the pathway in February.

In 250 metres your track comes down to a T-junction. Turn left here, passing a slurry pit on the left. You are approaching a long crest of downland where colourful gliders float on currents of air. In 300 metres you reach the old coach road that runs east – west below the Downs. It is now a cycleway. Turn right here and pass the old farm buildings of 'New Barn' on your left. After walking 400 metres along the old coach road, turn right. A footpath here follows the hedge on your right. You can look over the hedge to Berwick Church.

Alciston

View to Firle Beacon

In 225 metres at the field boundary, turn left. Follow the grass swathe to Alciston Church, seen ahead. At a high wall you have to turn right then left into a little field beside the church. Walk beside the churchyard to the entrance where steps take you up to the pathway to the porch.

From Alciston Church go back down the steps and follow the path to the lane through the hamlet of Alciston. Cross to the footpath opposite. More steps bring you up to open fields.

If you wish to linger in Alciston before crossing to the footpath above, you can turn left and walk up the lane to Court House Farm and the tithe barn. You also pass the medieval dovecote and the fishpond. Return to the proposed footpath and pass it on your left and the church on your right. Down the lane you will find the local inn. Now you are ready for the footpath!

Climb the steps up to the field and head northwest passing a small circular reservoir. You are descending gently as you cross diagonally left through open fields with views over what must once have been a flood plain. When you come to the hedge in 300 metres, go through to the next field and turn right. You can now hug the hedge on your right. At the field corner, avoid the footpath to the right. Go straight on down into the field ahead and turn left. Head northwest with a field boundary on your left. Cut across the corner and find a footbridge over a stream. Climb the slope in the next field and head north to a byway with the name 'Bopeep Lane'!

Cross the lane to the enclosed path opposite, passing a cottage on the right. The path opens to a small field with the A27 roaring ahead. Cross with care to the lane opposite. This leads back to Selmeston Church.

*If you have to return to Berwick Station, follow the very first instruction at the start of this walk. Once you reach **Stonery Farm,** you keep straight on to retrace your footsteps to the station.*

Walk 5: Lullington to Alfriston and Litlington

Three lovely churches stand above the River Cuckmere and offer a short riverside walk and a long walk with the addition of magnificent downland.

Starting Point: The rough Car Park on Chapel Road, above Lullington Church. The South Downs Way crosses the road here. **GR**532033
Map: OS Explorer 123 **Distance:** Approx. 4 miles or 7 miles
Terrain: Flat riverside and short hill slopes or longer climbs into the Downs
Local Information: The first National Trust building, the Clergy House is near Alfriston Church. It is a 14th century timber built Wealden house, open to the public from early March to mid-December.

When you look westwards towards downland called 'High and Over', you can see a white horse. It was first carved on the hillside in 1838 and again in 1920. It is 90 feet long and in good shape. During the Second World War this landmark had to be covered to hide it from enemy planes.
Warning: Alfriston Village is very popular. The lane through the village is congested with traffic on sunny days at weekends and holidays.

The Churches

Alfriston, St Andrew has been described as 'the Cathedral of the Downs'. It stands on a mound on the village green and can be admired from the Downs on all sides.

Alfriston

Alfriston

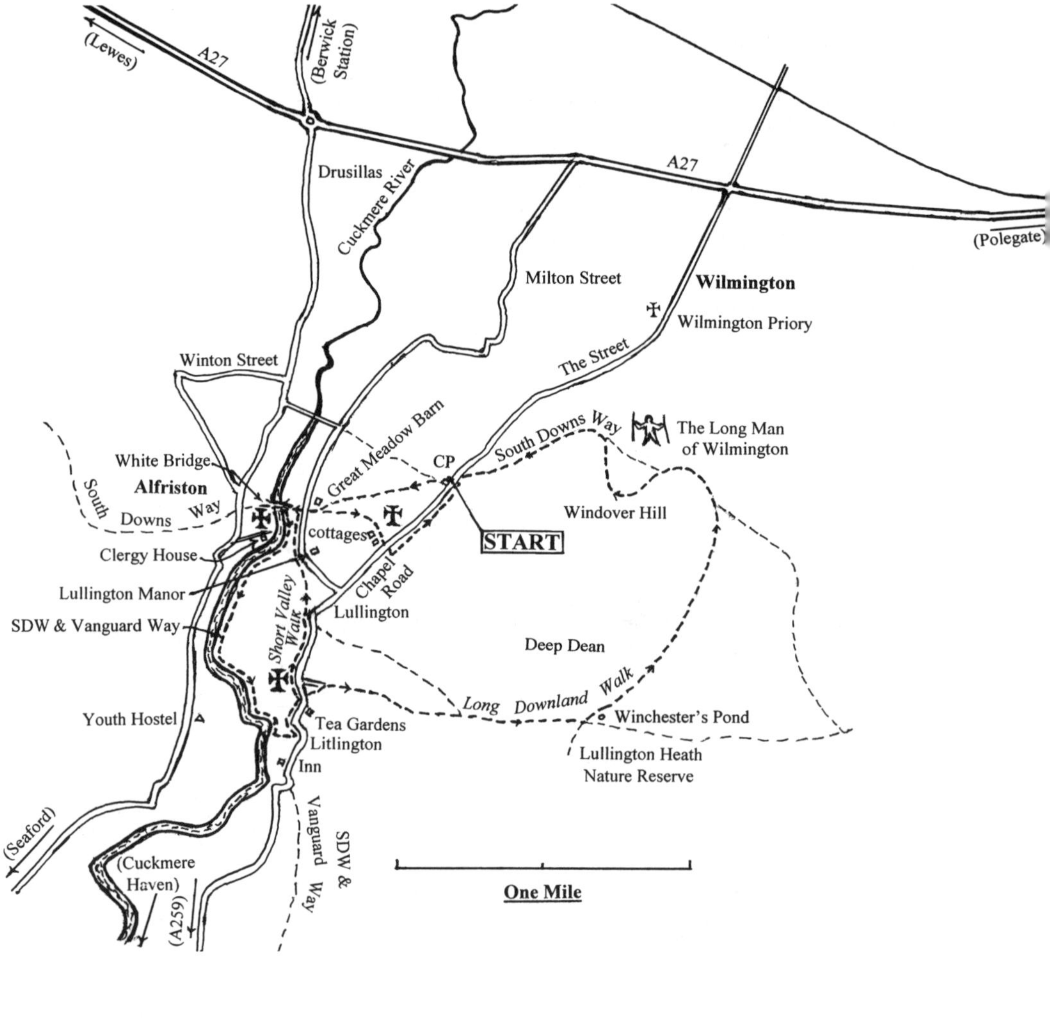
(Lewes)
A27
(Berwick Station)
Drusillas
Cuckmere River
A27
(Polegate)
Milton Street
Wilmington
Wilmington Priory
The Street
Winton Street
Great Meadow Barn
South Downs Way
The Long Man of Wilmington
CP
White Bridge
Alfriston
South Downs Way
Windover Hill
cottages
START
Clergy House
Chapel Road
Lullington Manor
Short Valley Walk
Lullington
SDW & Vanguard Way
Deep Dean
Long Downland Walk
Youth Hostel
Tea Gardens
Litlington
Winchester's Pond
Lullington Heath Nature Reserve
Inn
(Seaford)
SDW & Vanguard Way
(Cuckmere Haven)
(A259)
One Mile

Local flint and greensand stone were the building materials. The flint was knapped square and fitted so neatly that little mortar was needed. This fine church was built all of piece in 14th century just at a time of transition from the Decorated to the Perpendicular. In the shape of a Greek cross, it has a central tower with a shingled spire. The arches are tall and the church spacious. The pillars of the crossing are concave at their sides, as are the capitals. The roof is of king-post construction throughout. There are windows of both Decorated and Perpendicular styles here. The Jesse window in the south transept has glass by Kempe and Tower. Some old glass in the window in the north transept shows St Alphege, Archbishop of Canterbury in 1006. Two low windows on either side of the chancel have modern glass. The south window by Herbert Goodall shows St Christopher. The north window, 'St Peter the Fisherman', by Joseph Nuttgens depicts a young man hauling a net of fish. Through the net can be seen sky and trees. It is exquisite. In the chancel, figures carved on the Easter Sepulchre may be those of St Lewinna and her dog. This saint lived in the 6th century and she must be a link with an earlier Saxon Church. In fact the remains of a Saxon graveyard have been found at the top of Winton Street. Strangely no church in Alfriston is mentioned in Domesday.

Litlington

Litlington is a small Norman church with some windows of that period. A 'string course' running along the north and south walls is Norman. The south door is also Norman. The church was altered to Early English. The wooden roof beams in the nave are thought to be original. The chancel has a more elaborate roof. There is a double sedilia in the chancel so high it suggests that the floor is lower now. Outside, as you enter the porch you will see a 13th century sundial on the right hand side.

Lullington, the Church of the Good Shepherd. We have left the smallest until last. Here is the delightful part of a medieval church. It consists of part of a chancel, five medieval windows and a white belfry. A few mounds of stone on the west side are the remains of the nave. How pleasant to stand here in the open air and enjoy the view to the Downs.

The Walks

Both Walks

Go to the South Downs Way and turn left, heading west. In 50 metres leave the South Downs Way by a footpath on the left. This low downland path makes a

Lullington

beeline for Alfriston, seen below ahead. In 500 metres go through a tree-lined hedge to the next field, 'the great meadow' of Dirk Bogarte (see his autobiography).

Turn right and follow the hedge down to the nearby barn, **not** Plonk Barn as on OS Map. It is now Great Meadow Barn. At the time of writing the footpath continues on the south side of the barn. It may be moved to the north side, already used by walkers as it is less muddy. Both paths lead down to the Lullington road.

Cross with care to the footpath opposite. Go straight on over the flat meadow to cross the White Bridge over the River Cuckmere. Alfriston Church is on your left and the Clergy House just beyond.

From Alfriston Church return to the White Bridge and cross back to the east side of the river. Turn right. You are now heading south beside the river and pass Alfriston Church on the other side. You are back on South Downs Way which shares this wide grassy bank with Vanguard Way.

In one mile you pass Litlington Church away to the left. You have to stick to the riverside footpath, now more enclosed, before you can turn left to Litlington. This used to be a secluded spot in the Cuckmere Valley and still has an air of tranquility until the tourists come!

At the road turn left heading north for Litlington Church. Before you reach the church you might like to call in at Litlington Tea Gardens. I believe teas have been served here for over 100 years. It opens in April. If, on the other hand you prefer the inn, that is behind you back along the road.

From Litlington Church continue north along the road, passing Church Farm next door.

For the longer downland walk, *turn right opposite Church Farm and cross the road to the track opposite. It passes a barn with round brick pillars. After a sharp bend left then* *right, the track heads east for 1 mile with views behind. You can see the white horse mentioned above. You are climbing above a fold in the Downs on the left, Park Bottom. Pass a stile on the left into this 'Access Land'. You are also passing Cross Dyke on the right and entering Lullington Heath Nature Reserve.*

Soon after the access stile you come to cross tracks and turn left. Before turning, go a little further to see the 19th century dew pond, 'Winchester`s Pond', tucked away in the scrub. Now follow a new elevated track and head northeast for another mile with the valley of Deep Dean hidden behind trees and gorse on the left. You have open downland on the right.

A magnificent view over Cuckmere Valley opens on the left. Your track has become a mere mark in the grass, as you veer left above Deep Dean. You are approaching Windover Hill and come up to a pair of gates.

Go through and you are now on the South Downs Way. This makes a loop over Windover Hill. (You can cut across this loop to view the Long Man of Wilmington). Continue west on South Downs Way, pass a covered reservoir on the right. You come down to the ***Car Park*** *on Chapel Road at the start of this walk.*

Turn left. A short walk down the road brings you to Lullington Church on the right. Return to the ***Car Park****.*

For the shorter valley walk. After Church Farm, continue along the edge of the road for 200 metres. You now have a footpath on a raised bank beside the road for 250 metres. Then take the path on the left and walk across a water meadow with another view to Alfriston Church. Go behind the gardens of Lullington Court and turn right into a small field where you keep on course to reach the Lullington Road. Turn left.

A footpath in the field on the left runs parallel to the road but it may be muddy.

When you reach the familiar path at Great Meadow Barn on the right, cross the road to head east back up Great Meadow. Avoid the footpath on the left that brought you here earlier. Instead, keep straight on up to Lullington Church. It stands high on the left with some cottages on the right. I have been told that Dirk Bogarte as a child lived in one of these cottages.

From Lullington Church return to the footpath, pass the cottages on the right and turn left at Chapel Road. The **Car Park** is 300 metres up on the left.

White Bridge, Alfriston

5 Walks
Near Hailsham

The Wealdway near Jevington

Walk 6:
1. Folkington to Wilmington
2. Folkington to Jevington
(Two short walks to make a figure of eight)
3. Folkington to Wilmington and Jevington
(1 long downland circular)

So many ancient churches shelter in the lee of the Downs and testify to a simpler holier life in their lovely settings, carrying a breath of yesteryear.
Part of our way is on long distance paths, Wealdway and South Downs Way
Starting Point: Folkington Church at the end of Folkington Lane **GR**559038
Map: OS Explorer 123 **Terrain:** Some downland slopes, some flat fields, some enclosed tracks.
Distances: 2-3 Miles, a circular walk from Folkington to Wilmington
4 Miles, a circular walk from Folkington to Jevington
7 Miles, a circular walk from Folkington to Wilmington and Jevington

The Churches

Folkington Church, St Peter, close to woodland and looking out to the Downs, has a rustic charm. Sadly this tiny hamlet is struggling to keep its church in good repair. I hope visitors will give generously. The Saxon name, 'Folca`s tun', suggest that here was a farm belonging to Folca whose tribe may also have settled in Fulking. Our village is mentioned in Domesday as 'Fochintone'. The present flint church was built in 13th century and has some Early English windows in the nave. Two Perpendicular windows have also been added. Plain glass makes the church light. The roof with king posts and tie beams stretches across nave and chancel. There is no chancel arch. Some old box pews look remarkably cosy. The bell turret was added in 14th century. The octagonal font is Perpendicular.

Folkington

Wilmington Church, St Mary and St Peter was built in 1100 for the Saxon people of 'Winelton'. There was a covered cloister walk from the church to the Priory, now a

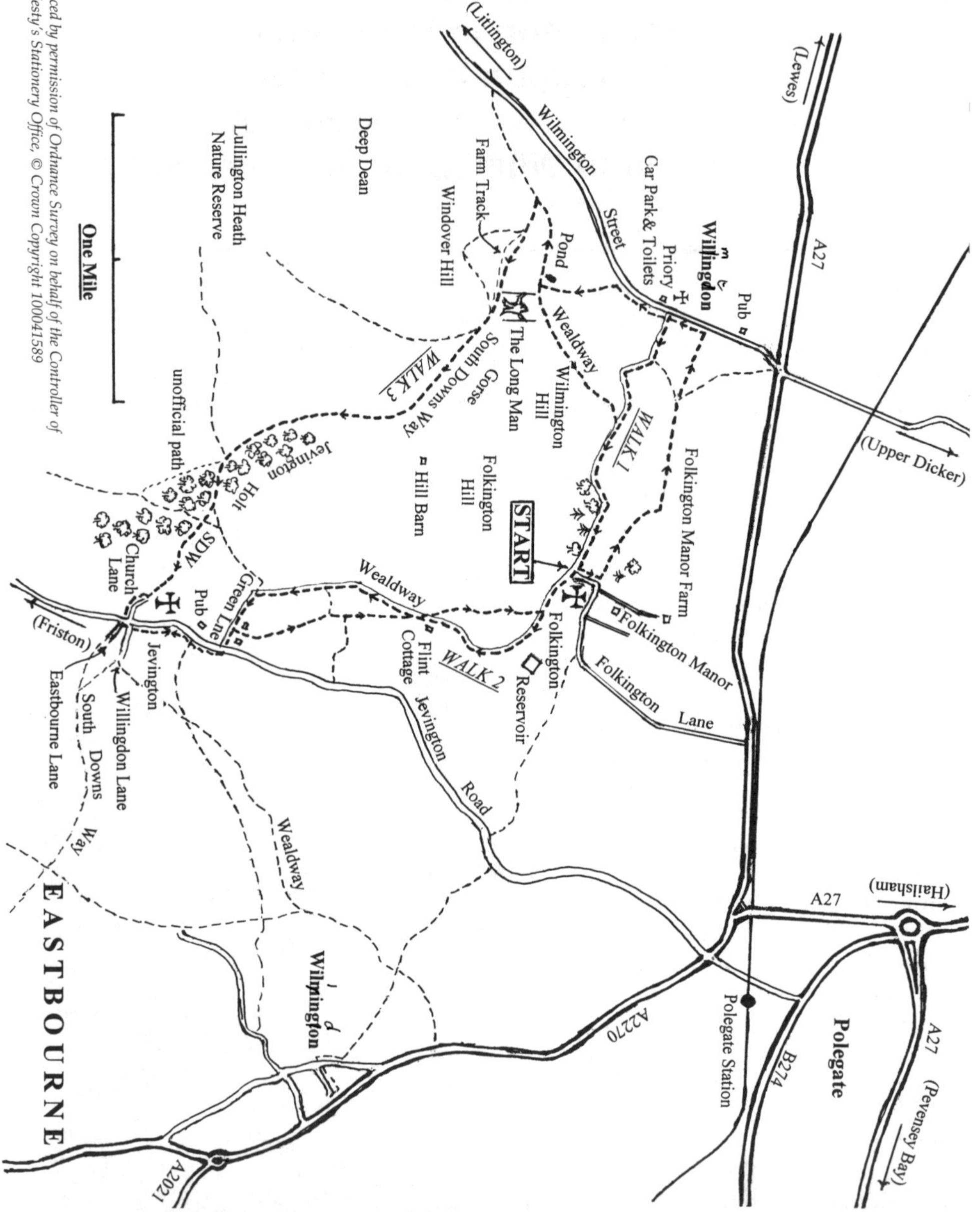
(Lewes)
(Litlington)
A27
Wilmington Street
Wilmington
Pub
Priory
Car Park& Toilets
Farm Track
Pond
Windover Hill
Deep Dean
Lullington Heath
Nature Reserve
One Mile
Wealdway
The Long Man
Wilmington Hill
South Downs Way
Gorse
WALK 3
WALK 1
Folkington Manor Farm
(Upper Dicker)
Folkington Hill
Hill Barn
START
Jevington Holt
unofficial path
SDW
Church Lane
Pub
Green Lane
Wealdway
Folkington
Folkington Manor
Folkington Lane
Flint Cottage
WALK 2
Reservoir
(Friston)
Jevington
Willingdon Lane
South Downs Way
Eastbourne Lane
Jevington Road
Wealdway
(Hailsham)
A27
Polegate Station
Polegate
B274
A27
(Pevensey Bay)
A2270
Willingdon
A2021
EASTBOURNE

ruin in a private garden. A Benedictine order from Grestain in Normandy settled here even before the Conquest. Apart from some rough outside rendering on the flint walls, the church is in pristine condition. The chancel has thick Norman walls and two original windows. It was used as a quire for the monks from 12th to 15th century. Outside, under the Norman windows there is a string course with carved triangles. Inside on the north wall is an early carving of a stone face. Over the years Wilmington Church has benefited from sympathetic restoration. The north chapel dates from 13th century. The Nave was rebuilt in 14th century. The south aisle was added in 19th century. The tall chancel arch in Early English style was actually built by the Victorians. A fire this century has inspired restorers to clear the 13th century north transept and insert a beautiful replacement of the window. The new window shows a phoenix rising from the ashes and St Peter with butterflies and bees.

Wilmington Priory

Jevington Church, St Andrew. Ancient footpaths lead to the door of this church. The Wealdway comes down from a Neolithic camp on Combe Hill and the South Downs Way passes tumuli as it approaches from the northwest. Saxons, led by Geola established a 'tun' or farm here. The name 'Geofinga Tun' gradually changed and is recorded as Jevington in 15th century. Our path to the church goes through a rare Tapsell gate. It is wide with a central pivot, allowing people to enter and leave at the same time. The church has a beautiful Saxon tower, built of flint and local sandstone in 900 A.D. Despite Victorian changes, original windows with arches of Roman brick can still be seen north and south on the outside. Inside, the tall Saxon arch has smaller Victorian arches on either side. A Saxon sculpture of Christ, found under the tower floor in 1785, has been set in the north wall of the nave. The chancel, nave and north aisle with small lancets are Early English. The nave has a 16th century roof with king posts and hammer beams. When the Victorian restoration was finished in 1873 and the church had been rescued from decay, the whole village celebrated. Houses and roads were decorated and children worked to make everywhere clean and tidy ready for the feast, partaken by all.

The Walks

Walk 1 Folkington to Wilmington (2 – 3 Miles)

From Folkington Church walk back down the lane for 100 metres as far as the bend to the right. Folkington Manor is straight ahead. Turn left into an alley on the edge of the Manor estate. You soon come out into fields with the A27 at a little distance below. Keep on course for 500 metres. A hedge on your left gets gradually further away.

Veer to the right when you come to open fields slanting up to the Downs on the left. You have reached the edge of your field. Go down to a nearby hedge where you turn left.

With the hedge on your right, head west for 1 kilometre to Wilmington. You can just spy the church ahead. Avoid paths to right and left. Keep straight on and go through a twitten to emerge on Wilmington Street. (There is a pub to the right).

Turn left for the Church, the Priory and the Car Park with toilets. Here you have a view to the Long Man of Wilmington, a figure carved on the hillside. No-one knows its history or who it represents.

Wilmington

Wilmington Church to Folkington via 'the Long Man'. *(Walk 3 also follows some of this route).*

From Wilmington Car Park, cross the Street to a raised path opposite. It is signposted to the 'Long Man'. Follow the signs and turn left in 250 metres. You have joined the long distance footpath, the Wealdway. It heads to the Long Man.

***After a gate** turn left and follow the Wealdway northeast on the edge of Wilmington Hill. In 1 kilometre you come down to another gate into the enclosed track below. Turn right for Folkington.*

For the most direct route from Wilmington Church to Folkington, cross the Street to an enclosed track opposite. It leads all the way back to Folkington and may have been part of a smugglers` trail. In places the hedgerow trees give way and you can glimpse the field path of the outward walk, below left.

After a gradual climb, you are joined by the Wealdway as it descends from the Downs on the right. Those who visited the Long Man join the track here.

Both short routes enter Folkington Wood where bluebells and the rare helleborine grow in the spring. You soon come down to Folkington Church.

Walk 2 Folkington to Jevington (4 miles)

Follow the track past Folkington Church. It veers left on the Wealdway and goes gently downhill heading southeast. You pass garden meadows and the mellow brick of old walls on the left and go through a pleasant avenue with downland ahead. The hard core under foot peters out and you have to climb on a chalky way enclosed by hedges, probably a route once taken by smugglers.

Keep on this track for 1 ½ miles to Jevington, avoiding paths to left and right. You pass a high, flat-topped reservoir on the left and later a lone flint cottage. Towards the end you come down to a T-junction. Turn left here and you are in Green Lane. Continue down to cottages and note the footpath on the left with the sign to 'Folkington'. This will be our route back.

The Long Man of Wilmington

When you reach the main road at Jevington, turn right. Follow the pavement for ¼ mile, passing the pub on your way. The pavement takes a turn to the right up to Folkington Church where seats and a tap of drinking water welcome ramblers.

To return from Jevington to Folkington, take the path through the tapsel gate

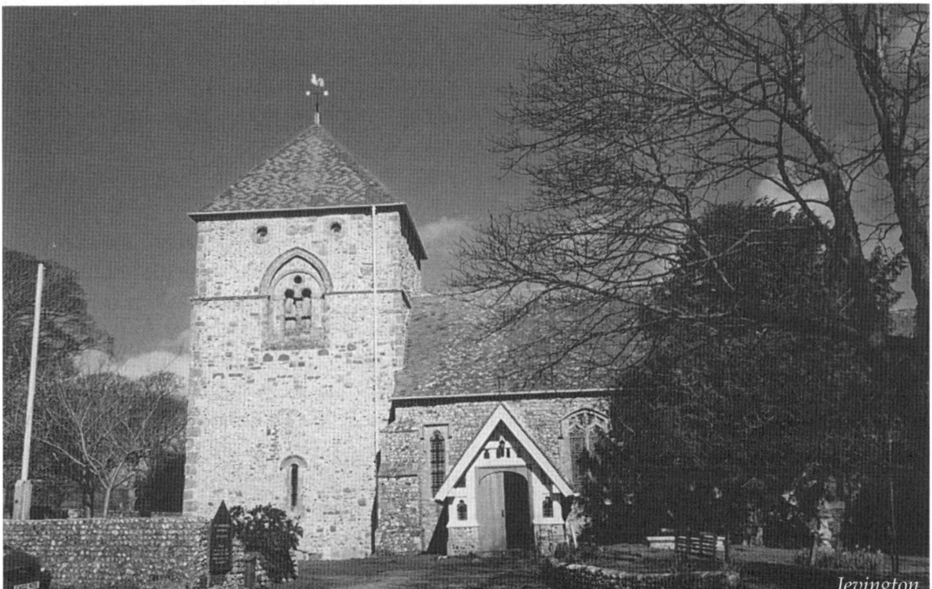

Jevington

and turn left on the Folkington Lane. (Those on the figure of 8, Walk 2 are retracing their steps for the next ¼ mile). Go past the pub then turn left into Green Lane. Find the footpath, signed to Folkington, now on your right. It passes a garden and then goes through horse paddocks. Cross a field diagonally left up to trees. Then keep on course to a cross track.

Go down into this sunken track and turn right. In 50 metres find a path on the left and climb out of the track. Keep on course again, aided by low wire fences. A view on the right opens to the sea with Stone Cross Windmill and Pevensey in front.

In ¼ mile you come to the familiar Wealdway. Cross this track diagonally right to a stepped path that leads up to downland with splendid views. You can see the hamlet of Folkington in trees below. The path curves down the right. At the bottom veer right again to rejoin the hard core track. Turn left and follow the track through the avenue back to Folkington Church.

Walk 3 Folkington to Wilmington and Jevington (7 Miles)

Follow Walk 1 as far as Wilmington.

From Wilmington Car Park cross the Street to a raised path opposite. It is signposted to the 'Long Man'. Follow the signs and turn left in 250 metres. You have joined the long distance footpath, 'the Wealdway'.

After a gate below the 'Long Man', turn right and pass a dew pond. Climb gently in a westerly direction for 200 metres.

Go through another gate and turn immediately left. Climb more steeply on a slightly sunken way with a wire fence on the left. There is a farm track down on the right. Keep hugging the fence on the left. This path takes you above the Long Man. You can look down over him and back over Wilmington to Arlington Reservoir below.

In ¼ mile you emerge to open downland and keep straight on. You are walking parallel to the South Downs Way nearby down on the right. Maintain your elevated route and look ahead to the succession of wooden way markers. They show the southeasterly course of South Downs Way. This is your way. Avoid turning right into the spectacular Deep Dean Valley. You will find a long gorse hedge away to the left soon keeps you company.

In ½ mile you pass Hill Barn, a stone ruin covering a large elevated patch on the left. Your route, South Downs Way veers imperceptibly south towards the wooded slope of Jevington Holt. In under ½ mile you reach this woodland on your left and continue beside it. Avoid a bridle way to the right. Instead, turn left to walk in the fringe of the wood. Then turn down into the wood, avoiding an unofficial path ahead.

You come to a triangle of paths at the lower end of the wood. Leave the main muddy track here and fork right, keeping to the South Downs Way. You pass a layered hedge on the right and come immediately to cross paths. Go straight on down to Jevington Church in the valley.

Follow instructions above under the heading: 'To return from Jevington to Folkington'.

Walk 7: Berwick Station to Chalvington, Ripe and Upper Dicker
Michelham Priory to Arlington and Arlington Reservoir

Just north of the Downs we find quiet byways to ancient villages, religious houses and more modern water holes.

Starting Point: (long walk) Berwick Station **GR**526067
Or (short walk) Car Park with toilets at Arlington Reservoir **GR**527075
Map: OS Explorer 123 **Terrain:** Mainly flat
Distances: 10 miles or 6 miles omitting Chalvington and Ripe.
Warning: Allow plenty of time to find your way across fields, especially on the long walk. A map and compass are essential.
Local Information: 1. Arlington Reservoir was formed 1969 - 1971 by cutting off a meander of the River Cuckmere with a dam made of clay faced with concrete. It is now a beautiful lake with a circular trail of 4 kilometres. It is also a nature reserve attracting many species of birds and butterflies.
2. St Bede`s School in Upper Dicker was originally a country retreat, built by Horatio Bottomley who founded the paper, John Bull in 1906. He was a popular self-made man and was elected an independent M.P. His unsound financial speculations caught up with him and in 1922 he was sent to prison for fraud. He died in 1933 and his ashes were scattered on the Downs above Alfriston where his racehorses had been exercised.

The Churches

Chalvington Church, may have been dedicated to **St Thomas a Becket** and later dedicated to **St Bartholomew.** It is a simple, late 13th century church consisting of nave, chancel, bell turret and modern porch. The Saxon name, 'Cealfing tun' means the farm of Cealfa, the calf. In Domesday it is called Calvintone or Caveltone but no church is mentioned. A church was here in1291 when Pope Nicholas 1V levied taxes. It is built of flint with stone quoins. The nave is considerably larger than the

Chalvington

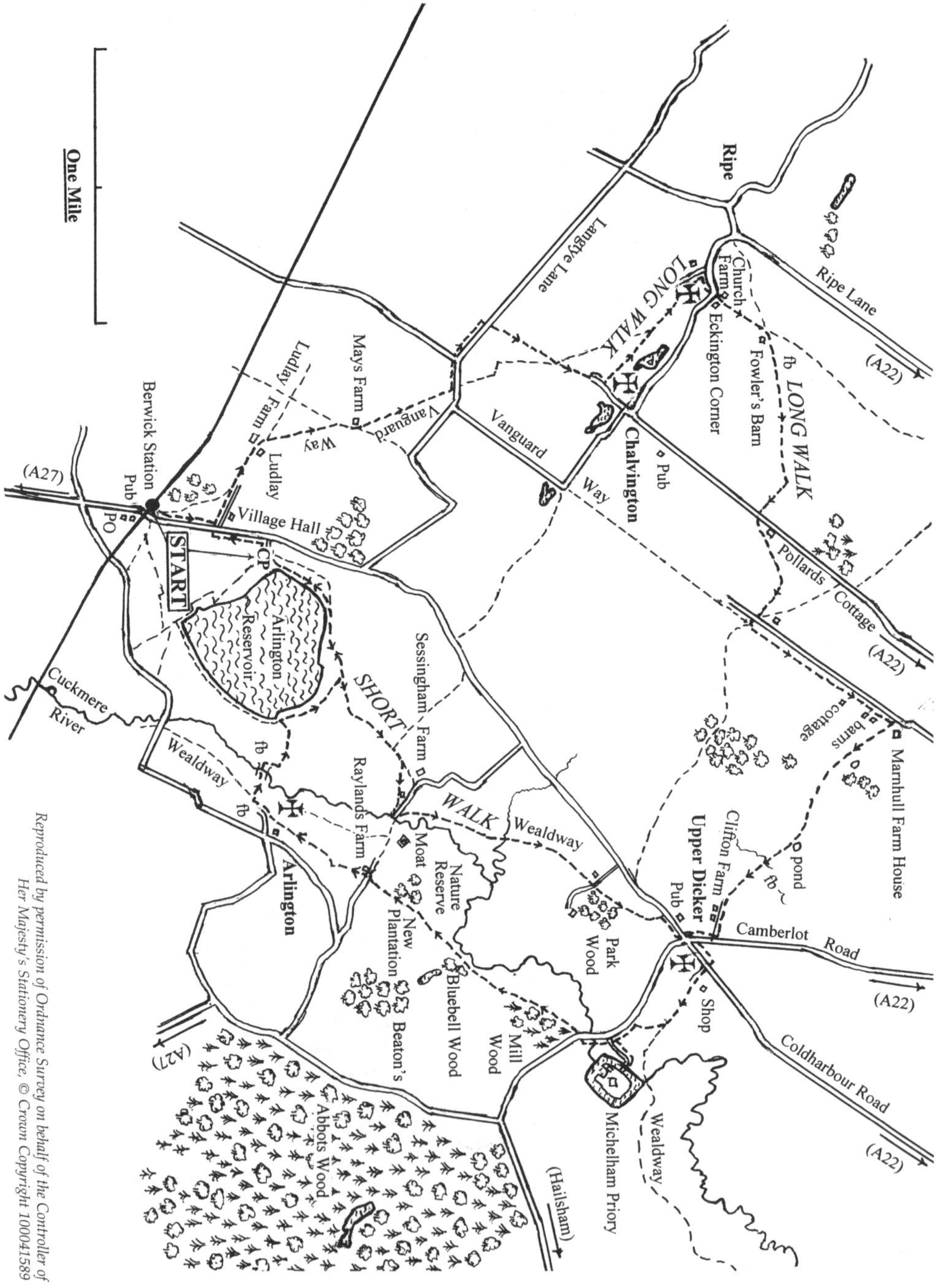
One Mile
Ripe
Langtye Lane
LONG WALK
Church Farm
Eckington Corner
Fowler's Barn
fb
LONG WALK
Ripe Lane
(A22)
Chalvington
Pub
Vanguard Way
Mays Farm
Vanguard Way
Ludlay Farm
Ludlay
Berwick Station
Pub
PO
(A27)
Village Hall
START
CP
Arlington Reservoir
SHORT
WALK
Sessingham Farm
Raylands Farm
Cuckmere River
Wealdway
fb
Arlington
Moat
Nature Reserve
New Plantation
Bluebell Wood
Beaton's
Mill Wood
Wealdway
Park Wood
Pollards Cottage
(A22)
cottage
barns
Marnhull Farm House
Clifton Farm
pond
fb
Upper Dicker
Pub
Camberlot Road
(A22)
Shop
Coldharbour Road
(A22)
Michelham Priory
Wealdway
(Hailsham)
Abbots Wood
(A27)

Ripe

chancel. The east window has intersecting tracery in Decorated style. Two tiny windows are above the chancel; one contains a piece of old glass. A panel in the northeast window of the nave has 13th century glass depicting an archbishop.

Ripe Church, St John the Baptist is under ½ mile away from Chalvington and linked by a delightful footpath. Once again, no church is mentioned in Domesday. In 1100 William Malfield presented the advowson to Lewes Priory. The church stands at Eckington Corner and in 1573 it was called 'Rype alias Eckyngton'. At the Dissolution in 1539, Henry V111`s henchman, Thomas Cromwell acquired Ripe or Eckington among his other vast estates. The present church has 13th century nave and south porch, 14th century chancel in Decorated style and 15th century Perpendicular tower. The west doorway has a Pelham buckle on either side (See Introduction). Windows in the nave and tower are also Perpendicular. A tall arch leads from the nave into the tower. The chancel arch is high and wide. The nave roof has two tie beams supporting king posts. Both nave and chancel are spacious. The chancel has a fine curvilinear east window of five lights. It contains ten separate remains of 14th century glass.

Upper Dicker, Holy Trinity stands on common land known as 'dyker'. The name may come from the Latin 'dicora' and here may refer to 10 acres or to the 10 rod dickers of iron paid in tax, a reminder of the old iron industry. The church is more recent; it was consecrated in 1843. The architect, Mr Donathorne chose a simple Norman style design, combining Sussex flint with Caen stone. The church is pleasant, light and welcoming.

The Gatehouse, Michelham Priory

Michelham Priory. The Saxon `micel ham` is a large water meadow. In 1229 Gilbert d`Aquila founded an Augustinian Priory of the Holy Trinity here at a bend in the River Cuckmere. Ordained priests gave up worldly things to become canons, known as the Black Canons. They divided their time between prayer and service to the community. Michelham Priory was near the main route between Battle and Lewes. Travellers would find shelter here in the priory. 1374 – 1417 Prior Leem kept the estate running smoothly. He is responsible for the construction of the moat, the longest in England and the gatehouse (1388). After him, the priory deteriorated and canons flouted all the rules. In 1537 Henry V111 seized the priory, the church was demolished, the wealth went to the king and the estate went to Thomas Cromwell. In 1540 after the fall and execution of T. Cromwell, the crown held the estate. In1556 the estate passed to private hands. Most notable, Herbert Pelham, grandson of Thomas Pelham of Laughton made Michelham his home in 1587. He greatly changed and enlarged the building Today Sussex Archaeological Society is in charge. The Priory is open from March to 31st October. There is a shop and a restaurant. Phone 01323 844224

Arlington Church, St Pancras stands on the site of a Roman cemetery. Roman bricks are above the Saxon round head window to the right of the porch. This window and the 'long and short' quoins of the nave are part of the Saxon church. A wattle and daub church may have been destroyed in fire. Signs of fires were found when the nave floor was excavated in 19th century. The Saxon north wall of the nave was removed in 13th century when a Decorated north aisle and arches were added. Besides the Saxon window, two Perpendicular windows are south in the nave. The north chapel is Norman with two lancet windows in the north wall. In the east wall a Decorated window replaced two lancets. The chancel also has a Decorated east window. The heads of King Edward 111 and Queen Phillipa are depicted at the top. There is a small leper window south in the chancel. It is Transition-Norman. The tower, of the same period 12th – 13th century, is quite short and has an eight-sided spire. The church owes much to Reverend Thomas Bunstan who took on the neglected church in 1889. He re-tiled the leaking roof, re-shingled the spire, lowered the floor in the nave to enhance the pillars of the arcade, reinforced the tower, restored the bells and removed the ceilings to reveal the fine roofs. Note the 15th century nave roof with king posts and rafters. He also removed an insecure gallery, rebuilt the porch using existing stone, redecorated walls, preserving the murals, opened up the north chapel that had been enclosed for use as a school and moved the school children to a nearby purpose built school house. He died in 1916.

Arlington

The Long Walk

See page 39 for the start of the Short Walk.

From Berwick Station head north, passing the village stores on the right and detached houses on the left. In ¼ mile you reach the Village Hall on the left. Turn left.

From the Car Park of Arlington Reservoir return to the road and turn left, heading south. Walk on the grass verge for ¼ mile to the Village Hall on the right. Turn right.

Pass the Village Hall on your right and walk up the pleasant, narrow avenue leading to Ludlay Farm. You pass the handsome farmhouse and pleasant garden on your right.

Go through a gate with footpath arrows and Vanguard Way sign and continue through trees to an open field. Stop! The footpath is not well marked.

Cross the field diagonally right but do not go to the far corner. Instead, veer to the right and make for a gap in the hedge about 100 metres from the corner. Here is a footbridge and stile into the next field. Keep on course up to Mays Farm ahead. You are still on Vanguard Way heading northwest.

At a track in front of the big grey brick house, turn right and you come to the farmyard. Cross the yard diagonally right but avoid the road on the right.

This is still Vanguard Way leading to a steep stile into a wide field. Cross the field diagonally left. Just short of the far corner, turn left into the next field. Follow the hedge on the right as far as the road, Langtye Lane. A lone house is across the road. *Vanguard Way goes off to the right.*

You turn left away from Vanguard Way. Avoid a path to the right and keep on the road to a junction. Fork to the right and continue on Langtye Lane for 200 metres. Here on the right is a gap in the hedge and a bridleway with a view to Chalvington Church.

Turn right and walk up the straight bridleway to the church.

At Chalvington Church pass the entrance porch on your left and go through gates to take the easy field footpath overlooked by the distant Downs on the left. In ½ mile you reach Ripe Church.

Go past the south porch then the tower of Ripe Church and continue along the little avenue, passing the old Rectory. The avenue opens onto crossways in the village. Avoid footpaths to the left but turn right on the lane to nearby Church Farm on the corner.

Turn left to enter Church Farm and veer right. Go past stables to the arena at the back. Pass the arena on your right and you take a bridleway heading north. It is enclosed with high hedges. In ¼ mile you pass the tumbledown remains of Fowlers Barn.

Turn right here into open fields and veer left to head northeast. Cross the left corner of the field to a footbridge over a stream. Go over to the next big field and turn right following the stream behind a rough hedge on your right. Ahead and left is a tall thick hedge. You have to go through this. The farmer has provided a gate at the lower end. The right of way, about 100 metres north does not exist but there is a fence 200 metres north. Take your pick!

When you have chosen your way into the next field, cross diagonally left to the far corner. Here you can cross the boundary and turn right into an enclosed path leading to a byway.

On the other side there stands a pretty cottage and a barking dog. Make friends with the dog and follow the cottage driveway to an arena at the back. Step over an improvised fence and look into the corner on the far left. Here is a narrow overgrown way, hampered by a stile through a prickly hedge.

When you have fought your way through these obstacles, head northeast over a field to a farm gate. Go through and cross to a farm gate in the next field. Markers show that you now hug the field boundary on the left for 150 metres. You then cross to the other side and follow the boundary on your right. Pass a small shelter on the right. At the road join Vanguard Way again.

Turn left for a welcome saunter on this shady lane. Immediately pass Mount Pleasant Farm on the left. In ½ mile, after a cottage then two barns, you come to the white-washed Marnhull Farm House. Turn right just before this house.

You are now heading southeast across open fields for 1 mile. Pass woodland up on the left then keep on course with the aid of yellow arrows on gateposts and using stiles with little footbridges in the hedges. Fortunately waymarkers abound. After the fourth field, you pass a wild life pond on the left then head for a strong new footbridge. You can at last see the buildings of Clifton Farm up ahead.

Once through the gate to the farm, follow the concrete road round to the left. It leads for 300 metres through buildings to Camberlot Road in Upper Dicker. Turn right on the pavement up to a staggered road crossing. Turn left into Coldharbour Road. You are on the long distance footpath the Wealdway

***The Short Walk joins here.** Both walks pass St Bede`s School.

Pass Upper Dicker Church on the right. The village shop with post office is next. Turn right here, still on the Wealdway. Pass the shop on the left then go through an alleyway to a field at the back of houses. Continue across the playing fields of St Bede`s School. You cross the left hand corner of the field then keep on course across horse paddocks. In 250 metres the Wealdway veers left. You have to turn right crossing another paddock to the farm gate and the main road to Hailsham. Turn left on this road and in 150 metres you reach the entrance to Michelham Priory on the left.

After visiting Michelham Priory (at least as far as the gatehouse where you can see the moat and water mill), return to the road and turn left to walk on the verge. The road narrows to a bridge over the River Cuckmere. In 50 metres turn right into a footpath heading southwest for the homeward walk.

Mill Wood is on your left and you hug this for 300 metres. You then come to a small field. Cross to the farm gate opposite and **beware**! Despite the notice asking you to close it, this gate does not lead to the footpath. Instead, take the farm track on the right of the gate.

The track veers to the right. The path then resumes its southwest course with the river on the right. Go through a little bluebell wood and emerge to a large sloping meadow above the river. Do not be tempted down to the bridge on the right but look ahead up to the far left corner of the meadow.

Arlington

You leave the river as it curves away and go up to this corner where you enter a nature reserve. (A detour to an old moat away to the right is not on our schedule!). Keep heading southwest to go under power cables. At an open field, the path has been slightly diverted to the right and you keep on course through a new tree plantation to reach a farm lane.

Cross diagonally right to an enclosed path past Raylands Farm on the right. Hug the hedge on the left. Veer right to walk across fields on a path leading straight to Arlington Church.

From Arlington Church go through the lychgate and you will see the pub on the village lane ahead. Turn right away from the pub and walk for a few metres along the road to a field. Follow the Wealdway again. It crosses the field slightly left and goes over a footbridge.

You leave the Wealdway here and make for the larger footbridge over the River Cuckmere. Look back to Arlington Church. Ahead, the banks of Arlington Reservoir can be seen.

Go up to the reservoir and turn right into woodland. The clear circuit track takes you northwest through the wood. In 300 metres you pass the bridleway familiar to the 'short walkers'. Here the circuit track curves west and south to return to the **Car Park**.

To return to the **Berwick Station**, go through the car park to the road. Turn left and follow the road for ½ mile.

Note: It is possible to extend the walk by taking the path round the south side of Arlington Reservoir.

Arlington Reservoir

The Short Walk

Arlington Reservoir Car Park to Upper Dicker and Michelham Priory

Go down through the picnic tables to the waters' edge and turn left. Here is a manicured path heading north. There are occasional tempting seats. Look east across the water to Arlington Church and south to the Downs.

Ignore footpaths to the left until in 1 kilometre you come to a marked bridleway. Turn left here away from the reservoir circuit. You are compensated by views over the gently rolling fields of the Low Weald.

Head northeast for 500 metres on the well-defined path, going under overhead power lines. Keep on course towards Sessingham Farm. Ignore the large white footpath sign and stay on this side of the hedge. Veer right and hug the hedge on the left. Pass the converted farmhouse and you reach another white board.

Find the footpath through trees ahead. Cross a footbridge and follow the overhung path for 30 metres when you turn left on the Wealdway long distance footpath.

This follows the course of the little River Cuckmere on your right. Avoid a path to the left and keep on course northeast. The river departs to the right and you have a backwater for company. In 1 kilometre you come to cottages and a crossroad at Parkwood Farm.

Cross the lane diagonally left to enter a field through a farm gate. Follow the edge of Park Wood on your right and admire the various trees: oak, ash sweet chestnut among them. After the wood keep on course across an elevated field and then a small golf course. Turn left into an enclosed path to rejoin the Berwick road, two miles north of Berwick Station.

Turn right for Upper Dicker and pass the pub on the left. At crossroads go straight on. You have joined the long walk here and follow instructions on page 37*.

Walk 8: Chiddingly to Hellingly

('ly' pronounced as in 'high')

We walk along the southern edge of Andredsweald the ancient impenetrable forest. Now agriculture has broken up the forest so that we wander through woods and fields and cross the many streams on footbridges.

Starting Point: Village Car Park opposite the church in the little access lane
GR544143 **Map:** OS Explorer 123
Terrain: Mainly flat, only gentle slopes. Occasional rough patches.
Distance: 7 Miles
Local Information:

1. Three well spaced inns can be found on this walk! (See map).
2. The Six Bells Inn in Chiddingly has retained its name but the church acquired two more bells for the Millenium and now has eight bells.
3. As an aid to pronunciation, note three local liars: Helling<u>ly</u>, Chidding<u>ly</u> and East Hoath<u>ly</u>. 'Three lies but all true'.
4. The name 'Gun Hill' recalls the days when Wealden iron went to make cannons.
5. Peke`s House is a private medieval building where the ghost of Sir Richard Milward is said to be seeking his daughter.

The Churches

Chiddingly

Chiddingly Parish Church is in a 'leah', a Saxon clearing in the forest. In Domesday the name 'Cetelingei' is given. There is no evidence of a Saxon church on this site. Carved Norman stones were discovered in the foundations when the Victorians rebuilt the chancel in 1804. The chancel arch is 13th century. The nave is square with a high kingpost roof. A magnificent tower arch is at the west end. Arcades dividing the nave from the aisles were built in late 13th century. Windows in the north and south aisles are early Perpendicular. The thick walls of the tower support a stone spire, one of only three ancient stone towers in Sussex. Dallington and Northiam are the others. This spire is octagonal with four distinctive pinnacles at its base. It overlooks a scattered community and eight tuneful bells ring

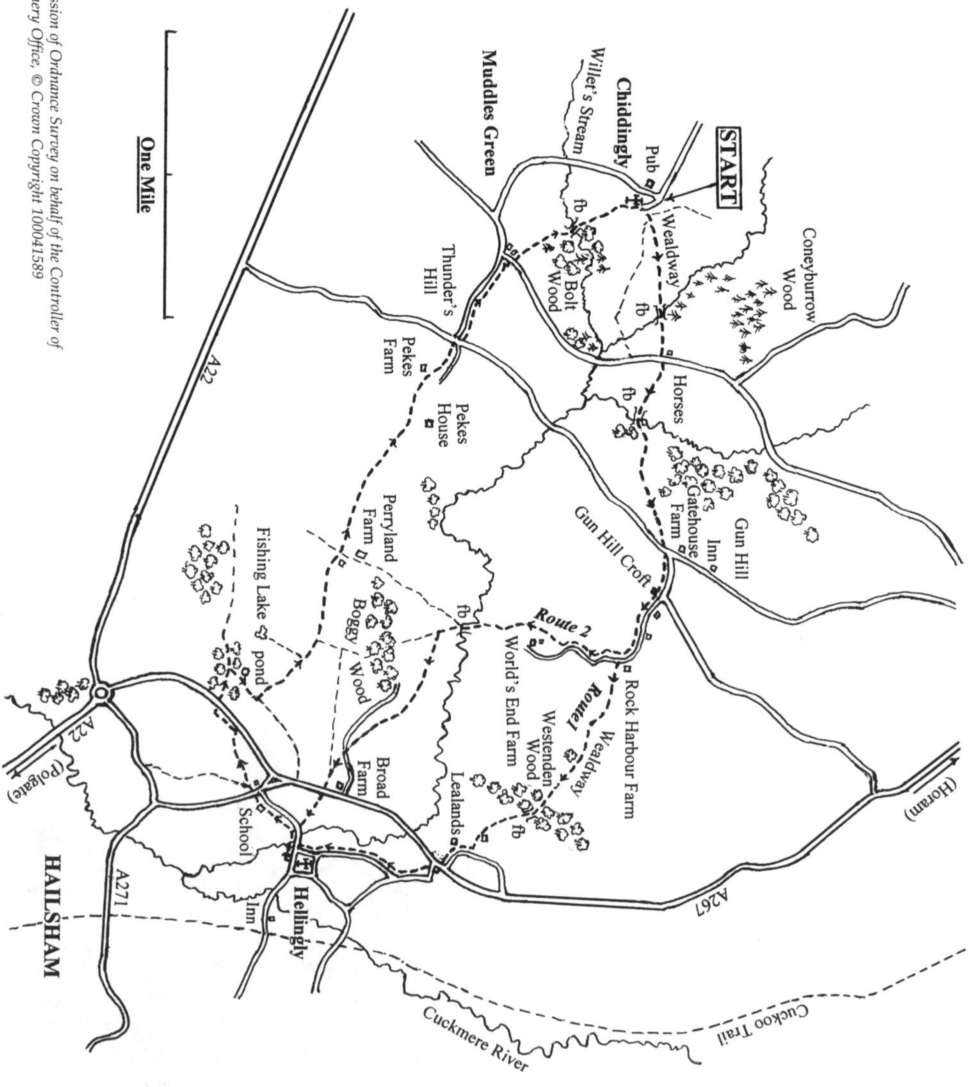

Reproduced by permission of Ordnance Survey on behalf of the Controller of Her Majesty's Stationery Office, © Crown Copyright 100041589

out. As at Ripe and Laughton, Pelham buckles are at the tower door (See Introduction). Apart from the porch, the church is built of local sandstone. The south transept was built in 17th century to hold the large alabaster Jefferay Monument. This early 17th century monument with erect figures is almost unique. Sir John Jefferay is actually reclining and leaning on his elbow, his wife Dame Alice is also recumbent in a lower segment but his daughter Elizabeth and her husband Sir Edward Montague stand proudly on either side. Another Elizabeth, the grand daughter kneels below. Sir John was chief Baron of the Exchequer under Queen Elizabeth. He died in 1578. The monument was dismantled and restored in 1996. There are other monuments to the Jefferay family who lived at Chiddingly Place, now Place Farm. The Peke branch of the family has a wall monument nearby. It shows Sir Awdray Harvey, his wife, seven daughters and two sons. For more details, see M. A. Lower`s 'Parochial history of Chiddingly'.

Hellingly

Hellingly Church, St Peter and St Paul stands on a Saxon site. Originally the ciric or Saxon cemetery was round. It was enlarged at an early date and became oval. Photographs taken from the air show the shape of the ciric, even vestiges of the four Saxon entrances. The oldest part of today`s church is the chancel. Here the Transition Norman windows are plain lancets on the outside and inside have banded shafts, The east window and north chapel parade are Early English. The tower, according to Pevsner is Georgian. It was rebuilt in 1836. The church was restored in 1869. The shape of the village has a delightful continuity with pretty tile hung cottages facing the oval churchyard.

The Walk

From Chiddingly Church return to the little access lane and turn right. You immediately come to footpath signs on the left. Enter the field and fork left on the Wealdway (WW). For the next 1½ miles you will be heading east on this long distance footpath. It is clearly marked with signposts, stiles, footbridges and footprints.

In the first fields look back to the church as you follow the tracks of walkers and go gently down to woodland. Cross a footbridge and continue to a quiet lane. Pass Orchard Cottage on the left.

Cross the lane diagonally left to a field entrance for horse riders. As you proceed through the field beside the hedge on the left you may catch glimpses of the riders. Follow the hedge down towards woodland. Cross a footbridge on the left and climb up through trees to an elevated field with woodland on the left. In ¼ mile you reach another road at Gatehouse Farm.

Farmhouse, West Street, near Gun Hill

Cross diagonally left to Swansbrook Lane and walk past a converted oasthouse. In 250 metres you come to a small grass triangle and a wide double entrance way. Avoid the first track to Gun Hill Croft. Turn right at the second entrance. The WW sign seems to be lost in undergrowth.

Here is a private track once known as West Street. (West Street Farm is among the names at the entrance). It leads to several houses including World`s End Farm. Follow the Wealdway along this track past the occasional farmhouse for 250 metres. After a pond and Rock Harbour Farm, the Wealdway goes off to the left.

You have a choice of routes to Hellingly:

1. The Wealdway goes up through trees to a field. Pass farm buildings on the left. After the last barn, veer right towards a gap in the facing hedge. In the next

field follow the wire fence on the left. In 500 metres at a small copse, cross to the left to follow the hedge, now on the right.

Avoid a path to the left. In another 70 metres, turn right into Westenden Wood. Follow the path down to cross a footbridge and climb out of the wood. There is a tall straight hedge in front of you.

Hug this hedge on your left and you come to the anomaly of Lealands. A house on the left has an incongruous flint arch with a clock. Keep on course through a rough piece of ground with a small grove of silver leafed poplars. Go down some steps to a shady lane, North Street.

Turn right and follow the lane. At a largish house on the right the lane bends to the left and leads to the A267. Do not go straight across. Take the short driveway on the right then cross with care to another lane opposite.

Turn right immediately and climb up out of the lane to a footpath with a view of the Downs. Make this short cut southeast over a field to rejoin the lane and turn right. At a road fork, follow Church Lane to the right and saunter down to Hellingly with its big church in the centre.

2. An alternative route to Hellingly with fewer stiles and minimal way marking:

Continue on the track, once known as West Street, for another 300 metres then turn right up to an opening in the hedge and a footpath. (If you reach World's End Farm on the track, you have gone too far).

Go diagonally left over a rough field and find a little footbridge to a wonky stile in the hedge. The next field slopes down gently to a stream, shaded by trees. On the way down you pass two farmhouses on your left. Before you reach the trees shading the stream at the bottom, go through a gap *in the hedge on the left.*

You have entered a rough little meadow. Turn right and follow the stream, Bull River hidden in trees, to a long new footbridge. The running water below will enter the Cuckmere near Hellingly.

Cross the footbridge to a wide sloping field. Boldly climb the slope ahead. At the top you can see Boggy Wood ahead and in the distance to the left the welcome sight of Broad Farm. Head for this distant farm, keeping Boggy Wood on your right. (At the time of writing, the farmer has left a clear cut path through his crop). You leave Boggy Wood behind and walk parallel to the farm track on the right. Gradually approach the farm track.

After one kilometre from the footbridge, leave the wide field and cross the farm track, passing a big metal gate on the left. Opposite a footpath takes you southeast. In 100 metres you are joined by a path from the right. Veer left to another metal gate. Go through to a rough path past horse paddocks on the right and an unfriendly bank on the left. Go through a short, narrow enclosed way and pass a house on the left. You reach the A267.

Broad Farm, an 18th century farmhouse is beside you on the left; its grand façade aloof from all the bustle of the 21st century. It belongs more to the life of a bygone Hellingly whose church looms large across the road.

Cross the A267 with care to the footpath opposite. Veer right over a field to a lane. At the lane turn left, cross a bridge over our familiar stream and continue to Hellingly Church up on the left.

The return route from Hellingly: with your back to the entrance to the church, turn right and go down to the road. Cross diagonally left to take the lane westwards towards A267. *If you chose route 2, it will already be familiar.* Go over the bridge and keep on the lane to pass a primary school on the left. At the nearby T-junction there is a house opposite. Just to the left of the house a farm gate leads into a field. Once inside the field you find a finger post. The footpath runs parallel to the main road on your right. At the second gap in the hedge on the right, go through to the main A267. Turn left to walk along the wide verge for 150 metres.

Cross with care to the footpath sign opposite. Here you have an overgrown bumpy surface to the narrow path under a band of trees. In 200 metres at a footpath sign, turn right to emerge from the trees.

Head northeast back towards Hellingly Church in sight across the fields. Pass earthworks and a pond on the left. Veer left to the corner of the field where another sign directs you onto a firm track for anglers. Turn left onto this track and follow it for 150 metres as far as large ornate gates. Leave the track here as it makes a right-angled turn towards another lake on the left. You go straight on and squeeze through the side of the large gates.

Hellingly

Keep on course on a softer track through open country with distant woodland. In fact Boggy Wood is away to the right. Pass a path off to the right. **Then take Care!** As soon as the grassy track stars veering left and southwards, get to the other side of the sporadic hedge on your right (you may already be on the correct side!).

In any case, you need to keep to a northwest course. The grassy path goes along the southern edge of a field where you can see the buildings of Perryland farm ahead to the right. The footpath continues on an enclosed way leading to cottages at Perryland – no sign of a pear tree now to provide fruit for that delicious drink!

At cross paths go through a gate and continue northwest on a firm rubble track. In one kilometre you reach Pekes Farm. Pass a pond and continue to the driveway to Peke's House – not even a glimpse of the house nor the ghost can be seen (see note 5 above).The driveway leads to crossroads on Thunder's Hill.

Turn left then immediately right into a lane signposted to Chiddingly. In ½ mile you come to another road junction (Muddles Green is to the left and tile hung cottages are opposite). Turn right then immediately left into an enclosed path. It passes gardens then enters Bolt Wood. Cross Willett's stream that divides Muddles Green from Chiddingly. In ¼ mile the path opens to farmland then playing fields. Chiddingly Church can be seen ahead. You can approach it from the cemetery on the right or continue through the sports field to a gate into the churchyard.

Walk 9: Herstmonceux Church to Wartling and Hooe

Three valiant churches overlook the marshes on the northern edge of Manxey Level where the many streams drain into the sea at Norman`s Bay.

Starting Point: Herstmonceux Church, 1½ miles southeast of the village.
GR643103 **Map:** OS Explorer 124
Distance: 7 ½ Miles **Terrain:** Flat with some gentle climbs. Short patches of boggy land. Look out for marsh birds.
Warning: Do not attempt this walk after prolonged rainfall! Much of the land has been reclaimed from the sea and some of the paths are neglected.
Local Information:

1. ¼ mile east of the church stands Herstmonceux Castle, a medieval brick building, complete with moat. It is now an international study centre, part of Queen`s University, Canada. For information on times and conditions of visiting, phone 01323 833816.
2. Nearby, further east still is the Observatory Science Centre. The Royal Observatory of Greenwich moved here in 1948 and you will see the six domes. To visit, phone 01323 832731.
3. Waller`s Haven was originally just another stream through the Levels. In the last century it was widened and a pumping station installed at Horse Bridge to facilitate drainage into the sea,

The Churches

All Saints, Herstmonceux has a large churchyard with glorious views over the levels to the Downs. Herstmonceux gained its name from the marriage of a member of the local family, 'de Herst' to a scion of a Norman family 'de Muncens' from Monceux in Calvados some time in 13th century. Before that, the name 'Herst' (wooded Hill) appeared in Domesday. With some truth a parishioner describes the church here today as a 'hotchpotch'. The looming tower in stone was built in 12th century in this fine strategic position for defence. It was here before the castle and must have overseen an earlier stone nave. It is in fact part of the west end of nave. The tower supports a later broach spire. The present chancel and north chapel are of brick. The chancel arch is Decorated. There is a fine brass to Sir William de Fiennes (1402) on the chancel floor. His son Roger began work on the castle in 1440. The north

Herstmonceux

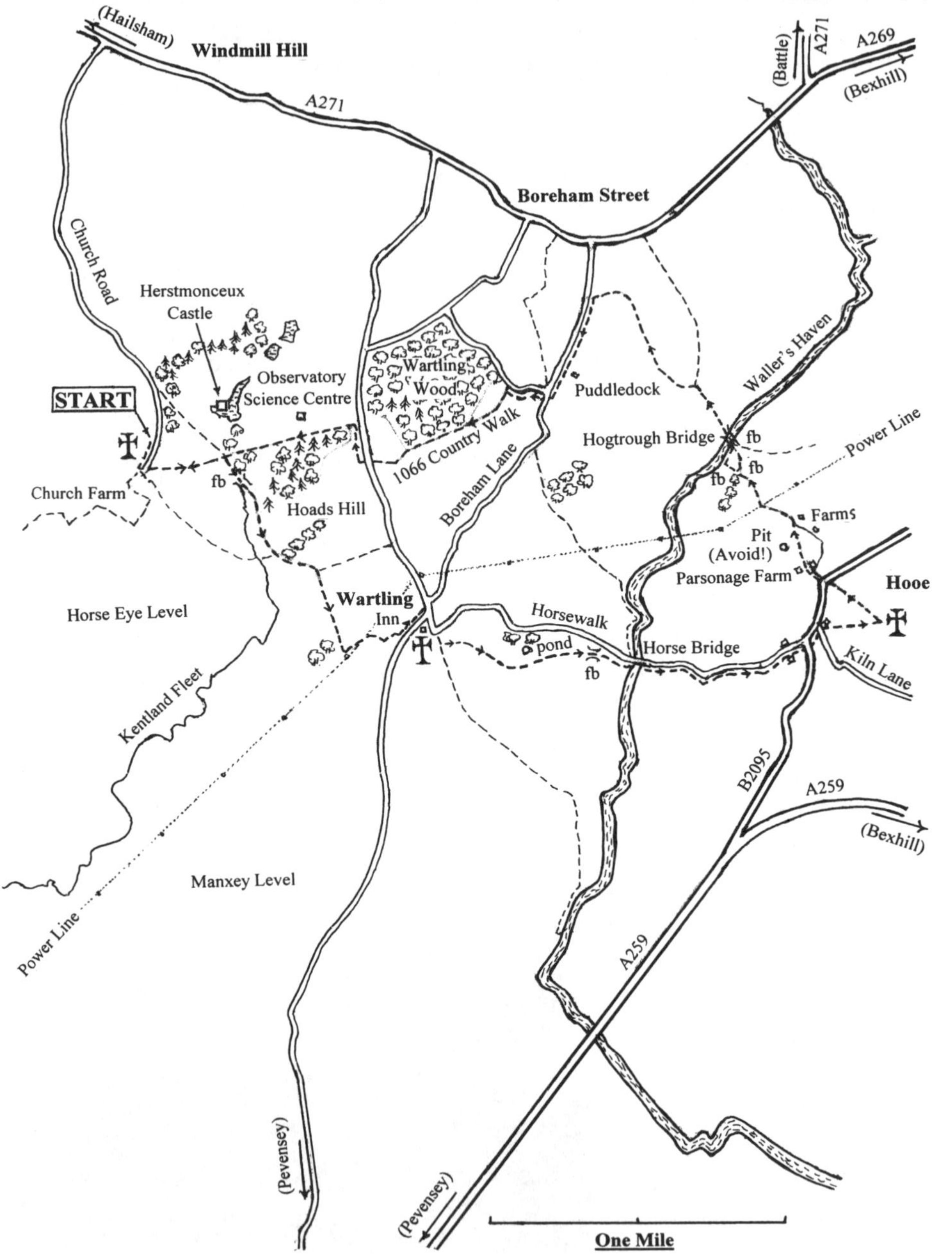
(Hailsham)
Windmill Hill
A271
(Battle)
A271
A269
(Bexhill)
Boreham Street
Church Road
Herstmonceux
Castle
Wartling
Wood
Observatory
Science Centre
START
Puddledock
Waller's Haven
Hogtrough Bridge
fb
Power Line
1066 Country Walk
Boreham Lane
Church Farm
Hoads Hill
Farms
Pit
(Avoid!)
Parsonage Farm
Hooe
Wartling
Inn
Horse Eye Level
Horsewalk
pond
Horse Bridge
Kiln Lane
Kentland Fleet
B2095
A259
(Bexhill)
Manxey Level
Power Line
A259
(Pevensey)
(Pevensey)
One Mile

'Dacre' chapel was added in 1450 and is one of the earliest examples of church brickwork in Sussex. A magnificent tomb was installed in 1534 with two effigies representing Thomas, eighth Lord Dacre and his son, Sir Thomas Fiennes. This tomb probably came from Battle Abbey when it was dismantled and the figures originally represented the Hooe brothers. The nave has a medieval king post roof. Both aisles have Victorian dormer windows. Many notable people have visited this church and some are buried here. See the church guide for more information.

Wartling

The Church of St Mary Magdalene, Wartling stands on a small hill with views across to Pevensey and Eastbourne. It was probably built on the site of a chapel attached to St Mary in Hastings Castle. The chapel existed in 1090. The present building dates back to the 13th century. The north and south walls of the chancel and the west end of the nave are of this period. The east wall of the chancel was altered around 1800 when the east window of the Good Shepherd replaced a lancet window. The belfry and the north aisle are 14th century. Outside the south aisle are a Pelham Buckle (See Introduction) and a Catherine Wheel, symbol of St Catherine. The daughter of Sir John Pelham, Katherine died in 1459. Perhaps the south aisle was built then as a chapel of remembrance. The north doorway is 15th century with a Victorian porch. The south porch is older, 1737. A recent addition is the remarkable lectern, carved in elm in the shape of a heron by Martin Wynn Pierce. It reminds us of the Wartling heronry. Two radar stations stood nearby during the Second World War. RAF servicemen are remembered in a tablet at the east end of the north porch.

Hooe Church, St Oswald is in a lonely elevated spot overlooking the marshes. The unusual name is from the Saxon 'hoh' meaning a spur of land. The Domesday version is 'Hov'. The church was known as 'All Saints' in 16th century, suggesting a Saxon origin. The font with a square bowl may be Saxon. The ancient dug-out chest is now believed to be 13th century. The northeast chapel survives from 13th century. The rest of the church was rebuilt in 15th century. Chancel, nave, west tower and south porch are all Perpendicular. There are remarkable corbels that would have held a wide heavy beam for a rood screen. Some of the glass at the top of the east window is 15th century. The delightful modern kneelers depict some of the houses of Hooe. Outside on the south side there are some grotesque heads as label stops. The tower has a northeast staircase turret.

The Walk

Continue south on Church Road, passing the church on your right. The road ends in Church Farm. Turn left into a tarmac yard, following '1066 Country Walk'. At nearby cross tracks with a 'College Private' notice on the left, go straight on into a strip of woodland.

Herstmonceux Castle

You soon emerge to **dramatic scenery**; Hermonceux Castle stands in its own grounds on the left and the large dome of an old observatory is up on the wooded hill ahead. '1066 Country Walk' goes straight on. We follow it down through the field for 50 metres to a signpost then turn right away from this main footpath. (You have to go round the signpost to find your arrow).

If you are in doubt about the marshes, you can keep straight on along 1066 Country Walk for ½ mile then turn right at Wartling Road for nearly a mile of road walking to Wartling Church.

For the marsh way to Wartling, go through a gap in the corner of the field and you will find way markers. Cross a stream, known as Kentfield Fleet. Arrows direct you so that you walk up along the lower slope of the hill on your left. Below are drained marshes. Avoid the unmarked paths below.

The path curves to the left round the base of Hoads Hill. You have a well-worn path here and it continues across a field, heading southeast. In 200 metres you emerge through the hedge boundary to a wide view over the marshes. *If in doubt, turn left and follow an enclosed track to Wartling Road. Turn right and walk for 500 metres beside the road to Wartling.*

Otherwise keep on course southeast but veering slightly to the right to find a wide opening in the field boundary below. On the way you pass a small copse on the left. In the next field avoid a distant house on the ridge to the left. Instead head towards power cables. Just to the left of the nearest pylon you will find a path entrance into a copse. Turn left to follow a rough track climbing up through trees for 150 metres. Eventually you emerge to the garden of a largish brick house. You are now up above the marshes. Turn left to pass between the house and a brick bungalow. Go down the driveway to the road in Wartling. Turn left for Wartling Church.

From Wartling Church return to the road and turn right to crossroads dominated by an inn on the corner. Turn sharp right beside the inn and you will see a narrow lane opposite, 'Horsewalk', known locally as 'Jacob`s Ladder'. *If you are in a hurry or wish to avoid further marshland, Horsewalk will take you directly to Hooe.*

For the scenic route, pass the inn car park and a little white board cottage on the left and enter the private farm track ahead. Almost immediately, you come to a footpath on the left and enjoy a view over land once under the sea. You cross fields diagonally left heading southeast. Keep to the top of the ridge until you come to a dirt track leading down beside a small wood. You pass it on the left as you descend to a gap in the hedges.

Once through the gap, you are heading due east over the level. There is a pond in the wood on your left. The path veers towards a plantation of willows on the left. Here are two farm gates. Avoid them both and step into the open field on the right. Follow the hedge on the left for 200 metres. There is a footbridge over a ditch and then you continue over the levels to Waller`s Haven. Turn left here to join the road at Horse Bridge.

You may want to linger on the bridge to admire the waters of Waller`s Haven before you take the steady climb eastwards for 1 kilometre to Hooe. At the top you pass two houses, one on either side of the road then emerge to the B2095. Cross to the wide grassy verge opposite and turn left.

At the nearby road junction, turn right into Kiln Lane. Beside the first house in this lane there is a post box then a narrow avenue. Cross to the entrance to this avenue where a concrete way marker on the ground confirms that this is a footpath.

This shady avenue leads to a field and the prospect of Hooe Church. Keep on course with the fence on your right then turn into the churchyard.

From Hooe Church retrace your steps a yard or two to the fenced fields and bear right. You are now following another fence on your left and heading northwest. You have to cross into the next field at a farm gate. As it had no hinges and no fasten, we had to push it over then pick it up again! Go up diagonally left to find a narrow gap in the hedge and the B2095 again.

Cross with care to the track opposite. *It bends to the right and is the easy way to the two farmhouses below.* First see if you can reach them on the public footpath. At the bend in the track look for a concrete marker hidden on the ground. The footpath goes between the white board house, Parsonage Cottage on the left and the neighbouring brick house. Cross a difficult stile into an overgrown garden. Follow the hedge on the left and tackle another tricky stile into a sloping field. From this slight elevation you have a good view over the fields north to distant villages on A271.

Avoid the little wood ahead. Instead, veer to the right across the little valley towards two well-spaced farmhouses. Head for a pedestrian gate next to the further farmhouse. Do not go through the gate *(unless you followed the track round).* Turn left on a straight, elevated path northwest.

Walk along this ridge for 150 metres then turn sharp right. Go under power lines and in the next field bear left down through trees.

Hooe

You come down to the levels beside Waller`s Haven. Cross two footbridges to reach the Haven, then finally Hogtrough Bridge with its concrete slabs and metal rails.

Once across the Haven, the path follows a small stream on the right to take you northwest still. In ¼ mile pass a field boundary on the left (the boundaries here follow the course of the streams). Just after this boundary, turn left away from the main path.

Hooe

Our new path is neglected. *If there have been no improvements by the time you are here, you may have to continue on the main path up to the main road and turn left. Walk along the main road for 250 metres to Boreham Street and turn left.*

With luck, someone will have heeded my protests and you can take the path I found neglected. It follows a reedy stream on the right. Keep to the path as it curves to the right and crosses a footbridge. You then veer left across reedy ground and climb out of the reed bed. Follow the hedge on the left until you find a way

Puddledock

through to the next field. Climb up to Boreham Lane where another unfriendly stile awaits you.

Turn left on this byway and go gently down for 500 metres. On the way you pass the quaint old cottage, Puddledock with a beautiful garden.

At the next lane turn right and go downhill for 100 metres. Turn left into a field at a '1066 Country Walk' sign. We follow this footpath for 1½ miles back to Herstmonceux Church.

First it follows a beech hedge, then the edge of Wartling Wood on the right and offers sea views to the left. After a short track inside the wood, it continues southwest across a field with a hedge on the left and brings you down into Wartling Road.

Turn right to walk up the road. Just before the drive into Herstmonceux Castle, turn left into more woodland. There are glimpes on the right to the Observatory. The path starts to descend on an enclosed way with spaced steps. Finally you emerge from the woodland to the familiar field with **dramatic scenery**. Herstmonceux Castle is on your right.

Keep straight on, retracing your steps through the strip of woodland to Church Farm and Herstmonceux Church.

Walk 10: Pevensey to Westham

The shortest walk in the book is packed with history in a landscape that has changed dramatically over the centuries. When the poor inhabitants of Pevensey were pounded by Romans, Saxons and later by Normans, a natural harbour reached inland for 5 miles

Starting Point 1: Pevensey Castle Car Park where you pay a small fee. There are tearooms, a pub and public toilets. **GR**646048
Starting Point 2: Pevensey and Westham Railway Station **GR**638044
Map: OS Explorer 124 **Terrain:** Well used paths on mainly flat ground
Distance: 1 Mile
Local Information: The outer walls of Pevensey Castle are part of a 3rd century Roman fort, called Anderida. These are the finest Roman remains in Sussex. The Normans built a fortress in the northeast corner of Anderida. 100 years later a medieval castle grew in the southeast corner.

The Churches

St Nicolas Church, Pevensey was built at a time of great prosperity. Pevensey was made one of the 'Cinque Ports' in 1207. (See Introduction). The church of local flint and greensand is spacious with all the elegance of Early English architecture. The tower is half way along the north side so that the bell ringers are in full view of the congregation. The chancel is almost as long as the nave. The prospect from the back of the nave to the chancel takes in pillars that are alternately octagonal and quatrefoil. The pillar holding the weight of the bell tower is double the size of the others. The font of Caen stone is Norman. There is a north aisle and a south aisle with a lady chapel.

Pevensey

St Mary`s Parish Church, Westham. As the name suggests, this basically Norman church was built on a 'hamm' or water meadow to the west

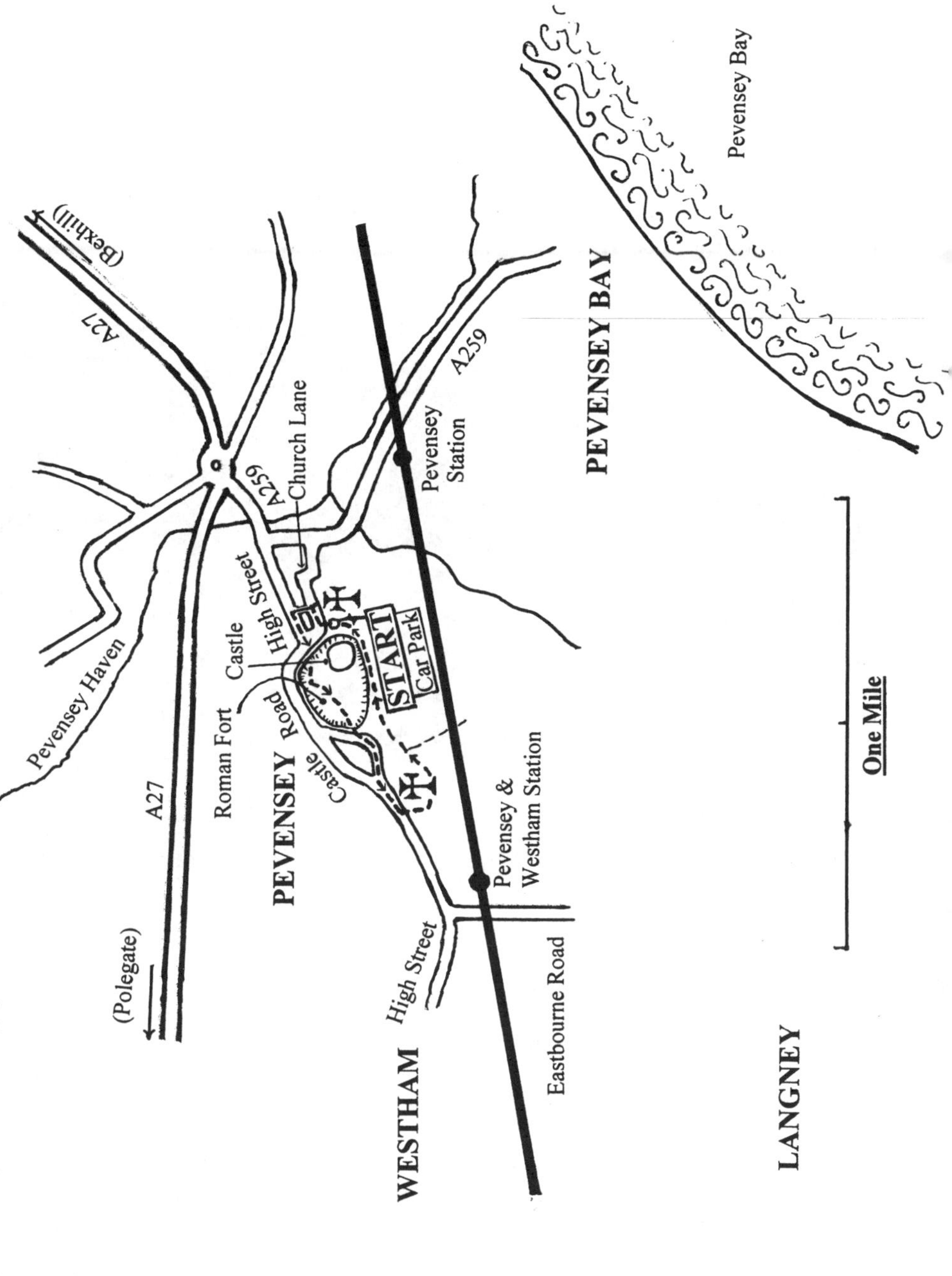
(Bexhill)
A27
Pevensey Bay
PEVENSEY BAY
A259
Church Lane
A259
Pevensey Station
High Street
Castle
START
Car Park
Roman Fort
Castle Road
Pevensey Haven
A27
PEVENSEY
Pevensey & Westham Station
(Polegate)
High Street
Eastbourne Road
WESTHAM
LANGNEY
One Mile

of Pevensey. The original church was cruciform and lacked a tower. Part of this early church survives in the south wall with three round-headed windows and in the round arch of the south transept. The east window in the Priesthaws Chapel in the south transept is Norman. This chapel was used as a private chancery. The massive tower was added in 1300. The north aisle has an Early English arcade. It also has the benefit of large Perpendicular windows. There is an outside tourelle, entered by a door in the north aisle. It probably led to an earlier flat roof. The chancel windows contain some medieval glass. Some of the oldest glass is in the upper part of the east window.

Pevensey Castle entrance

The Walk

Rail travellers start at Westham, go to the High Street, turn right for Westham Church and continue at the first paragraph, page 56.

From Pevensey Castle Car Park, go to the entrance of the car park and turn right into Church Lane to the nearby St Nicolas Church.

Cross to a short lane opposite the church and follow it to the High Street. The old Court House is on your right. Turn left and walk along the High Street to a bend in the road.

Cross with care to the archway entrance in the Roman walls. Go through to the open space in the Roman fortress of Anderida. Veer left on the tarmac path. The Norman castle is on your left. You pass the castle`s entrance bridge and continue down the path to leave the fort by a gate in the walls.

The inhabitants of Anderida spilt outside the walled town. In 410 A.D. the Romans left and the Saxons came, massacred the inhabitants and renamed the town Westham.

Keep on course along the road in Westham. You soon reach St Mary`s Church on your left. *(On the right for rail travellers who join here).*

Go behind the church and turn left to a footpath. At a junction keep straight on, towards Pevensey Castle on the left. The path goes through bushes to a wide sward below the castle. A recreation ground is ahead on the right. After a seat veer right towards this ground then go through a thicket on the left to return to the Car Park. *(Rail travellers go to the start of the walk: 'From Pevensey Castle Car Park...').*

5 Walks
Near Maresfield

View across the Ouse to Isfield Church

Walk 11: Fletching to Maresfield with an extension to Fairwarp

A wealden walk across gentle sloping fields and through patches of woodland that once formed part of the great forest. The hedgerows offer cover to wildlife and fruit in autumn. We visit two ancient parish churches, restored by the Victorians and one late Victorian church in Ashdown Forest.

Starting Point: The free car park in the road opposite the pub in Fletching.
GR429236 **Map:** OS Explorer 135 **Terrain:** Gently undulating
Distances : 7 ½ Miles (shorter walk) or 10 Miles (to include Fairwarp)
The shorter walk has more roads and leaves out Fairwarp. The longer walk on footpaths includes one mile along the Wealdway and a short precipitous descent in Furnace Wood.
Note: A compass will be useful in Park Wood.
Warning: We have to cross the A22 twice, once by underpass to Maresfield and later on a straight stretch that gives good visibility for the return crossing. We also cross the A272 near the golf course.

The Churches

The Parish Church of St Andrew and St Mary the Virgin, Fletching is a large building and begs the question whether there was once a small Saxon church here. 'Flescinges' appears in Domesday but no church is mentioned. The early Norman tower with double light windows must have stood above a very different church. Two windows above the south arcade are Norman. The present cruciform building of 1230 is Early English but has been much restored by the Victorians. The tall broach spire was added in 14th century and is a landmark far and wide. Horsham stone covers the nave and the 15th century porch. In 1880 the roofs were rebuilt, revealing the Decorated clerestory windows. The east window has most unusual geometrical tracery of 13th century. The glass by John Kemp is Victorian. There is 14th century glass in two lancet windows in the south transept and one in the north transept.

Fletching

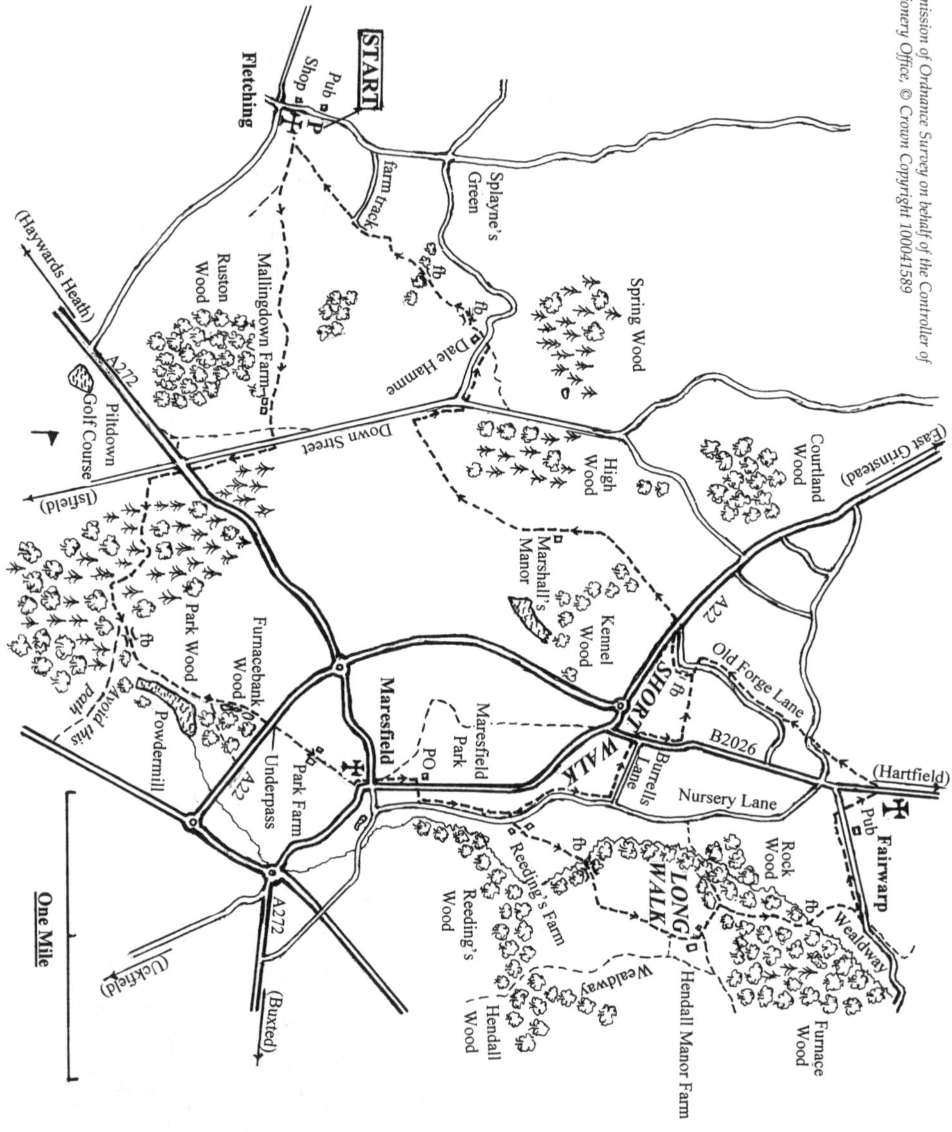
START
Pub
Shop
P
Fletching
farm track
Splayne's Green
Spring Wood
fb
fb
Dale Hamme
Mallingdown Farm
Ruston Wood
(Haywards Heath)
A272
Piltdown Golf Course
Down Street
(Isfield)
High Wood
Courtland Wood
(East Grinstead)
Marshall's Manor
Kennel Wood
A22
Park Wood
Furnacebank Wood
fb
Avoid this path
Powdermill
Maresfield
Maresfield Park
PO
Park Farm
Underpass
A22
SHORT WALK
Old Forge Lane
B2026
Burrells Lane
Nursery Lane
(Hartfield)
Fairwarp
Pub
Rock Wood
LONG WALK
fb
Reeding's Farm
Reeding's Wood
Wealdway
Hendall Manor Farm
Hendall Wood
Furnace Wood
A272
(Uckfield)
(Buxted)
One Mile

The glass had been buried in the churchyard and discovered in 1880. The south transept contains ancient monuments.

St Bartholomew`s Church, Maresfield. In1293 the village was called 'Meresfield'. The name describes this area, even as it is today: 'open land with shallow pools'. We pass some of the pools on our walk. Sadly, we cannot see the Norman church that stood here then. It was replaced in 14th century. During a restoration in 1879, a small Norman window was uncovered in the south wall of the nave and filled with Victorian glass. It is all that remains of the Norman church. The Norman font near the tower came from a lost chapel. There is also a Victorian font used for baptisms. The tower was added in 1412. The walls are 4 feet thick and hold a stone staircase. The restoration of 1879 was quite daring. The chancel was lengthened, and north and south transepts added. The east window was taken from the chancel to the south transept. The chancel arch was moved to the north transept. In this reconstructed chancel we see contrasting stained glass with subdued colours in the east window and bright colours in the north windows. For more details of the windows, see the church guide.

Christ Church, Fairwarp is built of local stone and consecrated in 1881. The tower and chancel, a gift from Sir Bernard Eckstein of Oldlands, were added in 1935. The building is known as the Church of the Forest. It is outside the village in a spacious churchyard with a car park to the tree-lined B2026 on the edge of Ashdown Forest.

The Walk

From the Car Park in Fletching, walk down the High Street to the Church. You pass the village stores on the right and footpath signs on the left. After visiting the Church, return to these footpath signs. Here the path leads just behind the Church through a very long churchyard. At the end turn left for a gate into a small field.

Fletching

Pass farm silos on the right and cross to the next field where paths meet. Take the path straight on with the hedge on your right. In 50 metres look for a stile in the hedge on the right. Ignore this. Instead, turn left into the wide open field. In the distance you can see the buildings of Mallingdown Farm a mile away. This is your destination.

Meanwhile, cut across the right hand corner of the field to find a metal stile in the boundary. To your right is White Barn Farm. Turn away from this and keep on an easterly course, parallel to the hedgerow on the right. You are going gently downhill with views over scattered woods.

In ½ mile cross a footbridge into fields with high hedges. Keep on course to enter a grassy hedge-lined track. It ends in a grass triangle with several gateways. At the time of writing, you have to climb over the low battered metal gate ahead. You then climb up the sloping field to Mallingdown Farm.

A high gate opens onto the driveway through the farm buildings. Walk along the driveway. The first building, once an oasthouse is now a holiday home. Leave the farm to continue through a narrow strip of common land, flanking the quiet byway, Down Street. *It is possible, immediately outside the farm, to turn right into this common land and follow an erratic path for 500 metres and then join Down Street on the left.*

It is easier to go straight onto Down Street and turn right. You then have 500 metres of road walking to meet the A272. Cross with care to the road opposite leading to Piltdown Golf Course. Before you reach the clubhouse which you can see ahead, turn left into Park Wood.

For 1 kilometre, follow the main track through the wood, heading east. It curves imperceptibly southeast and then northeast. There is one opening where tracks converge and you go straight on. Soon after, there is a small signpost indicating the left turn northeast. In another 250 metres you can see a way ahead out of the wood. Seize this opportunity. Do NOT follow the path to the right. You are still heading northeast.

The path out of the wood is enclosed. It crosses an insignificant hump back bridge then a wooden footbridge. Then you reach the southern end of a man-made lake, part of the Powdermill estate. A high fence excludes you from the lake. At the northern end a lower fence allows you to enjoy a prospect of the lake before you join the driveway used by fishermen.

Keep on course along the pleasant driveway through a green sward. Ignore the path to the right. Pass two smaller ponds and you approach the A22. The driveway swerves right here. You veer left and take the footpath in the corner. It leads underneath the main road to a farm track on the other side.

Follow the farm track past a cluster of handsome houses around a small green. Across the field to your left more fine old houses stand as if the 21st century did not exist. Take the footpath on the left into this field and leading to Maresfield Church.

From Maresfield Church go through the lychgate and cross the road to the Gothic Gatehouse. Despite all the 'private' notices, there is a public footpath here through an exclusive housing estate. I prefer to cross to the pub opposite and walk along the main road. You soon pass the shops and post office in a crescent on the left. On the corner on the right is a shop that at present features kitchen displays. Turn right here into a very short road leading to **Nursery Lane**.

For the longer walk on footpaths, see the end of this section, page 63.

For the shorter walk on roads, turn left and follow Nursery Lane northwards for 1 mile, ignoring side tracks. Turn left at the first road, Burrells Lane. It leads to B2026.

Turn right here and walk carefully beside the road for 300 metres then cross to the footpath opposite. This path, at first fenced, goes steadily downhill for 350 metres. It passes under overhanging trees and turns left at the bottom to cross a footbridge and emerge to **Old Forge Lane** beside a house on the left.

Turn left and follow the road as it curves right and climbs uphill to A22.

** The longer walk joins here.*

Cross with care to the track opposite. You are now heading southwest through trees with scattered houses. Keep straight on at cross tracks. Your track now passes through countryside and in ½ mile goes in front of a beautiful mellow stone Elizabethan house, Marshall`s Manor.

Keep on course along a grassy track up through woodland to open fields. The path southeast is well signposted so that you avoid private ways. Cross the wide field to woodland opposite. Go past the corner of the wood and climb gently uphill, crossing another field.

1 kilometre from Marshall`s Manor, you come out at the top end of Down Street. Turn right. In 100 metres turn left into the road leading to Splayne`s Green. The road goes downhill, passing another beautiful house called 'Dale Hamme', a large black and white cottage.

Pass this cottage, look for the inconspicuous footpath sign on the ground, then turn immediately left into a concrete drive. Go past the side of the cottage then veer right to cross a small field then a footbridge over a stream.

You also have several stiles to cross after leaving Dale Hamme. In the next field climb the gentle slope to the boundary. Here you have a good view across a wider field to a strip of woodland. Go straight over to the woodland and turn right. Look out for a narrow gap into the wood, now on your left.

Go down into the wood, cross a footbridge over a stream and climb out to the next field. Fields have been getting gradually bigger. Cross diagonally right to a farm gate in the corner. The stile is beside the gate.

You enter a hedge-lined farm track. When the track bends to the right, you turn left and cross open fields to Fletching Church, in sight ahead.

For the longer walk on footpaths, *follow Nursery Lane from Maresfield northwards for only 500 metres. The lane descends through woodland to undulating farmland. At the farm entrance to Reeding`s Farm, turn right. Pass stables in old buildings on the left. The path enters a field and forks. Take the left fork to go straight on. Do not enter the arena but stay in the field and follow the fence outside it. Pass the arena, a pony training area on the left.*

Cross to the next field and veer slightly left, following the line of the trodden path over a meadow to a small wood. Go down through the wood to take a footbridge over a stream and emerge to a wide, sloping field. Climb diagonally left on a fainter path to a track that continues your course northeast. You come to the long distance trail, the Wealdway at a Y-junction.

Veer left onto the Wealdway (WW) and head north. This track leads between Hendall Manor Farm on the right and a new brick house hung with tiles on the left.

Turn left to go round the outside of the garden of the new house. Follow the hedge on the left and make for nearby woodland. Enter Furnace Wood to scramble down a short steep slope to a path junction.

Turn right and walk through the wood, heading north still on the Wealdway. You have another sharp slope down but steps have been provided here. You come down to a woodland dell with a wooden footbridge over a stream. Cross the footbridge and avoid the unmarked track ahead. Instead, veer slightly to the right and enter a small meadow. The Wealdway passes through part of Fairwarp Nature Reserve here. Cross diagonally left and leave the meadow by a short track into more woodland.

At a T-junction of paths turn right and follow the Wealdway through the wood for ¼ mile to the tarmac lane.

Leave the Wealdway here and turn left to walk along the lane to the hamlet of Fairwarp. Pass the pub on your right then turn right into a driveway through the backs of houses. The footpath follows the driveway then keeps on course through woodland to Fairwarp Church.

You enter the churchyard from the south. The formal entrance is through ornate filigree iron gates on the left. They face the road B2026 and there is a footpath opposite. Cross with care to this footpath.

*Go through the unusual spring-back gate into heathland and follow the path southwest. This is open access land with paths in all directions. You have to keep on course avoiding all cross paths. In 300 metres you come to a tarmac lane. Turn right then immediately left into a wide path through trees with a wooden crossbar at the entrance. In 150 metres you reach Old Forge Lane. Turn right and go down to join the shorter walk. Continue to the end of the lane where it meets the A22. Follow the instructions at * on page 62.*

Walk 12: Buxted Park to Framfield

Two very different churches, one dominates parkland and one serves a little village, both are in the Weald so we enjoy a varied wealden walk

Starting Point: The Parish Church, Buxted Park **GR**486231
Parking nearby or a walk of one mile from the railway station in Buxted.
Map: OS Explorer 135 **Terrain:** Undulating **Distance:** 6 Miles
Local Information: Buxted Place has been a country seat since the 12th century. In 1830 the then owner, Lord Liverpool ousted the nearby villagers who moved to the present village. The site of the medieval village is across the estate road from the church. The house, now a country hotel and the church are lonely neighbours in Buxted Park.
Note: Much of this walk is on the Wealdway, a long distance footpath. Look for the symbol, '**WW**'. There are also other Wealden walks.

The Churches

The Parish Church of St Margaret is on a Saxon site. Caedwalla, King of Wessex gave the Manor to the Archbishop of Canterbury in 680 A.D. The name 'Boxstede' probably means 'beech place', 'boc stede'. In 1250 the present church was built in Early English style. It is unusual to have a church dedicated to St Margaret of Scotland. There is a unique painting of this saint in Binsted Church near Arundel (See West Sussex Church Walks). Buxted Church is large; it was the mother church of a large area including Uckfield and even Crowborough at one time. First came the lofty nave with barrel roof and ancient beams. It has 4 bay arcades to north and south aisles. The pillars are round, apart from two on the north side that are octagonal. The clerestory windows are on the north side only. An ancient chest (1260) is at the back of the north aisle. The chancel was built soon after the nave and probably replaces a smaller one. The large 5 light east window has the figure of St Margaret at the top. In the magnificent Elizabethan ceiling the frieze depicts urns holding hop flowers and marguerites. The Jacobean pulpit also has the marguerite motif in the carving. There is a small enclosed chapel south of the chancel where modern chairs of local wild

Buxted

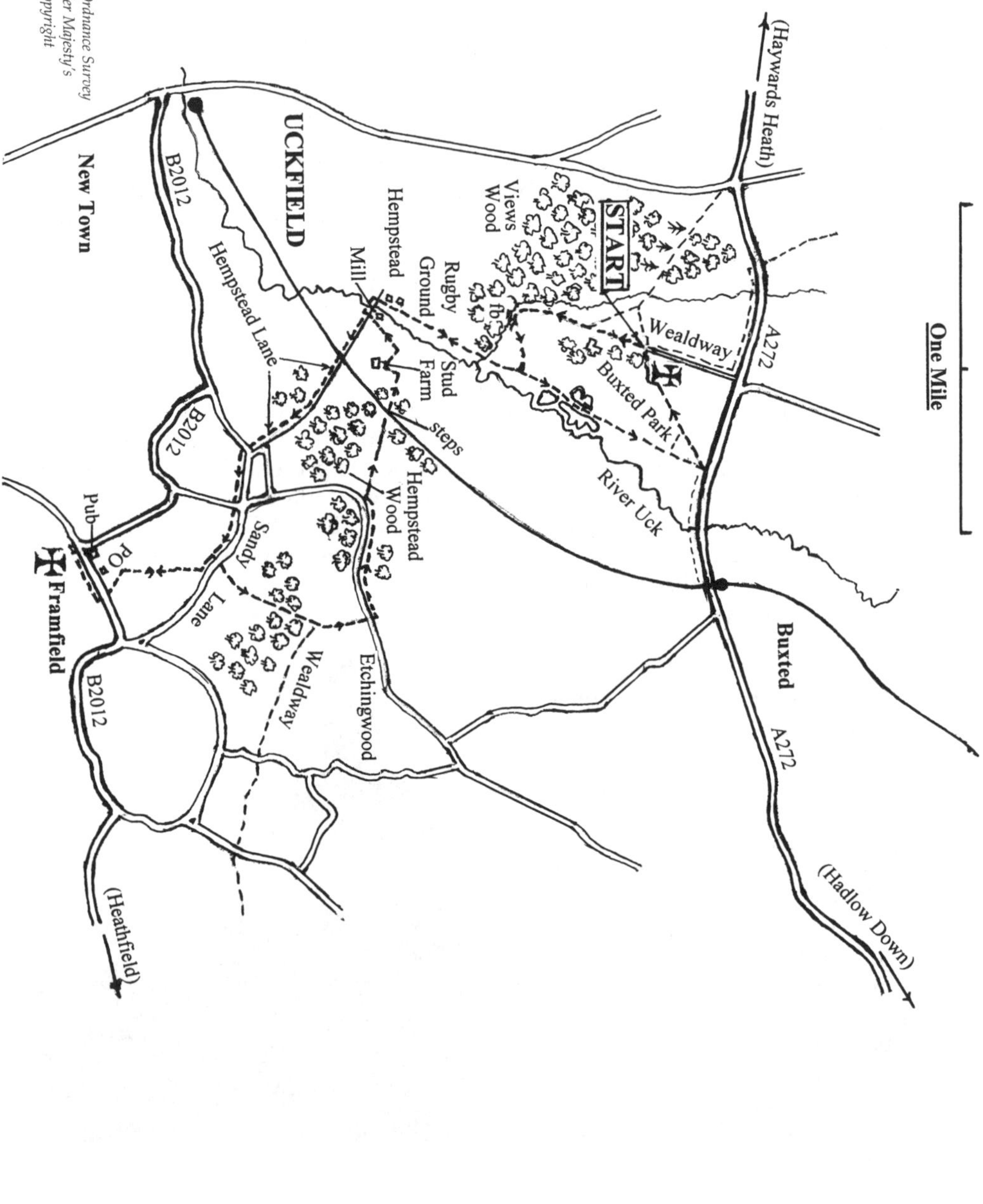
One Mile
(Haywards Heath)
START
Views Wood
UCKFIELD
Hempstead Mill
Rugby Ground
fb
Wealdway
A272
Buxted Park
Stud Farm
steps
Hempstead Wood
River Uck
Hempstead Lane
B2012
New Town
Pub
PO
Framfield
Sandy Lane
Wealdway
Etchingwood
Buxted
A272
B2012
(Heathfield)
(Hadlow Down)

cherry face a 17th century altar table. The 20th century has taken good care of this church; rescuing it from damp walls, also re-shingling and re-timbering the broach spire. Bell ringers still come to ring the famous 17th century 8 bells. There is a 2000 year old yew near the church.

The Church of St Thomas a Becket, Framfield. One of the last Saxon kings, Baldred gave the Manor of South Malling to Canterbury in the early 9th century. 'Framelle', mentioned in Domesday (1087), was part of that manor. The date of foundation of the first church here is unknown. The present building was started in 13th century with a chapel on the north side. Most of the church was burnt down in 1509. The chapel survived and is still in use today. The rest of the church: chancel, nave, aisles, south chapel and tower were rebuilt in late Perpendicular style using local sandstone with veins of iron. Among the few monuments, an interesting wall brass of 1595 depicts Edward Gage and his family. He founded the south chapel. See Walk 2 for details of the Gage family of Firle. In 18th century the chancel was neglected and disused. The vicar, Rev. Henry Hoare paid to have it rebuilt in 1842. He chose to base the design of the window on that of Tintern Abbey. The tower collapsed in 1667 and was replaced in 1892, complete with belfry. The handsome lychgate of ancient appearance, in fact commemorates the coronation of George V. It completes the picture at the approach to the church where timber framed old cottages overlook the churchyard.

Framfield

The Walk

From the church in Buxted Park, continue south on the drive, passing the large buildings of the hotel on your left. You leave the park grounds by a kissing gate and keep on course for another 300 metres. You are on the Wealdway (WW) and have views south. Go down into woodland and stop at the bottom. Do not cross the tempting footbridge. Instead turn sharp left and climb out of the copse. You are still on the Wealdway, heading east over common land.

In 200 metres you come to a thicket corner. Turn right into a fairly narrow, overgrown path, still the Wealdway. It takes you southeast for ½ mile. The sluggish River Uck soon joins you on the left and you pass Uckfield Rugby Ground on the right. After that you reach the houses of Hempstead, a village on the edge of Uckfield. You see a monumental hedge on the right and pass Hempstead Mill on the left.

At a T-junction turn left into a tarmac lane. Cross the river and look left across to where the water wheel once turned. Then the Wealdway departs to the left. You stay on the hedge-lined lane as it climbs gently up past a stud farm to the single track railway line. Cross with care. The lane continues through woodland. It is even harder to imagine that this was once the main road from Uckfield to Framfield. Here it is just a stony track up through Hempstead Wood.

In 500 metres you emerge to a tarmac lane. Turn right then immediately left to walk along the elevated lane. At crossroads cross half right to head southeast along Sandy Lane. After some cottages, **note the footpath** on the left but continue a little further and turn into a footpath on the right.

This descends gently southwards across open fields. Cut across the left corner of two fields. Turn left and in another 70 metres you are in the recreation ground of Framfield with a scattering of seats. Cross diagonally left to find the access road.

Go through to the main B2102, known here as the Street. Turn right and walk along the pavement for 200 metres. En route you pass the post office and stop at the pub on the bend.

Opposite you will see Framfield Church with its attractive Approach and ancient cottages. Cross with care at this bend in the road to Uckfield!

From Framfield Church return to the recreation ground and retrace your steps up over fields to Sandy Lane. Turn left then find **the noted footpath,** now on your right. Pass a farm gate then enter the enclosed path leading to a view over a valley bordered with trees.

Head north across the valley to enter the woods on the other side. Go gently down through spaced trees. At the bottom a small rickety footbridge leads to a wide field. Cross the field to a T-junction of paths and turn left.

You are now back on the Wealdway with a wood on your right. In 200 metres you reach the tarmac road. Do not turn right to Etchingwood. Instead, turn left and make your way up the hill heading west. In nearly ½ mile turn right into a footpath through a narrow copse.

In 70 metres you leave the footpath and turn left following the Wealdway. Cross a field diagonally right and southwest. Keep on course in the next field. Ahead is a strip of woodland above and hiding the railway line.

Go through the trees and down a flight of steps to cross the railway line and climb up as many steps on the other side. (You need to be sober for this crossing). You now emerge to a field behind the familiar stud farm and have a chance to mingle with the rescued animals, mainly ponies.

The Wealdway passes close to the farm buildings, keeping them on the left. There is a stiff farm gate onto a track and a broken stile opposite (I am reporting these). Cross this track and take the enclosed path to an open field. Go diagonally left to the far side of the field and another short enclosed path.

You emerge on the familiar lane at Hempstead and turn right. Cross the bridge and pass Hempstead Mill, now on your right. Turn right and retrace your steps past the huge hedge and the rugby field.

In ½ mile you rejoin the path at the kissing gate. This time turn right to leave the Wealdway and enter Buxted Park on the lake side. Follow the track between lakes. It is a straight route northeast through parkland. You see Buxted Place and the church up on the left. In 1 kilometre, just before a grey bunker, turn left to join the path up to the church.

Keep straight on for the main road, A272. Turn right for Buxted Station.

Walk 13: Isfield to Newick

Much of this walk is beside quiet rivers, none lovelier than the Ouse where meadows and woods have a timeless quality. The churches have a story to tell of earlier times when this bit of Sussex was busier.

Starting Point: Isfield Church **GR**444182 **Map:** OS Explorer 122
Terrain: Mainly flat, only gentle slopes. **Distance:** 11½ Miles
If you are willing to walk 1½ miles on a road, **Distance:** 8 Miles
For more details on the rivers, see the Introduction.
I recommend you bring a compass, especially for the full walk.

The Churches

Isfield, St Margaret of Antioch. Most churches reflect the history of their village and Isfield especially so. Its lonely position, the apparent affluence of the building, the lavish tombs in the chantry chapel can all be explained. A Roman road from Newhaven to London crossed the River Ouse to the west of this site. It may have been a pagan holy site. The church was established here later. The Normans built a motte and bailey castle at the confluence of the rivers Ouse and Uck. They also presumably built the church nearby. At that time the Uck was closer to the church. The River Ouse came to be a busy thoroughfare with locks to admit boats and barges carrying goods between Newhaven and Shortbridge. The river brought prosperity but by the end of 19th century it was no longer an important waterway. Locks were no longer maintained and mills were closed so the people moved away and the church was in solitude. Only the ghosts of Roman soldiers and Norman masters linger here. Hugh de Folkington held Isfield Manor 1171 – 1224. The south wall of the nave was built 1200 – 1220. In 1243 the manor passed by marriage to John de la Warr. The de la Warrs are most likely responsible for the building in 1300 of the chancel and the chantry chapel in Decorated style. The Shurley family took over the chantry chapel and filled it with their monuments. The most striking is the alabaster tomb of Sir John Shurley (died 1631), his two wives and nine children. The delicate carving is outstanding. A squint from the chapel to the chancel is directed to the Easter sepulchre. There is a fine window of 1951 by Christopher Webb. It shows local scenes including the cattle of Isfield Place Farm. On the outside wall of the chapel is a scratch dial, possibly earlier than the stated 1660. It informed the villagers of the time of mass. The tower appears to be the oldest part of the church but it may have been rebuilt in 15th century. It was definitely heightened in 1893 when the Sussex cap was removed and replaced with a spire. Oak beams were built into the new roof in 1598. Nicholas Culpepper of the famous "Herbal" was born in Isfield

St Mary`s Church, Newick is a blend of old and new and a tribute to successful Victorian restoration. There may have been a church here in 1080. One small window in the nave near the porch is Norman. The base of the font is Norman with a square bowl added in 14th century. The porch is 14th century and still has some original timbers. There are rings on either side to fit a chain to keep out cattle.

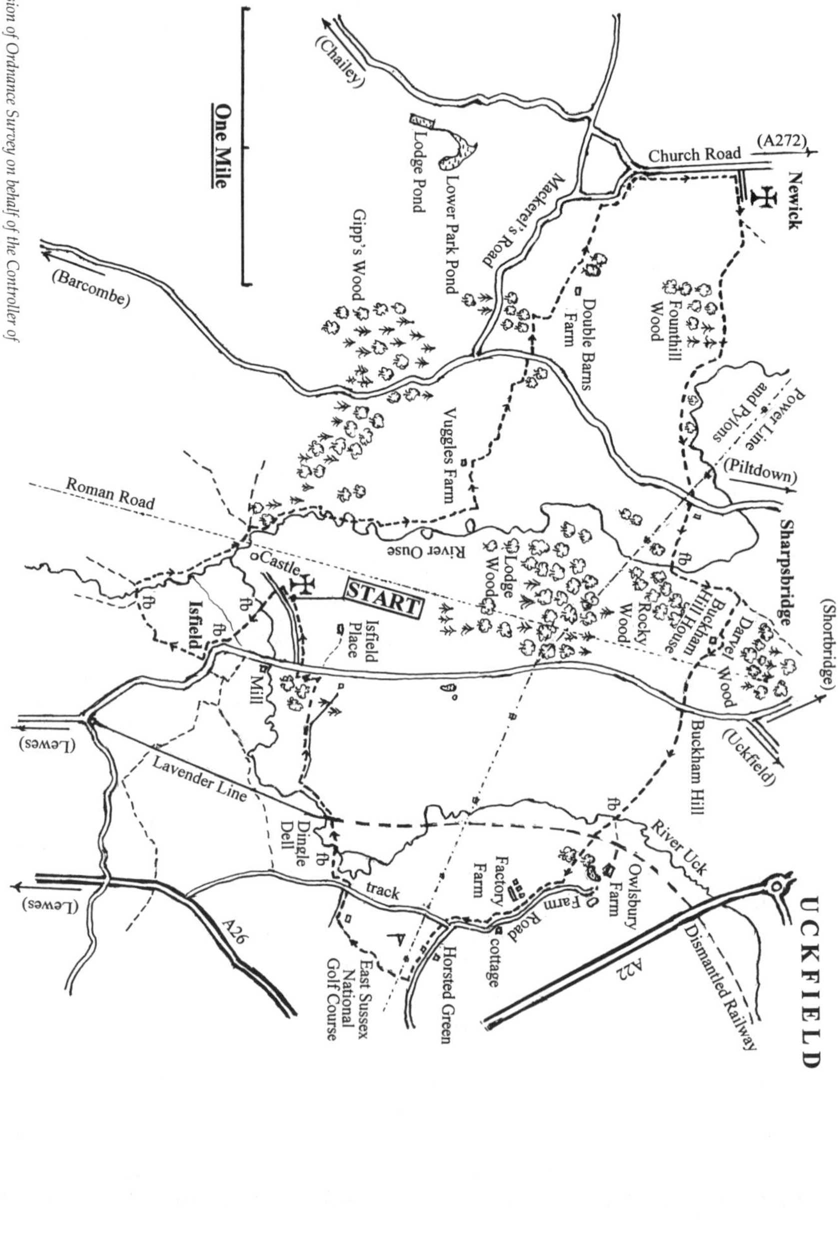
One Mile
(Chailey)
Church Road
(A272)
Newick
Lodge Pond
Lower Park Pond
Mackerel's Road
Gipp's Wood
Double Barns Farm
Founthill Wood
(Barcombe)
Vuggles Farm
Power Line and Pylons
(Piltdown)
Roman Road
River Ouse
Sharpsbridge
Castle
START
Lodge Wood
Rocky Wood
fb
Buckham Hill House
Darvel Wood
(Shortbridge)
Isfield
Isfield Place
Mill
(Uckfield)
Buckham Hill
(Lewes)
Lavender Line
Dingle Dell
River Uck
Owlsbury Farm
Factory Farm
Farm Road
track
cottage
(Lewes)
A26
Horsted Green
East Sussex National Golf Course
A22
Dismantled Railway
UCKFIELD

The handsome 15th century tower is built of local golden sandstone. The west door and window in the tower are Tudor. J. Oldrid Scott made the restoration 1886-7 with clear cut lines and generous space. He enlarged the nave and rebuilt the chancel. The chancel is enhanced with stencils and tiling. It has some medieval glass in the east window and has three Decorated windows. The windows of this church are varied and merit further study. Near the tower are two windows with glass engraved by Sally Scott. Newick lies about half way between Winchester and Canterbury. Pilgrims visiting shrines in these two cities would have rested at Newick where the Bull Inn has a relevant name. A 'bulla' was a Papal seal on a document.

The Walk

From Isfield Church cross the lane to take a footpath heading southeast over fields to the village. There are two good footbridges along the way, the second crosses the narrow River Uck.

At the road turn right and pass a converted barn and oast house on the right. In 150 metres turn right to join a footpath through a school field. The small school is on the left.

Isfield

Newick

In 200 metres you come to a driveway. Turn right and follow the drive as it curves to the left and passes a detached house and pond on the left. In another 100 metres you cross a footbridge over the River Ouse. This is White Bridge.

Turn right and follow the Ouse on your right for 1½ miles, a delightful stroll over wide open meadows and through coppice with just the river for company.

In ¼ mile the Uck joins the Ouse. In another ¼ mile you are looking at Isfield Church across the water – you have walked in a circle! Avoid a path to the left and carry on beside the river. Go through stretches of woodland, some established, others new plantations of willow and poplar. At one point you pass repair work on an old lock. Next you pass the drop of a weir and hear the fast flow of the water.

Cross a meadow to a narrow strip of land with a post to mark the way. The river is beside you on the right. Ignore the arrow on the Sussex Ouse Valley Way sign here. Instead veer left away from the river and follow a little straight stream on your left. You reach another post with the Sussex Ouse Valley Way sign and turn left to cross the stream. Make for the hedge opposite and turn right. Go through a metal farm gate into a small field. Hug the hedge on your left. Turn left through another metal farm gate. You can now see the way ahead to the west to Vuggles Farm.

Still on the Sussex Ouse Valley Way, turn right at the garden of the main farmhouse. Pass a deserted old oasthouse on your right then turn left and follow the edge of the garden on the left. Pass a small cottage then veer to the right for a gentle climb through a field towards a copse. The Downs are a distant presence on the left. In 450 metres pass the copse on your right and in 100 metres you come to the lane to Piltdown.

Cross the lane diagonally right to continue westward over fields. The Sussex Ouse Valley Way is well sign posted here. Pass a wood on the left. Turn right then left with a field boundary on the left. Head northwest passing Double Barns Farm at a distance on the right. After another copse, you keep to the hedge on the right until you reach steps down to Church Road.

Turn right to walk with care heading north along Church Road for 1 kilometre to Newick where you leave the Sussex Ouse Valley Way. Turn right at the sign to the parish church, unless you are seeking refreshments when you have to proceed further north into the village.

From Newick Church go through the churchyard heading east. After the boundary wall, descend gently across a rough meadow to Founthill Wood, a little over ¼ mile away. Follow the edge of the wood on your right ignoring two 'squeeze stiles' into the wood. Descend towards the unseen river and before you reach it, follow the path through a neck of the wood.

You have turned to the south and continue across fields above the Ouse, hidden behind trees on the left. In under ¼ mile there is a small hill. Turn left before you reach the top of the hill. *I have put in a request for a finger post here! At the moment there is a 'squeeze stile' and a gap in the hedge.*

Keep the trees on your left and head northeast for ½ mile towards pylons. At some places along the way you can peer down the steep slope to the river below. Go to the right of the pylon nearest the river and keep on course to come down to the lane to Piltdown again.

Cross to the footpath opposite. It leads past farm buildings on the left and takes you southeast to the field hedge. Go through the hedge on the stile and you are back in the enchanted valley of the Ouse.

To return to Isfield cross the river on the footbridge and turn sharp left. You are making for Daniel Wood where I saw a bold large fox. You go through a damp, shady strip of land to emerge to a field and a fork in the ways. Fork right on a footpath that leads southeast uphill through a field to Buckham Hill House. Pass the rock garden first then the house itself on your right and continue climbing to walk through the sunny gardens of converted barns. Look back over the Ouse valley before going through to the road at Buckham Hill.

Here you can shorten the walk by 4 miles by turning right and walking on the road gently downhill to Isfield for 1½ miles. Take care of traffic speeding on this straight stretch of road.

For the full walk cross to the footpath opposite. Pass a villa, complete with swimming pool on the left and continue downhill heading southeast through fields. In 500 metres you reach the River Uck. The noise of traffic on the A22 on the edge of Uckfield has been getting gradually louder.

Cross the footbridge over the river and avoid the path half left. At the time of writing there is no finger post for the footpath to the right. Nevertheless, you have to turn right towards another bridge over the river then bear left away from the Uck. You leave the narrow field and come to an old railway track. Cross diagonally right to a footpath and continue southeast through a small field and then enter a wood strewn with wood anemones in spring. Your general direction is southeast for the next mile.

You emerge from the wood to a grassy corner, again there is no finger post. There is a stile. Cross the stile into a field with a farm cottage ahead left and a monstrous building away to the right. Make for the left hand side of the monster. As you approach this farm factory, you find there are two farm gates onto the road. The one on the left was unlocked at the time of writing. Go through to the farm road and turn right to hurry past the farm factory on the right.

Can you believe it – a few yards down the road is a lovely cottage with open garden and an air of utter contentment! Pass this cottage on the left and continue down the road, a definite byway as it reaches Horsted Green.

Pass an inconspicuous track on the right and follow the road as it curves to the left passing a few detached houses. In 50 metres after the last house, turn right into a footpath heading south.

Keep to the left hand side of the small field, go under some power cables and you soon enter what seems to be an extension of East Sussex National Golf Course. This extension is not yet shown on Ordnance Survey maps. You will find new helpful waymarkers here.

Go straight on along a narrow drive past a pond on the left and the rolling slopes of the golf course on the right. The drive curves up to the left to the Manor House but we have to leave it. Go straight on along a grassy path towards a high hedge. Turn right to go through a gap in the hedge. Walk through a flat field for 75 metres then turn left. Go down through another rough little field to emerge at a tarmac driveway.

Turn right and pass two houses on the right, then the golf course again. Avoid all tempting paths to the south but stay on the driveway heading towards trees. Here it joins the inconspicuous track mentioned above. Turn left onto the track. Head southwest down the track for 100 metres.

Turn right into a field. Now the footpath follows the little River Uck on the right. Cross a footbridge and continue southwest with the river on your left. Go under a disused railway line. The river is still on your left. In 200 metres turn right away from the river making due west on a wide, easy track.

It is tempting to stay on this track but in 300 metres you have to turn left into a field. The path crosses diagonally right towards woodland on the left. Enter the wood and your way is circumscribed until you come out at the road opposite the gates of Isfield Place.

Turn left and walk with care along the road towards Isfield Village. In 150 metres you reach the narrow road to Isfield Church on the right.

Walk 14: Hartfield to Withyham

A glorious walk through parts of Ashdown Forest where there are so many local attractions We concentrate here on two very different ancient churches

Starting Point: Hartfield Church (parking on the High Street) **GR**479357
Map: OS Explorer 135 **Terrain:** Mainly flat, just gentle slopes. May be muddy in woodland. **Distance:** 3 Miles or 6 Miles
Local Information: The longer walk takes you through landmarks in the stories of Christopher Robin and Winnie the Pooh by A.A. Milne.
For more information on the Medway, see the Introduction under 'Rivers'.
According to Roger Penn (See the Bibliography at the end), a tributary of the Medway, the Steel Forge River is a name given to the stream that flows under Pooh Sticks Bridge.
Hartfield is a charming village with a Pooh Corner Shop, tea rooms and pubs

The Churches

The Parish Church of St Mary, Hartfield stands near the River Medway where a fort in Castlefields was probably guarding the river. In Domesday it is mentioned as part of the Hundred of Herteval, an area stretching from East Grinstead to Rotherfield and the border of Kent. The church was built in 13th century. The patronage passed from Abbot of Grestain in France to the Dean and Chapter of Chichester to Queen Elizabeth and finally to the Sackville family. The north wall with rough masonry and a blocked lancet visible on the outside are from this first church. In 14th century the church was enlarged, including the south aisle with Decorated windows. The Perpendicular tower with tall slender spire were added 14th – 15th centuries. There may have been a fire in 16th century necessitating further building and the removal of the chancel arch. In 19th century the spire was struck by lightning and was repaired with the addition of a conductor. An organ was installed in this century. In 20th century, at the Millenium floodlighting was introduced to bring out the beauty of the church at night.

Hartfield

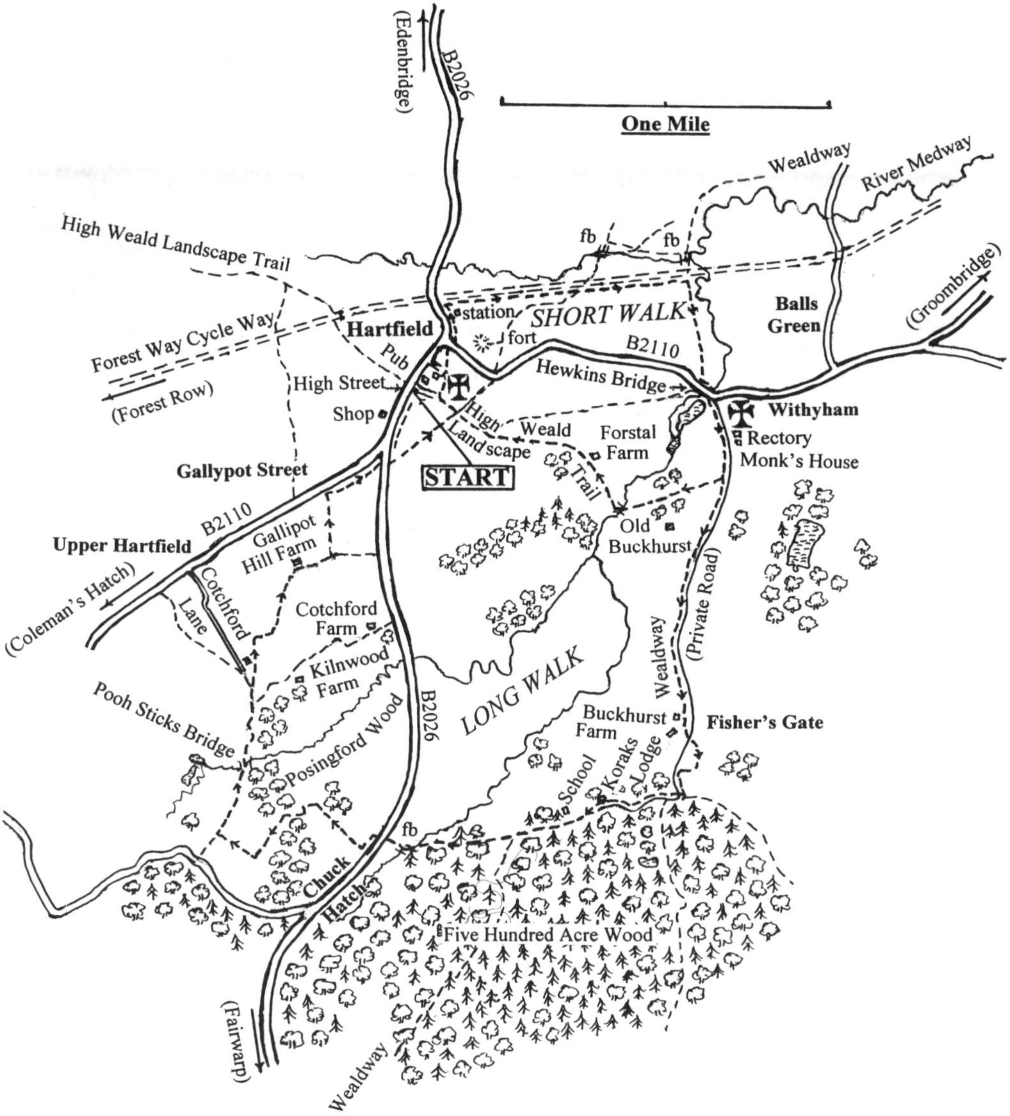
(Edenbridge)
B2026
One Mile
Wealdway
River Medway
High Weald Landscape Trail
fb
fb
(Groombridge)
Balls Green
Forest Way Cycle Way
Hartfield
station
SHORT WALK
fort
B2110
Pub
Hewkins Bridge
(Forest Row)
High Street
Withyham
Shop
High Weald Landscape Trail
Forstal Farm
Rectory
Monk's House
START
Gallypot Street
Old Buckhurst
B2110
Gallipot Hill Farm
Upper Hartfield
(Coleman's Hatch)
Cotchford
Lane
Cotchford Farm
(Private Road)
Wealdway
Kilnwood Farm
LONG WALK
Pooh Sticks Bridge
Posingford Wood
B2026
Buckhurst Farm
Fisher's Gate
School
Koraks Lodge
fb
Chuck Hatch
Five Hundred Acre Wood
(Fairwarp)
Wealdway

The Parish Church of St Michael and all Angels, Withyham stands on a lovely hill above trees. Streams below wander through woodland and into lakes before entering the Medway. The Rectory next door has kept the church company for 700 years. The church was first mentioned in 1291 in connection with the Crusades. After rebuilding around 1400, the church was struck by lightning in 1663. The nave north wall, the chancel south wall and the lower part of the tower were salvaged. To finance a second rebuilding, other churches had to contribute; Maresfield managed 7s 8d and East Grinstead gave £2 16s. Work went ahead at full speed. The south arcade was abandoned and workmen finished rebuilding the main church by 1672. The sundial on the south porch bears the same date. The Sackville chapel was ready by 1680. We can enjoy the spacious nave and the beauty of 17th century Gothic arches. The east window and the depressed arches of the windows in the Sackville chapel are of this period. This private chapel contains some magnificent monuments. In particular there is a poignant altar tomb of the boy, Thomas Sackville who died in 1677. His mourning parents lean over him. They are life size figures in white and grey marble by C. G. Cibber. The south aisle was built and the north arcade removed by the Victorians. The chancel window has 10 panels by Hardman. Much more of interest can be seen in this church.

The Walks

Both long and short walks start on the same route.

As you approach Hartfield Church from Lych-gate Cottage, fork left through the churchyard. Pass the north wall of the church on your right then veer further left to leave the churchyard and enter the private car park of the village school.

Go through the car park then turn immediately right to a rough village green. Cross diagonally left to the B2026. Turn right here, the road is signposted to Edenbridge.

Follow the pavement and pass the old railway station on the right. Before the bridge turn right and go down to the old railway line, now a cycle track, 'Forest Way'. Avoid going under the bridge on the left and avoid the path straight on. Instead, turn right towards Groombridge.

You are now heading east on a straight track, Forest Way lined with scattered trees and glimpses of the countryside on either side. The little River Medway is down on the left. Keep on this track for one kilometre. Go past the first footpath crossing. The second crossing is another long distance footpath, the Wealdway.

Turn right onto the Wealdway and cross an open field heading south. Keep on course in the next field. You can see the tree covered hill ahead where Withyham Church stands. In ½ mile you reach the B2110.

Turn left on the B2110, cross Hewkins Bridge and turn immediately right up a road to the Church. The Wealdway continues south on this private road. Pass the Church and the Rectory on the left and follow the Wealdway.

Short Walk In ¼ mile turn right onto yet another long distance footpath, 'High Weald Landscape Trail'. You are now heading southwest towards woodland. Pass Old Buckhurst and its tower on the left and enter the wood. You soon come out of the wood to reach a farm track.

Turn right on the farm track and cross a bridge over a fast flowing stream. Forstal Farm can be seen ahead. Head north passing the 'farm', a house and garden on the right. Keep on course to the field boundary where an open gate gives access to the next sloping field.

Veer slightly left and walk uphill. The spire of Hartfield Church comes into view. Head northwest towards the disappearing church as trees block the view. At crosspaths veer right hugging the tall hedge on the right until you can go through to the church.

Long Walk Continue south along the private road, still on the Wealdway. In one mile you reach the cottages of Buckhurst Farm. Pass these on your right then divert to the left. Your path goes down into a dell then veers right to rejoin the private road. You are now in Five Hundred Acre Wood ('Hundred Aker' according to Christopher Robin).

The private road continues southwest then west through the wood but not deeply into it. Avoid turnings to the left and keep strictly to the well marked Wealdway (WW). The tarmac ends soon after the high gateway of Koraks Lodge on the right. You then keep on course uphill on a track beside the high fence of this lodge estate.

Just after a large hut on the right, veer left. You leave the Wealdway here as it turns sharp left. You keep straight on along a path still on the edge of the wood. In 500 metres cross a footbridge over a stream. Veer to the right to go up an enclosed track to the B2026.

Turn left to walk beside the road until you come to the sign 'Chuck Hatch'. There is a footpath opposite.

Turn right here and follow the path across a sandy arena to a farm track. Cross to a field on the left and enjoy the view over fields and woods. *According to OS you walk round the edge of this field.* On the ground it appears you cross diagonally left. In any case at the far corner you enter Posingford Wood. Head southwest through the wood avoiding work tracks. The footpath tends to have a firmer base than other tracks.

The path approaches an open field and turns left uphill. You can avoid this climb by crossing the open field with the help of kissing gates. Re-enter woodland, go straight on for 50 metres and you reach a T-junction with a wide track. Turn right.

You are now on the main route to Pooh Sticks Bridge. Follow the wide track westwards through the wood. You emerge at a byroad, pass a house on the right. There is a sign on the left pointing across the road to Pooh Sticks Bridge. Turn right into the track heading north. In ½ mile you come down to cross Pooh Sticks Bridge and continue on the track.

You come up to houses on Cotchford Lane. (The right fork leads to Cotchford Farm, home of A.A. Milne). Fork Left and walk for 25 metres along Cotchford Lane. Pass a turreted house and turn right into a footpath marked to 'Harfield'.

The path opens to meadows and takes you up through wild flowers and sorrel. Turn to admire the view behind. You come up to a select scattering of houses on Gallipot Hill. Here your path is enclosed – you cannot go astray. In 200 metres turn left away from the main path.

Head north through woodland and fields for 500 metres to B2110. Turn right and follow the pavement down to Hartfield.

Pooh Sticks Bridge

Hartfield

Lychgate Cottage, Hartfield

Walk 15: Mayfield to Rotherfield

We cross many streams, woods, meadows and countless stiles in the High Weald to reach handsome villages with their grand churches.

Starting Point: Car Park nearly opposite the Post Office on the south side of Mayfield High Street **GR**588269
Map: OS Explorer 135 **Distance:** 10 Miles
Terrain: Undulating with some delightful woodland ways, also some lanes
Warning: We cross the A267 twice and walk for 150m on a verge beside it.

The Churches

The Church of St Dunstan, Mayfield. In 960 St Dunstan, Archbishop of Canterbury built a wooden church in Mayfield. He also built a residence there. The original Saxon buildings have gone but 14th century remains of an Archbishop`s Palace, including a fine medieval Great Hall still stand in the nearby convent and school. St Dunstan was a poet, scholar, musician and metal worker. Legend has it that the Devil appeared to St Dunstan in the form a beautiful maiden. St Dunstan spotted the cloven hooves, seized his red hot tongs and clamped them on the Devil`s nose. The Devil leapt howling all the way to Tunbridge Wells where he made Chalybeate Waters! The Normans built a stone church in Mayfield but it was destroyed by fire in 1389. Only the 12th century tower survived. The shingled broach spire was added later. 1410 – 1420 a large Perpendicular church was built, starting with the chancel. The arcades in the nave are of 4½ bays. There is a fine king post pitch pine roof. 1503 – 1532 the roof was raised and the clerestory added. The south porch is vaulted and has a chamber above it. Carved bosses in the porch roof include two beasts curved round each other and a grotesque head. Most windows in the church are of 19th to 20th centuries. The lancet window near the tower is the oldest. The design is taken from an ancient drawing of St Dunstan in the British Museum.

St Denys` Church, Rotherfield has an illustrious history**.** In 792 Duke Bertoald of South Saxony built a wooden church on his estate at Ridrefeld as a thanksgiving for a cure for illness. Anglo-Saxon 'hrither' means a horned beast. Ridrefeld was the 'feld' or open country of horned cattle. King Alfred mentioned Rotherfield in his will in 899. Rotherfield may have been in the path of the Danes who were defeated at Halland and routed at Saxonbury Hill. Rotherfield is mentioned in Domesday 1086. William 11, who came to the throne in 1087, granted the demesne to the de Clare family. The last male de Clare was killed 1314 at Bannockburn. His sister inherited the estate. In 1450 the lordship of Rotherfield went to the Nevills, Lords of Burgavenny (named Abergavenny in1724). The old Saxon building was replaced by a Norman church in 1060. The northeast corner, the Nevill Chapel is the oldest part of the church. It has original huge beams across the roof and wooden bosses of carved faces including two 'Green Men'. The late Norman nave

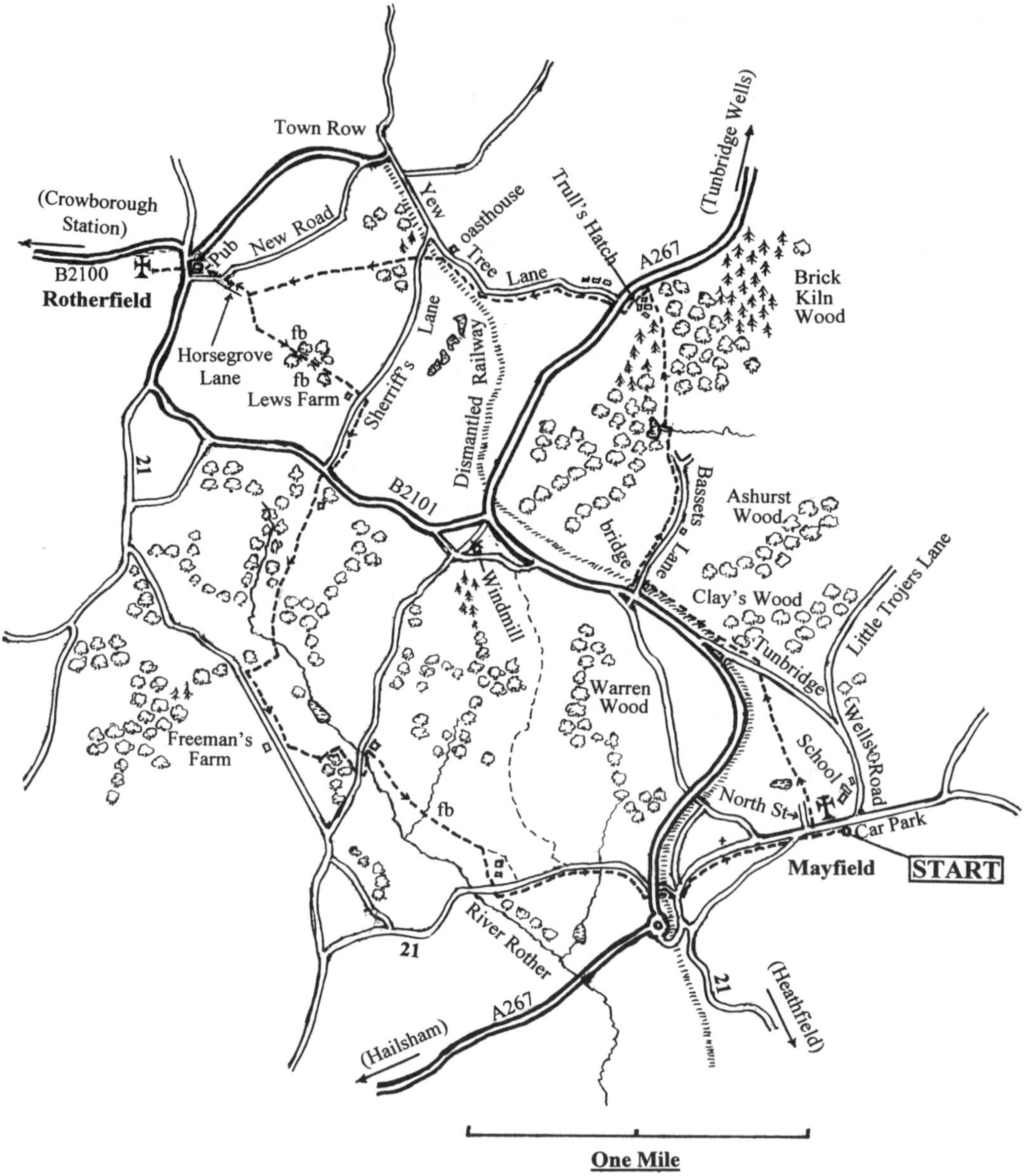
Town Row
(Crowborough Station)
B2100
Rotherfield
Pub
New Road
Yew Tree Lane
oasthouse
Trull's Hatch
(Tunbridge Wells)
A267
Brick Kiln Wood
Horsegrove Lane
fb
fb
Lews Farm
Sherriff's Lane
Dismantled Railway
21
B2101
Bassets Lane
bridge
Ashurst Wood
Little Trojers Lane
Clay's Wood
Windmill
Tunbridge Wells Road
School
Warren Wood
Freeman's Farm
North St
Car Park
Mayfield
START
fb
River Rother
21
A267
(Hailsham)
21
(Heathfield)
One Mile

was oblong with a flat roof. The fine wagon roof with arched rafters was added later. The north aisle, added in 1250, has round pillars. The 14th century south aisle has octagonal pillars. The huge chancel arch is Early English. In the south side of the chancel the sedilla and piscina are exceptionally fine. In 1893 medieval wall paintings were discovered; they originally covered the whole church. The chancel arch has a 15th century Doom painting with Christ on a rainbow. The battlemented tower and the two-storeyed north porch are Perpendicular. In 1987 the great storm blew down the wood-framed spire. In 1989 a steel spire with chestnut shingles was lifted in sections and placed by helicopter on the tower.

The Walk

Cross the High Street, Mayfield and turn left for the church.

Just past the church turn right into North Street, this must be the narrowest street in Sussex. It starts as an alley curving behind shops then straightens to pass between cottages and the churchyard, heading north.

Go down to sports fields and take the diverted path to the left. Pass a pond then an arena for horse riding on the left. Keep to the hedge on your right until you come to an opening. Cross to the other side of the hedge and keep on course through horse fields.

Ahead is a ragged hedge. Go through the gap and continue towards houses on Tunbridge Wells Road. Turn left and walk for 50 metres along this quiet residential part of the road. The road bends left but you go straight on northwest through a newly opened right of way along the dismantled railway. You can hear traffic on the A267 on the left and look out to meadows and woods on the right.

In 500 metres you go under a road bridge and have to climb up out of the railway line and onto Bassetts Lane. Turn away from the road bridge and head north. This is a country access road to cottages and a farm. You have good views over the wealden landscape. In 450 metres at the end of the tarmac lane, take the footpath on the left down into woodland.

The footpath becomes a good track north, crosses a stream and bends to the left to pass a pond. It reverts to its steady course north through Spitlye Wood. In one kilometre you pass the cottages of Trulls Hatch on the left. In another 150 metres you are at the A267 again.

Turn left to walk beside the road for 150 metres. Fortunately there is plenty of space for pedestrians, even an informal path through trees. You come to the front entrance to Trulls Hatch on the left.

Turn right and cross the main road with care to Yew Tree Lane opposite. Follow this lane for one kilometre. Pass a few detached houses, go down to a bend. Ignore the footpath on the left where a woodland track leads to a lake for angling. Keep on the lane. You may catch a glimpse of Rotherfield Church over fields to the left. Pass a converted oasthouse on the right. Now look for a path on the left. It is signposted to Sherriff`s Lane.

Turn left and cross the grassy way, once the railway line to go through a little copse and emerge as promised at Sherriff`s lane, 100 metres in total.

Rotherfield

Mayfield

Cross to an enclosed path opposite. You are heading southwest on a clear track through trees. In ¼ mile you emerge to meadows. Keep on course up to the right hand corner of the first meadow. Now follow the hedge on the right in the next field. At a break in the hedge you again catch a glimpse of Rotherfield Church spire. At the field corner you reach houses at the edge of Rotherfield.

Follow a short leafy lane, Horsegrove Lane to its junction with New Road. Cross to the footpath opposite. This starts as an alley, opening to Jubilee Fields and the inviting back garden of an inn. Pass the inn on your right and cross the High Street to a yard opposite. There is a surgery on the left and a gate in the corner on the right. This gate leads into the churchyard.

From Rotherfield Church retrace your steps back to Horsegrove Lane and the field at the edge of the village. Avoid the path that brought you here. Instead, turn immediately right and hug the hedge on the right to reach the southwest corner of the field. Here is a very high stile (that I hope to rectify) into the next field. Individual young trees have been planted there. Cross diagonally left heading southeast towards the first young tree then continue down towards an enclosed strip of marshy ground. Keep this on your right and you come to a wood. Keep on course through the wood.

As you enter the wood, you cross two footbridges. Come out of the wood and veer right to re-enter and leave the wood again finally. Veer right across a field where horses graze and you come to stables at Lews Farm on Sherriff`s Lane.

Turn right on the lane and walk past the farm. Sherriff`s Lane climbs a hill here. In 500 metres you come to a T-junction with B2101 which has the unlikely name, 'Bicycle Arms Road'.

Cross to the track opposite and pass houses, including a large greenhouse, at Holme Park. Head gently downhill southwest for one kilometre. Your way is a lovely avenue that allows views over the folding meadows to patches of woodland. Go down through Lumps Wood and cross a stream at the bottom on stepping stones. We have found the upper reaches of the River Rother. Continue on your track as it turns right and goes up to a tarmac lane.

Turn left and walk along the lane for 500 metres as far as Freemans Farm on the right. Turn left at a footpath sign. Cross the field diagonally right to the far corner. Cross a stile to the next field and follow the wood on your right. Go downhill towards the little river at the bottom. Turn right so the river is below on your left and enter the wood. A house and garden are on the other side of the stream. A rough path goes for 200 metres through the bottom of the wood and leads to Argos Hill Road.

Turn left to go down this lane for 50 metres. Go over the River Rother and turn immediately right just before a cottage. Pass the cottage garden on your left and avoid a cleared path straight on to the little river. Instead follow the path on the left that rises up above the river.

You come to a meadow and keep following the river in a dip on the right. As the river starts curving to the right, you strike out over the slope ahead and come to another strip of woodland. You enter it on a long footbridge. You soon leave the wood for fields and follow the hedge on the left for an elevated route southeast. In ¼ mile you come down to an enclosed path. An alternative path branches to the right across the field. Take this open route towards a nursery building. Pass this then the plants of the nursery on the left and rows of trees on the right. You reach a short slope down to a lane

Turn left and follow the lane for ½ mile to Mayfield. *This lane is marked on the map as part of cycle route 21.* On the way you pass the entrance to the nursery, two footpaths to the left and one to the right near the bridge over the river. You then come up past houses to a bend. After the bend you have to cross the A267 again – at least there is an island in the middle.

Once across the A267, you go up the zigzag way to a road junction. Cross to the signpost opposite. Turn left for the '¼ mile to Mayfield'. Follow Station Road uphill past comfortable houses then the Catholic Church on the left and you join the High Street.

5 Walks Near Wadhurst

View from the Pantiles to the Parish Church, Tunbridge Wells

Walk 16: Ticehurst to Etchingham

We traverse fields, woods, hills, rivers and lanes to find two exceptionally fine churches. The long walk touches on Bewl Water.

Starting Point: Ticehurst Church **GR**688301
or Etchingham Railway Station **GR**714263
Rail travellers start at Etchingham Church then go to the beginning of the walk
Map: OS Explorer 136
Terrain: Undulating, some road walking, muddy in places.
Distances: 13 Miles to include Bewl Water **or** 9 Miles on the Short Walk
Local Information:

1. King John`s Lodge dates back to 14th century. The garden is open daily and refreshments are available (Phone 01580 819562)
2. Three rivers meet in Etchingham: the Rother and its tributaries the Limden and the Dudwell. See the start of the Introduction for more on rivers. The community shop in Etchingham has welcoming beverages.
3. The long walk passes Pashley Manor, a Tudor house, where there is a café for garden visitors in the summer (Phone 01580 200888).
4. Bewl Water is a reservoir built 1973-5, the largest in south east England.

For information on the rivers, see the Introduction.

The Churches

Ticehurst Parish Church, St Mary`s. 'Ticcenes hyrst' in Saxon suggests a wooded hill where young goats are kept. The first record of 'Tychenherste' is in 1180 when Adam was the 'presbyter'. The present church dates from 14th century. The base of the tower is even older. It is a distinctive tower with an embattled turret and a short breach spire. The buttressing is neat and shapely. In 1851 the Revd. Arthur Eden did much to restore a dilapidated building. He was vicar for 57 years so had the satisfaction of seeing the success of his work. The chancel was all but rebuilt in 1856. All windows were careful replicas of those they replaced. Most are Decorated or Perpendicular in style. The east window was restored in 1856 and the glass replaced in 1897. The central light gained first prize in a Paris Exhibition. The north wall of the sanctuary has some medieval glass portraying Doom. Among the sinners carried to Hell are a bishop, a king and a pope. The porch entrance is through the replaced 14th century arch. A niche over the porch entrance contains a stone carving of the Virgin Mary. At the apex of the vaulted roof of the porch is a shield of the Etchingham family who may have been influential in building the early church. The nave roof is high and spacious. In nave, north and south chapels the roofs are on crown posts with tie beams. A list of memorials in this church is in the visitors` corner. Of interest to us are the memorials to the May family who owned Pashley Manor from 16th to 19th century. (We pass Pashley Manor on our

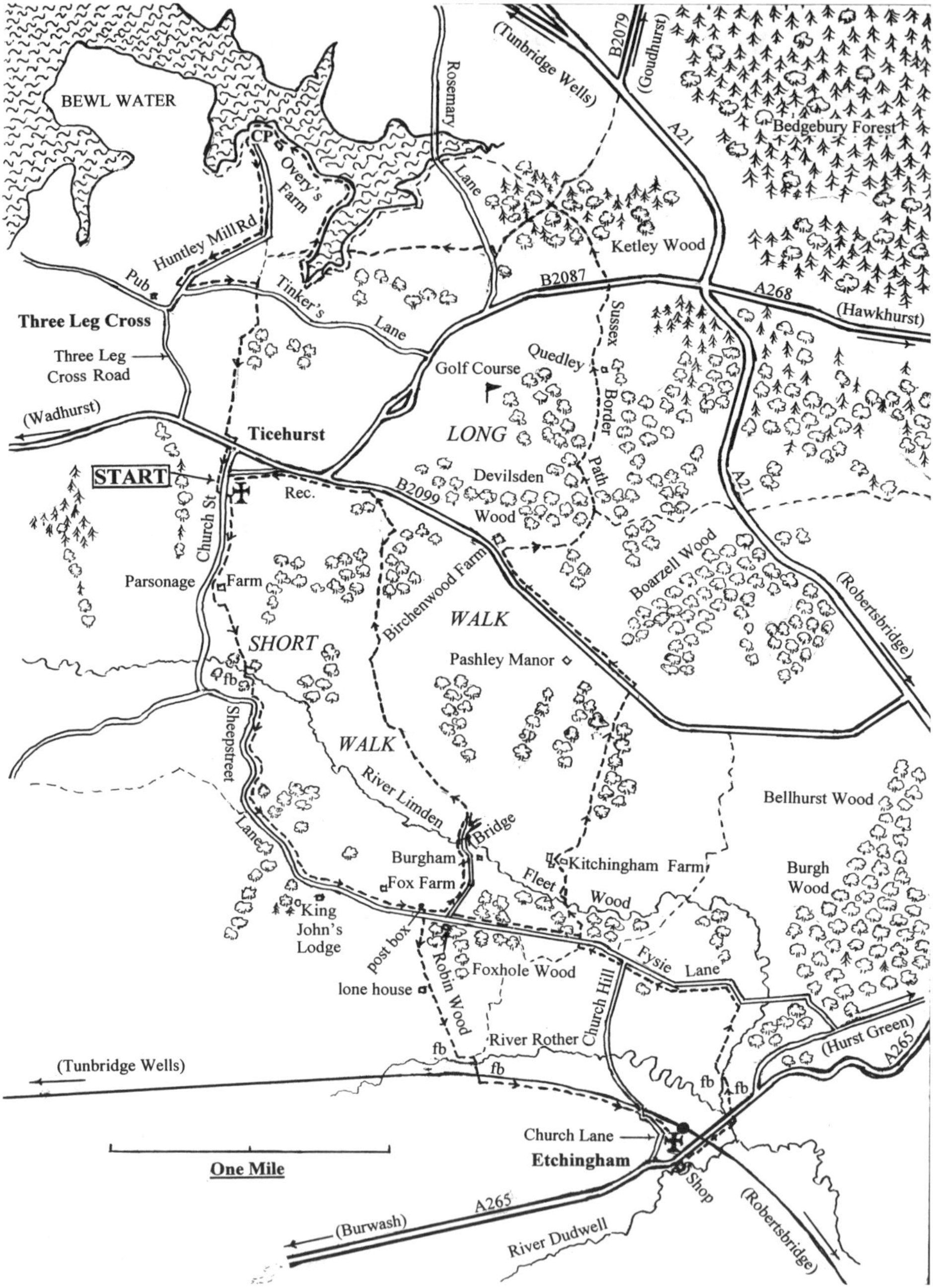
BEWL WATER
CP
Overy's Farm
Rosemary Lane
(Tunbridge Wells)
B2079
(Goudhurst)
A21
Bedgebury Forest
Ketley Wood
Huntley Mill Rd
Pub
Tinker's Lane
B2087
A268
(Hawkhurst)
Three Leg Cross
Three Leg Cross Road
Sussex Border Path
Quedley
Golf Course
(Wadhurst)
Ticehurst
LONG
START
Rec.
Devilsden Wood
B2099
Church St
Birchenwood Farm
Boarzell Wood
Parsonage Farm
WALK
SHORT
Pashley Manor
(Robertsbridge)
fb
Sheepstreet Lane
WALK
River Limden
Bridge
Bellhurst Wood
Burgham
Kitchingham Farm
Fox Farm
Fleet Wood
Burgh Wood
King John's Lodge
post box
Robin Wood
Foxhole Wood
Church Hill
Fysie Lane
lone house
River Rother
(Hurst Green)
A265
(Tunbridge Wells)
fb
Church Lane
Etchingham
One Mile
Shop
A265
(Burwash)
River Dudwell
(Robertsbridge)

walk). An organ now stands in the former Pashley Chapel south of the chancel. Many churches dominate their village; none more so than St Mary`s. Large, imposing and sturdy, the church offers its spacious land to all who enjoy the green churchyard.

The Parish Church of the Assumption of Blessed Mary and St Nicolas, Etchingham. The Manor House, where the Rivers Rother, Dudwell and Limden meet has been destroyed in 19th century when the railway was built. Simon de Achyngham held the Manor in 12th century. A descendant, Sir William de Echyngham is responsible for building the church we see here today. He built it with local sand stone in 14th century in Decorated style. The church fortunately has escaped restoration. It was a collegiate church of the Cistercians (see the next walk). They valued simplicity and later iconoclasts found little here to smash. On the floor of the chancel there is a brass memorial, dated 1389, to the noble founder. His head has been obliterated. It may be the oldest brass in Sussex. Nearby is a three figure brass of his son`s family. On the floor of the south chapel is a small brass of Elizabeth Echyngham (died 1452). The church has a short central tower with a pyramid roof and the original bronze vane. The chancel is longer than the nave. The choir stalls in the chancel are misericords, raised seats that give the impression the sitter is standing. The carving on these seats is as clear today as it was 700 years ago. One shows a fox dressed as a priest, preaching to some geese. The nave is square with arches of different heights. Clerestory windows high in the nave contain heraldic arms of local families. The east window of the north aisle contains fragments of medieval glass.

Ticehurst

The Walk

Pass Ticehurst Church on your left as you walk down Church Lane for ½ mile heading south.

Pass a converted school, several individual houses and finally Parsonage Farm on the left. Turn Immediately left into a field. Follow the wooded field boundary on the left. In the next field cross diagonally left enjoying a view over farmland below. Just to the right of the corner, cross into the third field. Go down to a farm gate and enter a rough wooded glen. Turn left and follow the stream, the tiny River Limden on your left for 50 metres. Climb a short steep bank on the right and walk away from the river to cross a small field to the road.

Turn left and walk along Sheepstreet Lane for 1 mile. You have fine views over Limden valley on the left. On the way you pass individual houses including King John`s Lodge which offers accommodation and provides a plant nursery.

Look out for Fox Farm on the left. In another 150 metres, just past a small postbox on the left, turn right at a concrete way marker on the ground.

You are now heading south along a driveway with Foxhole Wood on your left. In ¼ mile veer left away from the driveway. Veer southeast to enter an enclosed path. Pass a lone house on the right then in another 100 metres you emerge to a boggy field. Hug the hedge on the right to continue to the field corner then turn left. In 50 metres turn right to cross two plank footbridges with wooden rails.

Cross the railway line with care then turn sharp left. The public footpath keeps close to the railway on the left and passes through wet, marshy patches. Some walkers have found firmer ground on the grassy strip to the right. They have to return to the railway line to cross a stile to the next field.

This leads to a quiet lane in Etchingham, Church Lane. Turn right, passing cottages on the left. At a bend in the road, turn left into a rough path that leads straight to Etchingham Church. The shop is opposite the nearby children`s recreation field.

Etchingham

From Etchingham Church go to the road, A265. Turn away from the recreation field and towards the station. Pass the station on the left. Cross the level crossing and you have left the village behind you. Go over the bridge across the River Limden. Turn left almost immediately and go down into the meadow. The narrow river is on your left. You have to veer left to cross two footbridges over the river. In ½ mile you reach Fysie Lane.

Turn left and start climbing. Pass the junction with Church Hill on the left. Ignore the first footpath on the right. *The Short Walk is below on page 89.**

For the Long Walk, turn right at the second path (¼ mile after Church Hill). Here is a farm track signposted to Kitchingham Farm. Go down through Fleet Wood. Pass oast houses and keep on the track as it swings to the left and goes through the garden of a delightful old black and white, tile hung cottage. You then pass a barn under conversion on the left. At the end of the track, climb through a canopy of trees to turn left towards woodland.

You are on an elevated path hugging woodland on your right and enjoying views across the valley on the left. In 500 metres your path continues through the wood. You emerge to B2099 with Three Gates Farm on your right.

Turn left and walk along the verge of B2099. In ¼ mile you pass Pashley Manor on the left (see above). In another ½ mile, turn right at Birchenwood Farm. You have to pass through a narrow alley before emerging to the welcome sight of rolling fields.

Veer left onto a wide grassy path that leads down towards Devilsden Wood. Look out for footpath arrows and veer further left. At the outside corner of the wood you join the Sussex Border Path.

Turn left and enter the dark dank wood. Follow the Sussex Border Path down to cross a brook and up the other side. Eventually you come out of the wood to reach a golf course.

You can see a stile on the other side of a swath of grass but have to brave the golf balls. Cross to the stile and continue northwards passing Quedley Farm on the left. Follow the driveway up to the main road, B2087.

Cross diagonally left to a bridleway, still the Sussex Border Path, and walk down through more woodland. In ¼ mile at cross paths in the wood, turn left and southwest away from the Sussex Border Path. In another ¼ mile you reach Rosemary Lane.

Turn right, passing a rest home then a driveway on the left. Turn immediately left into a footpath heading due west with the field boundary on the left. This well used path leads for ½ mile down to Bewl Water.

Go down to the field corner on the left, enter the tree fringe and turn right on an official track to the nearby water. There is more mud than water in this corner of the reservoir. Turn left on the footpath and go through trees with the edge of the water on your right. The path bends to the right to take you to the other side of this channel. Avoid a footpath to the left and keep following the bank as the channel widens. Pass two rows of poplars up on the left and a three-headed converted oast house. When you reach a small car park on the right, go through a farm gate and turn left on the track.

Bewl Water

The track takes you south away from Bewl Water. The track becomes Huntley Mill Road. In nearly 1 mile you reach Three Leg Cross where there is a pub at crossroads. Turn left just before the pub and head east along Tinker`s Lane. In ¼ mile a footpath crosses the lane.

Turn right and follow waymarkers through a copse then fields and on southwards to enter an alley at Ticehurst. Turn left at the main road, the High Street, then first right for the church.

* **The Short Walk** carries on a little further along Sheepstreet Lane. In ¼ mile you reach Fleetwood Cottage on the right and Robin Wood cottage opposite. Look for the concrete signpost on the ground on the right. Turn right into a concrete track with the signpost 'Burgham'. Go down this steep track with woodland on the right and scattered cottages on the left. The track bears left and goes down to Burgham hamlet. Here you veer left again, pass an oasthouse on the right then keep on the track to cross a bridge over the little River Limden. Follow the left concrete track almost to its end and turn left. There are now arrows indicating the footpath.

Here a grassy track heads northwest up an open field for nearly ½ mile. After a stile you hug a hedge on the left. Keep on course after going through a farm gate. You are now approaching Stroodspit Wood. Cross over to the other side of the hedge and you have a glimpse of houses up ahead. Keep on course with the hedge on your right. The hedge widens into a small wood. Keep this on your right until you find the grassy path curves to the left, crossing the elevated field to another small wood. Veer right and walk beside this wood on your left to houses at Upper Platts on the B2099.

Turn left and follow the road down to Ticehurst. Turn left at 'no entry' sign for traffic and walk up St Mary`s Lane for the church.

Walk 17: Mountfield to Salehurst and Robertsbridge

A delightfully varied walk through rolling fields, past a stately home then crossing the river in the footsteps of Cistercians to a huge church, next through an historic country town and finally back through parkland.

Starting Point: Mountfield Church **GR**735203
Or Robertsbridge Railway Station **GR**733234
Rail travellers go to 'Willow Bank', bottom of page 93 and turn right. When you reach Mountfield Church, revert to the beginning of the Walk.
Map: OS Explorer 124 (It is not essential to bring 136 despite an overlap)
Terrain: Undulating. **Distance:** 7-8 Miles

Local Information:
1. See the Introduction under 'Rivers' for more on the Rother.
2. Footpaths in the grounds of Mountfield Court pass close to this early 18th century home of the Egerton Family. The Counts of Eu were the first feudal overlords of the Manor of Mountfield.
3. **Robertsbridge** is not mentioned in Domesday. The Abbot of the nearby Cistercian Abbey built a bridge about ½ mile west of Salehurst, drawing traffic westwards. In 13th century the bridge is mentioned as 'Pons Roberti'. By mid-16th century Robertsbridge had taken shape. Many timber-framed houses in the High Street are 15th or 16th Century.

The Churches

All Saints, Mountfield stands on a gentle elevation among trees and overlooks green fields with a glimpse of Netherfield tower to the southwest. It stands on a ley line or ancient track. Nearby Gypsum Works are well hidden. The church welcomes visitors with open doors so all can share the beauty of this Norman building. The walls of nave and chancel are early 12th century. There are two small 12th century lancets and a blocked Norman door in the north wall of the nave. The larger window there is 15th century. On the south side of the nave there are three windows of 14th and 15th centuries. The chancel has a Norman arch. The squints on either side of the arch were made in 13th century. There are faint wall paintings above the arch; they are 12th, 13th, and 16th century. Three 13th century windows with Victorian glass are in the chancel. The east window is in the style of 14th century with glass of 1972. In 1896 the gallery was enlarged to make way for the organ. The tower in two stages was added late in 12th century. The magnificent font is also 12th century. Leaves, Tudor roses and scallop shells were carved on the side panels in 16th century. Scorched earth found under nave and near the tower is believed to be part of an earlier Saxon church, probably destroyed after the Norman Conquest. The low tower is Early English. The wooden porch on a brick base is 14th century.

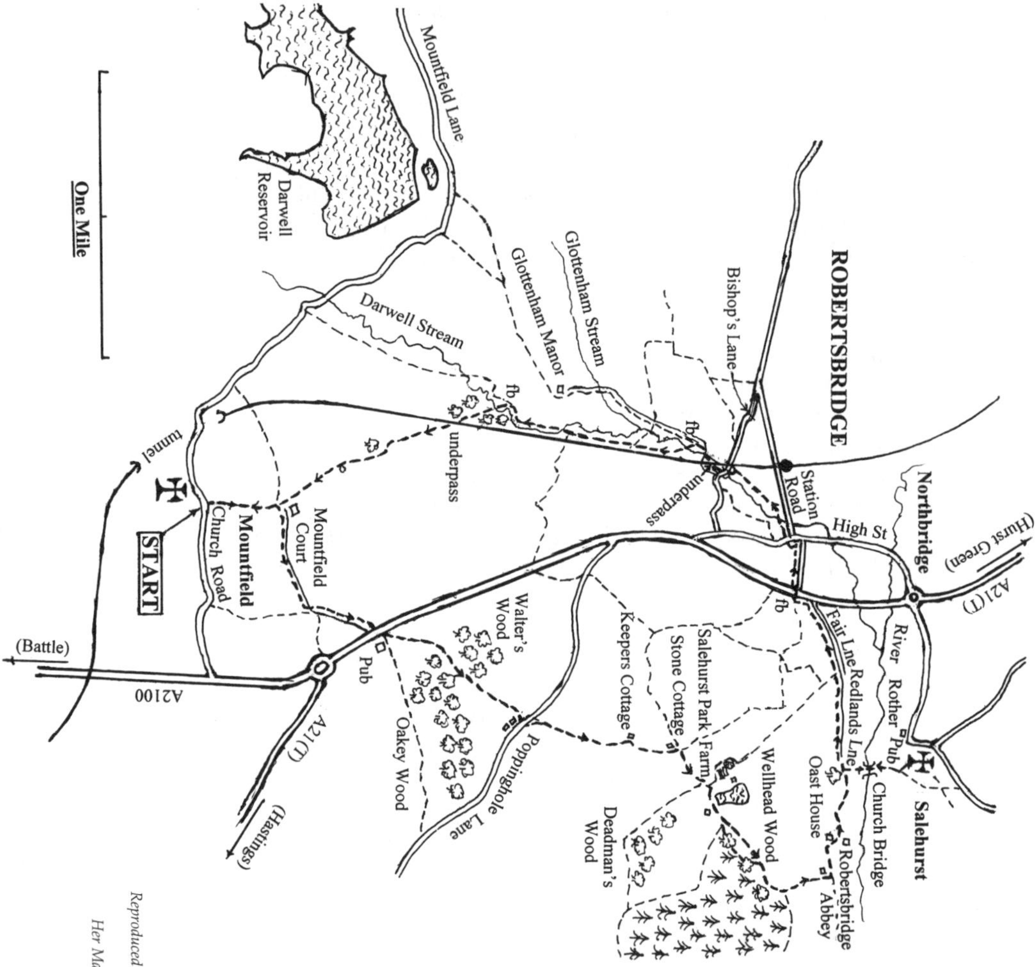
ROBERTSBRIDGE
One Mile
Darwell Reservoir
Mountfield Lane
Glottenham Manor
Glottenham Stream
Bishop's Lane
Darwell Stream
fb
underpass
fb
underpass
tunnel
START
Mountfield
Church Road
Mountfield Court
Station Road
High St
Northbridge
(Hurst Green)
A21(T)
River Rother
Pub
Salehurst
Church Bridge
Robertsbridge Abbey
Oast House
Redlands Lne
Fair Lne
fb
Wellhead Wood
Salehurst Park Farm
Stone Cottage
Keepers Cottage
Walter's Wood
Deadman's Wood
Poppinghole Lane
Oakey Wood
Pub
A2100
(Battle)
A21(T)
(Hastings)

Robertsbridge Abbey was founded around 1176. It is dedicated, as were all Cistercian buildings to the Virgin. It was flourishing in the Middle Ages. Sadly, Henry V111 dissolved the Abbey in 1539. Today the remains are hidden in a private house, once the Abbot`s House. Before the Dissolution, the Abbot had already started to divert a stream, the Lyme. Sir William Sidney acquired the land and created more channels for his new iron works. He is one of many new landowners who benefitted from the Dissolution to become a wealthy iron master.
St Mary The Virgin, Salehurst. Our approach to this church follows the footpath across the River Rother on the medieval road to London. Salehurst Parish was populous then and the Cistercians had their prestige to consider, so they built a large impressive church. In1226 Simon de Etchyngham acquired the advowsons of Salehurst, Mountfield and Udimore from the Collegiate Church of Hastings. He started rebuilding Salehurst and most of the present Church is of this period. The chancel, nave and lower part of the tower are all Early English. The aisles were added later in Decorated style. The nave may be the longest and loftiest of its period in Sussex. The west tower is an integral part of the church. As you enter through the west porch, you see three huge arches that support the tower. Above the porch the brilliant west window in Decorated style has five lights. Most stained glass in the church is 19th century. The window in the Lady Chapel is by Kempe. The south aisle windows are exceptional; a series of birds from a medieval pattern book owned by Samuel Pepys have been painted on the glass.

The Walk

From the entry drive at Mountfield Church go down to the lane below. This is Church Lane. Cross to the public footpath along the private drive opposite. Walk along the drive heading north for 500 metres. You come to crosspaths in front of Mountfield Court.

Turn right to walk along another drive east-northeast. In ½ mile you reach the main road, A21 and cross with care to the pub opposite. Pass the pub on your right and turn right immediately. Here beside the pub is an enclosed footpath through an unsavoury yard and leading to open fields at the back.

As you emerge from the yard, stand still. The path ahead is not for you. Instead, go through the nearby gate on the left. (At the time of writing there is no signpost). Head northeast across an open field towards woodland.

Suddenly you are beset with signs urging you not to stray from the footpath! Steer a course through a narrow field with Walter`s Wood on the left and Oakey Wood on the right, at the same time crossing diagonally left. Go through willow bushes to open fields, rolling and pleating into the distance. Continue northeast.

After crossing a field boundary, you will see two houses ahead. Keep to the left of these and you will find the way through to Poppinghole Lane. Turn to the right then immediately left to resume you northeasterly course over fields. You can see the tower of Salehurst Church in the distance.

After a short downward slope you come to Keepers Cottage. Pass this on your left. You are on the drive now. In 300 metres you reach cross tracks at Stone Cottage.

Turn right on the track to Park Farm and you come to more crosspaths. Veer to the right but not sharp right. Your track passes a large pond on the left and brings you to a single storey Pipes Cottage.

Pass the cottage on your right and go uphill towards woodland, Wellhead Wood. Avoid the path to the right and follow the track that enters the wood heading northeast. Some walkers have chosen to step to the left outside the wood, walking parallel to the track to avoid the mud inside.

Come out of the wood to a farm track. Avoid turning right. Instead head north along the track towards a house. Turn left onto a footpath that skirts the garden of the house and comes to a T-junction.

Turn left onto a new track and follow it as it bends right then left. Stop on this bend with an oasthouse on the left and an old building on the right. The remains of the Cistercian Abbey are in and around the private house on the right. Continue along the track for another 250 metres. Turn right on a path, once the old London road.

It leads to a footbridge over the River Rother then uphill on an enclosed track to Salehurst Church and the nearby pub.

Retrace your steps from Salehurst over the Rother and back to the new track, known as Fair Lane. Turn right to resume your trek to Robertsbridge. As you approach the A21, veer left to cross a footbridge over the bypass here and you are in Robertsbridge.

Walk down the street, a continuation of Fair Lane to the High Street. (The post office and other handsome timber framed buildings are to the right).

Turn left then right into Station Road. Pass a car park on the left. When you come down to a road called **Willow Bank**, turn left. *Rail travellers walk up Station Road and turn right at Willow Bank.* There is a footpath on the right that crosses Piper`s meadow in a southwesterly direction.

Salehurst

At the railway line, do not go through the first underpass. Instead, turn left into Bishop`s Lane. In 50 metres you reach a small road on the right that also leads under the railway line. This is the way you want. You are on the road to Glottenham Manor, now a nursing home.

In 75 metres after the underpass, turn left on a footpath to walk beside the Darwell Stream. Cross the stream and follow the railway on the left. In ½ mile pass Glottenham Manor on a low hill on the right.

Avoid a left turn over the railway but keep the line on your left and boggy land on the right. Head southwest away from the railway. At a field corner turn left to a footbridge. (The main path stays with the Darwell Stream).

Cross the footbridge and head southeast away from the stream and towards the railway again. First you go through a lovely bluebell wood. The path climbs through the wood and brings you out beside the railway line. In 50 metres go through the underpass to the magical parkland of Mountfield.

Avoid the avenue on the right. Cross a farm bridge over Bottom Hole Brook. Veer right and climb through scattered trees with cattle roaming free and enjoying the pond down on the left. Climb more steeply up to a gate.

Go through to the drive. Pass Mountfield Court on the left. Come to the familiar crosspaths and retrace your steps back down to Mountfield Church.

Robertsbridge

Walk 18: Wadhurst to Tidebrook

This is a charming walk through wooded slopes and quiet valleys.

Starting Point: The Car Park off Washwell Lane or a nearby side road.
GR639317 **Map:** OS Explorer 136 **Terrain:** Undulating
Distance: 8 Miles
Warning: There are no refreshment spots on this walk until you return to Wadhurst. Take a Picnic!

The Churches

The Parish Church of St Peter and St Paul, Wadhurst. An early settler, Wada came to a wooded hill and gave the name Wadehurst. The name has changed little but the village has grown and thrived. The large church dominates near and far. The tower is Norman, part of the original building. The tall broach spire was added in 14th century. It has survived fire and storm – just! The walls of the Norman nave were removed in 13th century when the aisles were added. The pillars are alternately round and octagonal. The south aisle has undergone several changes. It has been widened and then rebuilt in 1592. North and south aisle windows were restored in 1858. In 15th century the chancel was enlarged. The east window has late Victorian stained glass. The 15th century was a busy time; the tower arch was built then, the north transept and the clerestory windows were added then. The porch with a priest`s room was built then and the huge oak beams of the nave roof are probably also 15th century. Wadhurst made its wealth out of the iron industry. It has a record number of iron tomb slabs. Dating from 1614 to 1790 there are 30 iron slabs, set mainly in the church floor. They testify to the importance of the iron industry to Wadhurst. See the church guide for the stories behind these tombs.
Tidebrook Church, St John the Baptist was built by Rushforth in 1856 on land given by John Joseph Newington of Towngate. The first vicar came in 1858. Pevsner describes the building as "...a remarkably good job. Lancet style with a bellcote over the west end of the chancel". Collar beams support the roof. Plans are afoot today to add a meeting room and an elevated outside walkway. The church is on a slope below the road.

The Walk

Walk down Washwell Lane with the church behind you. The residential road changes to a quiet lane with playing fields on the left then sinks into the tree covered slope.

In 500 metres turn right into a footpath above the lane and continue southwest across open fields. At a junction of paths go straight on. (You are crossing our lane at a lower point). Once on the path opposite, pass a large house, Foxes Bank away to the right. There is woodland on your left. Carry on downhill into Snape Wood.

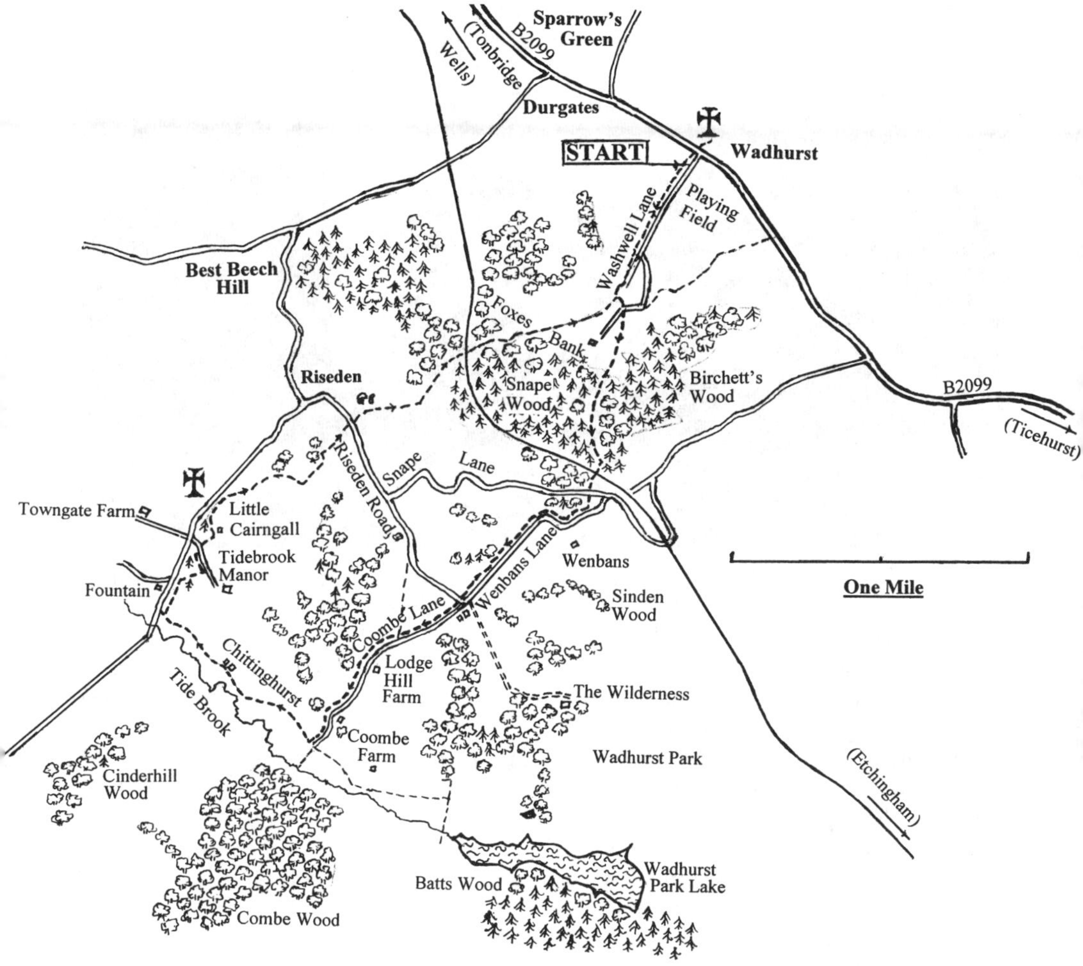
Sparrow's Green
(Tonbridge Wells)
B2099
Durgates
START
Wadhurst
Playing Field
Washwell Lane
Best Beech Hill
Foxes Bank
Riseden
Snape Wood
Birchett's Wood
B2099
(Ticehurst)
Snape Lane
Riseden Road
Towngate Farm
Little Cairngall
Tidebrook Manor
Fountain
Wenbans Lane
Wenbans
Coombe Lane
Sinden Wood
One Mile
Chittinghurst
Tide Brook
Lodge Hill Farm
The Wilderness
Coombe Farm
Wadhurst Park
Cinderhill Wood
(Etchingham)
Batts Wood
Wadhurst Park Lake
Combe Wood

Wadhurst

Tidebrook

Follow the way markers. Cross a forestry track and continue southwards for ¼ mile. The path curves to the left before reaching the railway line. Cross with care to the footpath on the other side. It leads to Snape Lane.

Opposite is another footpath into a small field. It has been diverted away from the house on the left. Bear to the right as you cross the field and enter more woodland. Climb up to Wenbans Lane.

Turn right on this lane and pass Wenbans Cottages on the left. Keep on this straight road for ¼ mile to a junction; Riseden Road is on the right and a private road to Wilderness on the left.

Go straight across to Coombe Lane where you pass two white cottages on the left. Look across to wonderful views to the left. You pass the idyllic buildings of Lodge Hill Farm. Here is a tiny oasthouse. In another ¼ mile you come down to a cottage of Coombe Farm. The lane bends to the left but you have to go straight on, squeezing between a fence on the left and a hedge on the right.

Descend on this path. Just before it enters woodland, you turn right into a welcome open field. You are now on a northwest course for 1 kilometre.

A narrow stream, hidden in trees below on the left has given its name to the parish: 'Tide Brook'. Go straight across the field to a gate on the other side. Go through the gate to a lane. It passes through the private buildings of Chittinghurst and leads to the road through Tidebrook.

Turn right and walk along the road, passing Tidebank Cottage then a side lane on the left where the Fountain Pub used to be. Turn right here and go up some worn steps in a wooded fringe above the road. Keep on course across a sloping field to enter the drive to Tidebrook Manor. Turn left on the drive.

The drive curves down to the left. You bear right towards a gate. Avoid the gate, join the path on the left and resume your way through woodland. You soon pass through the garden of a cottage, Little Cairngall. (The owners object to mud on their drive so perhaps they will apply to have the path diverted). Just past the garage a space in the hedge allows for a narrow footpath that leads down on the left to a steep grassy slope. Here a finger post points the way to Tidebrook Church below. Cross the road with care.

Snape Wood

From Tidebrook Church cross back to climb the grassy slope. Turn left at the finger post. Avoid the house up on the right. A stile in the fence takes you to their drive. Cross to enter more woodland and shortly emerge to the corner of a small field. Ignore arrows. Follow the field boundary on your right. Cross to a slight track in the next field and turn left.

Follow the track northeast to pass woodland on your left. In ¼ mile you reach Riseden Road. Cross to paths opposite. Avoid the path on the right and follow the hedge on the left. You reach a wide dramatic view over a wooded valley.

Stop! Do not be tempted across the lovely slope to the right. Keep strictly to the trees on the left as you descend and in 400 metres you will find the path through the wood below. This path leads to the railway line, well hidden in the thick wood.

Cross the line with care and climb up on the other side. In 50 metres you come to cross tracks in Snape Wood. Avoid the track opposite and that on your right. Instead, follow the track to the left, marked with an arrow. It goes through the wood for ¼ mile before veering left and down to a welcome green field.

Avoid permissive paths straight on. Turn right following the edge of the wood on your right. You have to enter a narrow enclosed path to go down to the familiar junction of paths of the outward walk.

Turn left and cross the field diagonally right towards the spire of Wadhurst Church. Go down to Washwell Lane, turn left and retrace your steps to Wadhurst.

Walk 19: Burwash to Batemans and Brightling

Hills, woods, streams and stately homes all feature in this walk, not to mention two churches with fascinating histories and a beautiful village.

Starting Point: The Car Park opposite the post office in Burwash.
GR675246 **Maps:** OS Explorer 124 and !36 **Distance:** 10 Miles
Terrain: Hilly, wooded, muddy in places. Sorry! No pubs. Bring your own!
Local Information: Three beautiful houses built on the proceeds of iron:
- Bateman`s (1634), home of Rudyard Kipling 1902 – 1936, now in the hands of the National Trust which also manages the watermill on the little River Dudwell.
- Socknersh Manor 17th century, timber framed. A Collins family worked Socknersh Furnace in 16th century. They may have re-built the Manor. There are traces of an earlier medieval house in this idyllic setting.
- Brightling Park (1699). Thomas Fuller bought the mansion in 1697 and rebuilt it. It is still in private hands.

John Fuller (1757 – 1834) inherited the Brightling Estate and proceeded to scatter follies all around. We see the Obelisk or Brightling Needle 646 feet above sea level and 65 feet high and the Pyramid, 25 feet high, the grave of 'Mad Jack Fuller' in Brightling Churchyard.

See the Introduction under 'Rivers' for more on the River Dudwell.

The Churches

The Church of St Bartholomew, Burwash. The first known church was built here in 1090. Only the tower remains from that Norman building. The belfry windows are two-light and separated by balusters. The spire was re-shingled in 1725. You go through the porch and under the tower to enter the church. In 1190 a south aisle was added and in 1250 a north aisle. They were both widened in 14th century. In 1250 the old Norman chancel was replaced by a larger structure. The wide chancel arch has an unusual 'string course' running over it and continuing to the north and south walls. The 16th century font has a Pelham buckle on it (See 'Norman Invasion' in the Introduction). A 14th century slab on the wall of the Lady Chapel has the inscription

Burwash

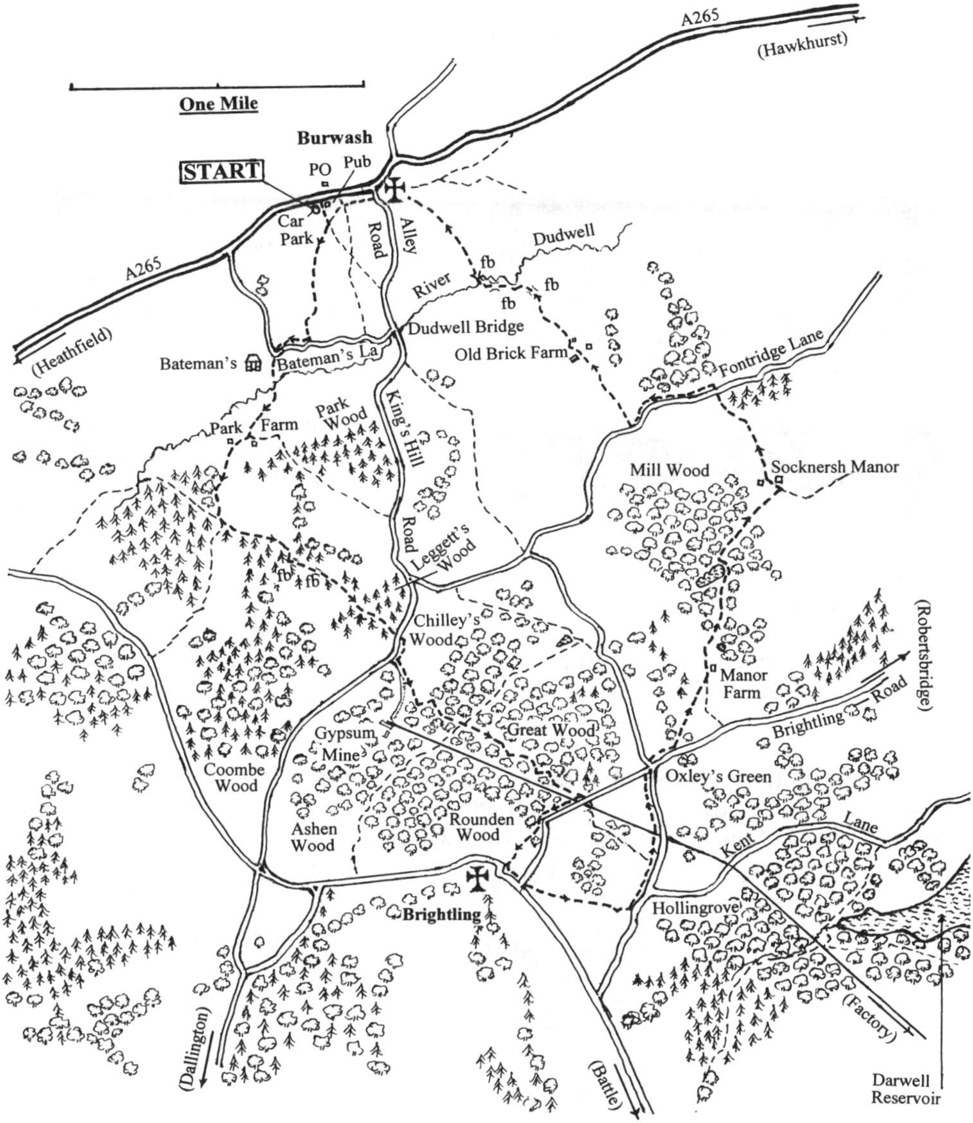

Reproduced by permission of Ordnance Survey on behalf of the Controller of Her Majesty's Stationery Office, © Crown Copyright 100041589

Brightling

'orate p. annema Johne Coline' – 'Pray for the soul of John Collins. His family owned the forge at Socknersh. This may be the oldest piece of Sussex cast iron grave slab. The church has changed little since the Middle Ages. In 1856 the building was restored, keeping faithfully to the original.

The Parish Church of St Thomas a Becket stands high on Brightling Hill. There may have been a wooden Saxon church here first. As at Burwash this building was erected soon after the Norman Conquest. This church has undergone many changes since then, resulting in arches of different heights. The south walls of the nave, chancel and chapel were built in 13th century. The east window of the chancel and the east window of the chapel are Early English. The tall pointed 14th century chancel arch dominates the east end. It contrasts with the smaller arches of the 13th century chancel arcade. The north aisle and arcade were added in 14th century. The roof of the north aisle has braced rafters. Both nave and chancel have wagon roofs. The low tower started in the 13th century in Early English style and had battlements added in 14th century. There is much more of interest in this church and you will find it in the Church Guide.

The Walk

Find the footpath in the left hand corner of the Car Park and scramble down into a sloping field. Follow a hedge on your right downhill. At crosspaths turn right to the other side of the hedge and head southwest for ½ mile. You have a view across to hills in the south and an obelisk, one of Jack Fuller`s creations. It makes a good landmark for you to aim towards.

Near the bottom, you pass a pond on the right. Come down to Bateman`s Lane and turn right. Bateman`s, the lovely home of Rudyard Kipling soon comes into view. (See 'Local Information' above).

Bateman's

Turn left at the junction in front of the house. You are heading south on the private road that crosses the little River Dudwell. It leads to Park Farm where there is an oasthouse among other buildings. Ignore all paths to right and left. Keep straight on through a farm gate. Pass stables on your right and make for the footpath ahead left.

You climb up into bluebell woods. At first you have to negotiate a collapsed path. After that there is nothing worse than slippery mud – worth the effort for the view behind!

In 500 metres at crosspaths, turn left and go southeast. Now you have the luxury of a woodland trail for another 500 metres. You then have to turn right to a way-marked footpath down through the wood to a stream.

Cross two footbridges. Immediately after the second footbridge turn sharp left. Walk up through a gully in Leggatt`s Wood. Your footpath is confirmed with way markers and you continue southeast to King`s Hill Road.

Turn right and walk beside the road for 100 metres to the entrance to Brightling Gypsum Mine. Just on the left is a narrow footpath that runs beside the boundary of the mine. Take this path and you soon come out to a sloping field. Turn right.

Hug the woodland on your right as you descend steeply to a field corner at the bottom. Just left of the corner you enter Beaks Wood. Follow the woodland path for 300 metres to cross paths and keep straight on, southeast, now in Great Wood. You stay in Great Wood for 1 kilometre. You are climbing much of the way and steps have been provided at two steep points. As you approach the edge of the wood, veer left up to a stile and continue to the Brightling Road.

Avoid the footpath opposite and turn right to follow the road over a bridge. *An enclosed aerial line below carries gypsum to the factory at Mountfield.* Climb up the road for 170 metres. At the bend turn right to a footpath and go through trees to a green swathe. Veer left and continue climbing through this swathe. You are walking parallel to the road. Near the top, swing to the right and walk over to a brick cottage with the church beyond. At the elevated road turn left. Brightling Church is opposite.

For the return walk, pass Brightling Church on your right and continue along the road as it bends left. You now appreciate your height above the countryside ahead. Go down to a nearby road junction with a signpost; Robertsbridge is to the left and Battle to the right. Avoid both roads.

Cross to the footpath opposite and you are heading east across an open field with views to the sea and Darwell Reservoir below. The path becomes enclosed as you descend into Hollingrove, a tiny hamlet. Turn left at the bottom onto Kent Lane.

Immediately turn left again past a converted chapel. You are now heading north on a byway. Pass an occasional cottage, one of them thatched. Go under a bridge carrying the gypsum line.

At cross roads with Jack Fuller House on the corner, turn right. You are on Brightling Road. Pass detached houses on the left. In 200 metres, just after the Forge, turn left passing a pond on the right. At the time of writing there is no footpath sign at the start of this path but I hope to change that.

Follow the footpath northeast through scrub land keeping to the hedge on your right and passing a wooden seat. In 250 metres go through the edge of a private garden and come down a bank on your right into an estate road.

Turn left. Pass Manor Farm and an oasthouse on the right. You are now heading north for one mile on the private estate road, a right of way for walkers. The road takes you through Oldhole Wood and past a lake on the left. It then veers right through Mill Wood.

Ahead you can see Socknersh Manor and crossways. Turn left and climb up the driveway between the estate office on the left and the Manor on the right. Here are verges where primroses, violets and narcissi flower in the Spring. Continue to the main entrance to the estate at the top of a ridge.

Socknersh Manor

You emerge at Fontridge Road and turn left, passing the entrance to Glydwish Hall on the right. The next turning to the right is the driveway to Old Brick Farm. A finger post on the other side of the road confirms this is a right of way.

Turn right saunter down the driveway northwest. A line of trees flanks the driveway on the left and a rotunda stands in the field on the right. You see the farm below and a view over the valley of the Dudwell to Burwash up on the other side.

Go straight through the farmyard of Old Brick Farm and head for a nearby pond. Veer to the left before the pond, go through a farm gate then hug the hedge on your right. You are on a northwest course towards water meadows.

At the end of the hedge you can see a footbridge ahead to the right. This takes you across a narrow stream Veer left over the meadow to another bridge beside the River Dudwell. Walk alongside the river for 200 metres. Here a third footbridge takes you over the river.

Once across, bear left towards the tower of Burwash Church. In 100 metres you have a choice of ways. Avoid the entrance to a field on the left. Instead, go to the right of a thick hedge and climb into an open field. The elevated path keeps a little distance from the thick hedge down on the left. At the top left hand corner of the open field, go through to a smaller field where you veer left and uphill toward the church. A kissing gate takes you into the churchyard.

From Burwash Church turn left to walk along the High Street (A265) and back to the Car Park. *You have now followed Pevsner`s advice: 'The High Street of Burwash ought to be walked to appreciate it'.*

Walk 20: Tunbridge Wells to Frant

From an elegant Georgian spa town we escape to the forest wilds and a village too remote for Domesday. We also visit two splendid churches.

Starting Points 1. The Railway Station, Tunbridge Wells **GR**584392
2. Frant High Street **GR**591356
Map: OS Explorer 135 **Distance:** 10 ½ Miles **Terrain:** Undulating
Local Information:
1. Chalybeate Spring was discovered by Dudley Lord North in 1606 when he was staying at Eridge Park. The Nevills, landowners encouraged him to keep away from their park and he chose the remote edge of their estate as the centre where he advertised the health benefit of the waters. A fashionable spa town grew up around this spring. Tiles were laid for the benefit of Queen Anne. These tiles of baked mud gave the name to the centre, 'Pantiles'. We walk through the Pantiles and later pass by the original spring.
2. Quiet lanes lead to the Broadwater Warren Nature Reserve, a large heath and wood, acquired by RSPB in 2007. It is in the process of restoration. At the time of writing there are no way marks and we follow the most clear route, described by RSPB warden. In season there are wood larks, tree pipits, nightjars, woodcocks and finches.

The Churches

The Parish Church of King Charles the Martyr, Royal Tunbridge Wells

Open from 11 a.m. to 3 p.m. on weekdays, thanks to volunteers.

A chapel was built here 1676 – 84 to serve the distinguished summer visitors who came for the benefit of the spring waters. In 1606 Dudley Lord North discovered seven springs including the Chalbeate Spring. It became an attraction for fashionable aristocrats. The colonnaded walkway, the Pantiles (1698), also built for visitors is near the church. The original church was a rectangle. In 1678 one of Wren`s Plasterers, John Wetherell worked on the ceiling to create low circular domes. In 1688 the church was enlarged to double its size, the second part a duplicate of the first Another of Wren`s plasterers, the skilled Henry Doogood made the second magnificent ceiling in its octagonal dome in 1690. There were outside staircases to the panelled galleries so that the

The Pantiles

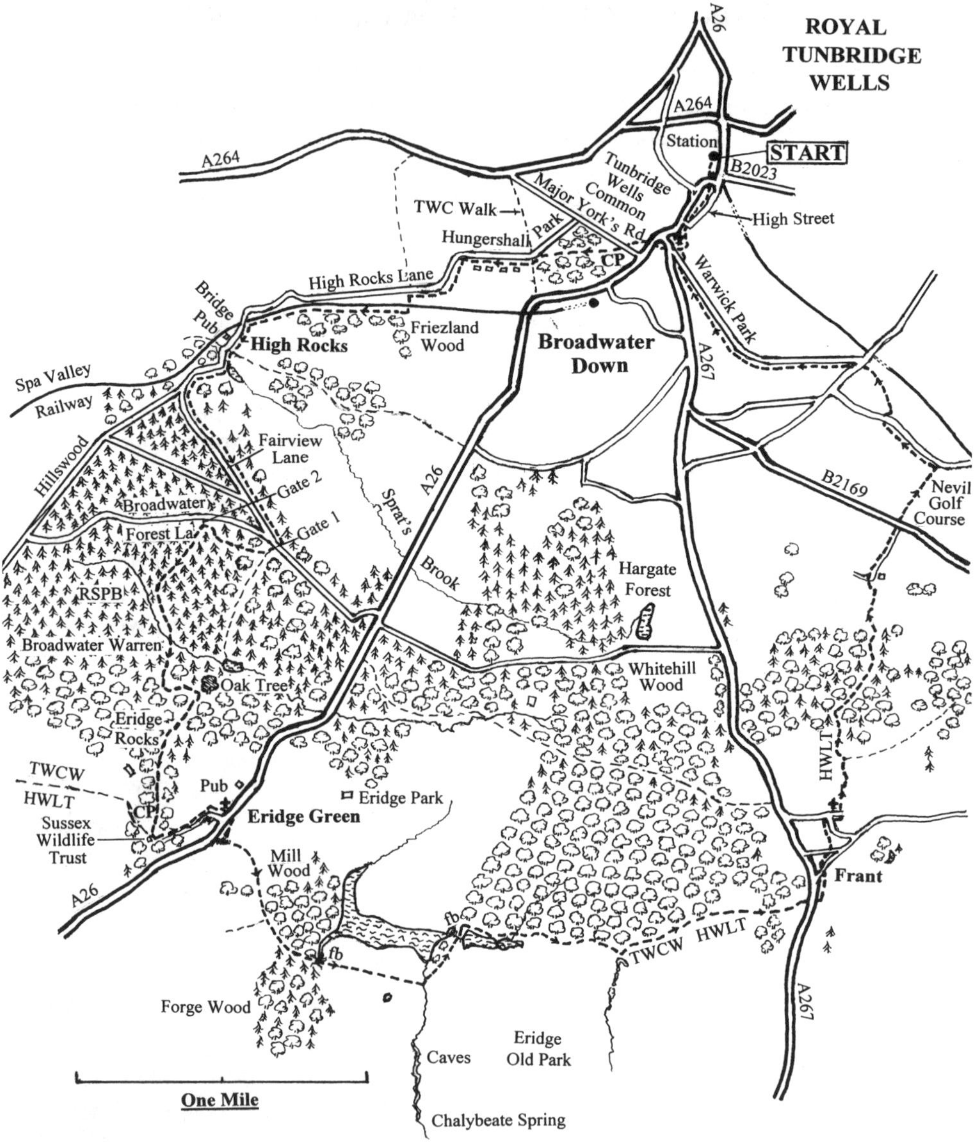

HWLT = High Weald Landscape Trail
TWCW = Tunbridge Wells Circular Walk

lower orders could attend services without mixing with their superiors. The staircases are now inside the church. In 1835 Princess Victoria and her mother used the north gallery. In 1882 the east gallery was removed for the addition of a chancel. The windows all have rounded heads. In 1907 a large font of Pentelikon marble was introduced. The first baby to be christened was a gypsy. All parts of the building have blended to form a beautiful interior. Outside there is a clock tower and a cupola.

Eridge

Eridge Church, Holy Trinity is a small, mid-Victorian church on the Nevill Estate. The Nevills, known as Lords of Burgavenny have held the manor for 900 years. During that time they employed hundreds of estate workers many of whom worked here for generations. The second Earl of Abergavenny (the later title) rebuilt all the estate houses. Some are quite elaborate but the traditional weather boarding of the Wealden village cannot be found here!

Frant Church and locality. Set in the northern end of the Pevensey Rape, the wilderness of Frant escaped discovery by the Normans, so is not mentioned in Domesday. The name means a ferny heath. Gilbert de Clare of Rotherfield (see Walk 15) built a chapel here in 11th century. A stone church replaced it in 13th century. Unskilled builders enlarged it in 15th century. It had a square nave and two chancels. Other local churches were also built in stone between 1340 and 1420. They all survived but Frant had to be rebuilt. Vicars at Frant were subordinate to rectors at Rotherfield. Fine craftsmen were employed in building a grand new nave at nearby Bayham Abbey. This Praemonstratensian Abbey was founded in 1208. The people of Frant valued this rich neighbour with its tradition of charity and hospitality. When Cardinal Wolsey closed it in 1525, the people of Frant, led by the vicar re-opened it and appointed a new Abbot. They were punished by Henry V111! Frant prospered in 17th century thanks to the iron industry. There were 20 iron works in the neighbourhood. Links to Bayham are lost; no footpaths head that way. Instead roads and tracks opened to Tunbridge Wells. In 1822 Frant Church was rebuilt. John Montier, a carpenter and joiner designed the new church. Only the tower was

Frant

preserved, re-covered in stone and heightened. The pillars of the new church are of cast iron and the Perpendicular windows have iron glazing bars. Perhaps Montier wanted to strengthen this church! Certainly, the embattled roofs give an appearance of strength. In 1867 it was extended, gaining a larger chancel and a south aisle. A visitor to Frant, Auguste Gern, who had helped build the organ for Notre Dame de Paris, set to work to provide the church with a magnificent instrument. The value of this organ was fully appreciated when it broke down in 1960s and had to be restored; there are 20 miles of wiring and 1626 pipes. Fernani Germani, organist to St Peter`s, Rome, came to play on the masterpiece once it was restored in 1968.

The Walk

At Tunbridge Wells Station go out past the ticket office and turn left to the nearby main road. Turn left again and walk uphill to cross with care to the High Street. Wander down past shops and cafes, heading south. At the bottom the cupola of King Charles the Martyr beckons. Keep straight on along the narrower lane to the church. You can go either side to find the entrance.

If you take the steps ahead then turn right, passing the church on your right, you come to the busy A267. A request pedestrian crossing at traffic lights is on your left. Cross to the Pantiles opposite where shops, cafes and the Tourist Information Office may waylay you. Walk along the cobbled surface and up steps. The bath house is behind you. Pass the first gap, Woods Passage on the right. Go through the second gap, Flat House Passage to the main road A26.

Cross the main road by a pedestrian crossing on the left and you are on Tunbridge Wells Common. Here is a straight, well defined way southwest. Keep on course after an intersection and you come to Major Yorks Road. Cross with care to the Car Park entrance opposite. Pass the car park on your left and continue along the tarmac path, now a 'restricted byway'. It is a pleasant, shady path with some bracken under scattered trees.

In 600 metres you leave the Common at crossways. Go straight on across the long distance trail, *Tunbridge Wells Circular Walk* to the lane opposite, Hungershall Park Road. Pass sumptuous houses on the left with a view across the fields of Nevill Park. This lane curves south down to Cabbage Stalk Lane. Continue along High Rocks Lane where there is no pavement. In 250 metres keep a sharp lookout for a footpath sign on the **right**. Turn **left** here to go under the Spa Valley Railway.

Turn right, joining *the Tunbridge Wells Circular Walk* through woodland. Walk beside a stream on the right, the little River Groom and the railway beyond. In ¼ mile you pass the edge of High Rocks on the left. Come up to a lane with the railway bridge below **right**. Turn **left** away from the bridge and walk along the lane to reach the inn and restaurant at High Rocks. *For a small entrance fee you can go up into the Stone Age camp opposite the inn.*

Continue along the lane past the inn car park on the left and the Tunbridge Wells Circular Walk that departs to the right. You are on the appropriately named Hillswood Road. In 500 metres turn left into the wooded Fairview Lane. Pass a road turning to the right and in another 200 metres you come up to the main road at a T-junction.

Cross with care to the metal gate opposite. This is Gate 1 of the RSPB reserve, Broadwater Warren. Enter the reserve via a stile beside the gate. Go straight ahead on a path. **Stop** in 25 metres and turn right to follow a sandy path that runs parallel to the main road. In 500 metres at a T-junction, turn right towards another metal gate. This is Gate 2 of the reserve. Just before the gate, turn left. Another wide path curves left then heads southwest gently down through heath and trees. Keep on course for nearly one kilometre, crossing a little stream on the way and avoiding all crosspaths. At the end the path curves left. Turn left and follow the path northeast then southeast, a distance of 250 metres. You come to oak trees. **Stop!** At a large oak on the left, turn right.

The path here leads southwards out of the reserve and into land of Sussex Wildlife Trust. At present there is no apparent boundary. You pass a succession of shapely rocks that form a high natural wall on your right. In 500 metres you come to the SWT Car Park where there are some information stands. Turn left at the road and you have joined the *Tunbridge Wells Circular Walk also the High Weald Landscape trail.* They take the same route here.

We follow these paths to the edge of Tunbridge Wells, so look out for their symbols on posts.

Ahead are the estate houses of Eridge Green. Pass these and you come to the A26. The little Church of Holy Trinity is to the left. Turn right and walk along the pavement for 100 metres, passing more estate cottages. Then cross with care to the footpath opposite. A lovely view opens ahead; sloping fields sprinkled with woodland.

Hug the hedge on the left and go down to the field corner. Keep on course in the next field. Then swing to the right to head south and follow the edge of Mill Wood. Cross a footbridge to an enclosed path. Avoid the path to the right. The enclosed path leads to a track.

Cross the track to enter the wood. Go through the wood where there are more footbridges to cross. As you emerge from the wood, you pass a sign, 'Broadoak Fisheries' on the left. The footpath ahead takes you southeast over an elevated expanse of meadow above a large lake on the left.

In the age of iron and blast furnaces, this area could be alight with flames and ringing with hammers. Now all is quiet. Clumps of trees are on the hill tops of Eridge Old Park ahead. In the meadow you will see clover, reeds, yellow vetch and the odd brilliant pink flower of the rare vetchling grass in the summer.

You come down to a strip of woodland and a footbridge over a stream. *The famous Chalybeate Spring is to the right also caves, the haunt of smugglers past.* In the next meadow the path veers left. Woodland is on your left and there is another lake ahead. Cross the footbridge over the stream of water plunging from this smaller lake to the first large lake and turn right. You pass this smaller lake on your right.

You are heading east through scrub where ragwort grows. Keep on course through more woodland where there may be damp patches under foot. The path ends after a low slab bridge. Avoid the field gate into the sloping field ahead.

Instead, turn left into the edge of the wood. The field is on your right. Pass a

Eridge Park pond

stand of information on this ancient hunting forest. Veer right and head east, passing through a gate in a high deer fence. Avoid the permissive path ahead and start the climb up to Frant. Your steep path ends in an overgrown alley and emerges at A267.

Turn left and in 150 metres, cross the road that leads to Bayham Abbey. Continue climbing over the Village Green to the High Street. Frant Church is facing you at the end of this short street. The pub is on your right.

From Frant Church, go through the churchyard to find the same long distance paths at the back. Follow the hedge on the right and head north downhill. You have a view to Tunbridge Wells ahead. In 250 metres keep on course at a cross track and avoid the path to Ely Grange on the right.

In another 100 metres enter Chase Wood and walk with care as you descend on the clear path through the wood. In 500 metres you cross a footbridge and come out to continue along a field edge. You come to a private lane leading to a small cottage on the right. Turn left on the lane then immediately right into an enclosed farm track.

The farm track leads to Bayham Road, B2169. (Frant Station is to the right). Cross with care to the path opposite and walk on the edge of Nevill Golf Club. Pass the clubhouse and car park on the right and you reach Benhall Mill Road.

Turn left to walk along the pavement for ¼ mile. The wall on your left ends in an attached little house. Cross to the footpath opposite here. It is hidden in the layby. I shall be requesting a clearance for this neglected footpath! Follow it through bushes. You are above the unseen railway line in a dip then a tunnel on the right.

The path widens and joins a track bringing you out to Forest Road. Cross diagonally left to Warwick Park. You enter this wide road at a junction. Pass the tennis club on the right as you descend on this comfortable residential road. At the end turn right and find the steps back up to the High Street and return to Tunbridge Wells Station.

5 Walks
Near Battle

St Clement, Hastings

Walk 21: Crowhurst to Battle and Catsfield

The highlight of the '1066 Country Walk' must be the section that passes the famous battlefield. All is peaceful now as we explore the lovely countryside near Battle and go through a wooded nature reserve near Crowhurst.

Starting Point: Crowhurst Church **GR**758123
(I was advised to use the village hall car park near the school. You may need permission for this. Otherwise find a verge). **Or**
Crowhurst Railway Station **GR**760129
Map: OS Explorer 124 **Terrain:** gentle slopes **Distance:** 8 Miles
Note: At the time of writing, some paths after Catsfield have no signposts. I shall inform East Sussex County Council. Meanwhile, bring a compass!
Local Information:
1. The romantic ruins south of Crowhurst Church are of the old manor house (12th – 13th century).
2. Catsfield Place, now a school was rebuilt in 1685, probably by Nicholas Pelham. See Introduction under Norman Invasion for more on the Pelhams.

The Churches

Crowhurst, St George. An early 19th century rhyme describes the church:

And the village church low towered and small
Stands close to a ruined mansion wall,
On a grassy bank, in a peaceful nook
Just above a rush – fringed brook.
Half hid by the very largest yew
I ever saw in my life - or you.

The name goes back a long way. 'Croghyrst' is mentioned in 771 when the Bishop of Selsey acquired land here. After the Conquest the Manor passed to William Fitz Lambert. His descendant Walter de Scotney was executed for attempted murder in 13th century. The church became a prebend of the Collegiate Church of St Mary in the Castle, Hastings. In 1412 Henry 1V granted the Manor of Crowhurst to Sir John Pelham. A church, dedicated to St George was then built in Early English style. There have since been four restorations. In 1726 the chancel was repaired. In 1794 the nave was rebuilt. In 1856 the chancel was rebuilt to its original size. 1960 –1970 the floor and roof were repaired, the church decorated and heating and organ overhauled. The tower and west doorway are Perpendicular. Pelham buckles are on both sides of the west door. The yew tree may be the largest in Sussex.
Battle Abbey. William the Conqueror had the Abbey built on the site of the 1066 Battle. The high altar marks the spot where Harold fell. Little remains of the Abbey Church but excavations show its size and shape. **The Gatehouse** at the town

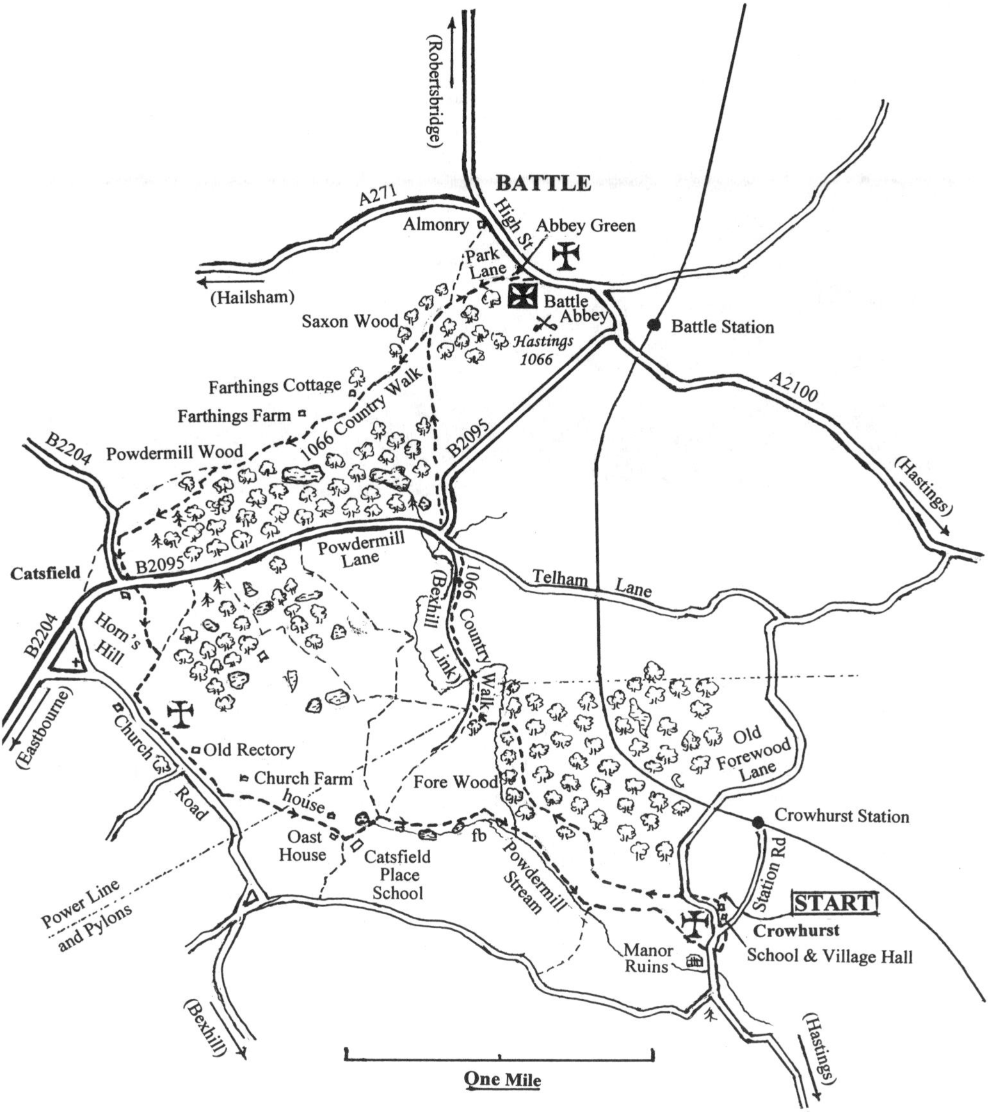
(Robertsbridge)
BATTLE
A271
High St
Almonry
Abbey Green
Park Lane
(Hailsham)
Battle Abbey
Saxon Wood
Hastings 1066
Battle Station
Farthings Cottage
Farthings Farm
1066 Country Walk
B2095
A2100
B2204
Powdermill Wood
(Hastings)
Catsfield
B2095
Powdermill Lane
(Bexhill Link)
1066 Country Walk
Telham Lane
B2204
Horn's Hill
(Eastbourne)
Church Road
Old Rectory
Church Farm
house
Fore Wood
Old Forewood Lane
Crowhurst Station
Oast House
Catsfield Place School
fb
Powdermill Stream
Station Rd
START
Crowhurst
School & Village Hall
Power Line and Pylons
Manor Ruins
(Bexhill)
(Hastings)
One Mile

Crowhurst

entrance to the Abbey was built by Abbot Alan in 1338. It combines 'power with the filigree delicacy of the Decorated style ... one of the finest in England', according to Pevsner.

Battle Parish Church, St Mary, north of the Abbey was built by Abbot Ralph in 12th century. The partly blocked arch in the south chapel is from that first church. The square font is Norman. The chancel was extended in 13th century and has three Early English windows. The aisles were lengthened in late 12th century. The five – bay arcades are Transitional. They have alternate round and octagonal pillars. The north chapel was enlarged in 14th century. The tower, south porch and south chapel are 15th century. The three-light window in the south chapel is Perpendicular.

The Church of St Laurence, Catsfield stands near the manor still, as described in Domesday. The name in that chronicle, 'Cedesfille' may be a distortion of the Saxon 'Cattsfeld'. The church retains some of its Norman features such as the herringbone masonry in the south wall of the nave. The present 12th century tower may be a replacement of an earlier one. In 15th century a timber broached spire was added. The shingles have been replaced several times but the wooden frame has survived. In 13th century the chancel in Early English style was added. The lancet windows and piscina are original. The plain octagonal font (1310) is on a modern pedestal. The chancel arch is a Victorian copy. The north aisle, designed by Carpenter was added in 1847. William Marwick, whose family owned Catsfield Place in 17th – 18th centuries, was interested in Natural History and some of his observations are included in Gilbert White`s book. The parishes of Catsfield and Crowhurst are now united. I hope the parishioners will be inspired to walk between the two churches and make the footpaths clearer!

The Walk

From Crowhurst Station *head south down Station Road for half a mile and turn right for the church, passing the school on your right.*

From Crowhurst Church head northwest – that is uphill away from the school. In 150 metres turn left into a footpath with the sign '1066 Country Walk'. Keep on course across a field and veer right to enter Fore Wood, an RSPB nature reserve. Here is a pond and tempting seat just inside the wood.

Keep strictly to the well marked way northwest and avoid all paths that lack the sign, '1066 Country Walk'. In ½ mile you emerge from the left side of the wood and go westwards across a field to another wood. Turn right into this smaller wood. You join a lane and soon reach a junction at Powdermill Cottage.

Fork right here and follow the tarmac lane in a northerly direction, still on '1066 Country Walk'. In 1 kilometre you reach a T-junction at Telham Lane. Turn left and you come to the busy B2095.

The 1066 Country Walk continues up the slope opposite. Cross with care to this footpath then walk above the main road on the right. In 250 metres cross a track to resume your northerly course for 1 mile through fields up to Battle. This is the way William the Conqueror came to defeat Harold. You pass the battle site on the right.

On the way up to Battle you meet a **branch of the 1066 Country Walk** on the left. You will take this branch on the return walk. Meanwhile, keep on track northeast with a hedge of trees on your right. As you approach Battle, you enter a lane, Park Lane and pass a car park on the right.

Suddenly you are in the centre of Battle. Pass the Gatehouse on the right. This is both the entrance to the Abbey and the site of the Tourist Information Centre. William built the Abbey on the site of Harold`s death. Cross the High Street and turn right to visit St Mary`s Parish Church.

From the Parish Church retrace your steps to the Gatehouse and return down Park Lane. Continue down to the familiar fork in ways. Fork right to follow the other **branch of the 1066 Country Walk**. This leads down to woodland on the right.

Here you have an enclosed path going southwest in and out of woodland for one mile. On the way you pass Farthings Farm away up on the right. You then turn left away from the main track. You are still on 1066 Country Walk. You climb up through dark woodland then turn right to continue southwest. (OS does not show the bend in the path here).

Cross a rough space with some trees and emerge to a field. Turn sharp right, hug the field boundary on the right and you come up to B2204. Turn left and keep on this road. Say goodbye to the 1066 Country Walk as it goes off to the right.

You come down to a busy road junction. You have to cross with care to the footpath opposite. There is a central grass triangle that might help you make this awkward crossing in safety.

The footpath leads up through a field, passing the garden and tennis court of a large house on the right. In the next field go up the modest Horn`s Hill and veer left to go over the top to a new view. Below is Catsfield village.

Catsfield Methodist Church

Catsfield

On the right is the spire of the Methodist Church. Go down to the field boundary and turn right down to Church Road, opposite the village school.

Turn left and walk a short way up the road to the Parish Church on the left. You can take the slope or some steps up to the church.

From Catsfield Church continue along Church Road heading southeast. A footpath is on the left bank above the road. Pass the Old Rectory on the left then turn left into the driveway of Church Farm.

Turn immediately right into a footpath across little fields heading east towards a pylon. Pass the pylon on the right and find a stile in the wire fence opposite. Go under the power cables and emerge at the top of a rise.

Below you can see **Catsfield Place**, now a school. This is our goal. (There are no waymarkers at the time of writing). First, head for the nearest cottage and take the narrow, rough path behind it. You come down to a neglected farmyard below the remains of an oast house and cottage.

Pass the farm cottage on the right and you come to a track. Turn left along the track and pass the school behind the hedge on the right. Pass a pond on the left then veer right on the track to crosspaths. Here is a rare finger post.

Take the path furthest right. It goes through trees and follows the course of a stream on the right. The stream manifests itself in a series of ponds. Pass all these ponds on the right and keep heading east across a small field. In ½ mile you are relieved to find that you are approaching Fore Wood.

Turn right and follow the wood on the left at a distance. Turn left at a footbridge but do not enter the wood. Instead, turn right and follow the Powdermill Stream on the right heading southeast for ½ mile over delightful meadows.

After a footbridge turn left and uphill. Make for the farm gate and soon you can see Crowhurst Church. Go down to the lone arch of the Manor, possibly a victim of Norman vengeance. (See Local Information above). Continue to the road and turn left. Turn left again for Crowhurst School. *Or keep straight on along Station Road for Crowhurst Railway Station.*

Old Manor House, Crowhurst

Walk 22: Dallington to Warbleton Priory

Medieval monks established themselves in a valley hidden in the Wealden Forest. We seek the site of this priory, still remote and tranquil.

Starting Point: The verge beside the lane, midway between Stream Farm and Dallington Church. **GR**656187
Map: OS Explorer 124 **Distance:** 4 ½ Miles
Terrain: Some hill slopes, some lanes, some footpaths.

The Churches

Dallington Church, St Giles may once have been dedicated to St Margaret of Antioch. The first mention of a church in Dallington comes in the Hastings Priory charter of around 1180 – 1204. Sadly the church was crumbling and rotting by the 19th century and architects decided to demolish and rebuild in 1864. The tower and spire were spared. The tower was apparently the work of the Pelham family in 15th century. The Pelham buckle is carved on one of the shields. (See Introduction for more on the Pelhams). The spire is one of three ancient stone spires in Sussex. The others are Chiddingly and Northiam. This one must be unique in having a copy nearby; one of Mad Jack Fuller`s follies, 'the Sugar Loaf' is an imitation spire. He could see his handiwork from his home, Brightling Park and presumably kid his visitors it was the spire of Dallington Church! (See Walk 19 under Local Information for more on Jack Fuller).

Warbleton Priory was built in 15th century by Augustinian Canons from Hastings seeking refuge inland from the sea and the French. One of their order, Robert Michell became Rector of Warbleton Church (1500 – 1522). The bells of the priory church, Holy Trinity rang out over the countryside at dusk to drive away the evil spirits from the forest. In 1536 a Royal Act compelled the Canons to leave their monastery. Only the Prior received a pension and went to live at Salehurst (See Walk 17). The Priory was stripped of its lead and all its valuables and the proceeds went to the Royal Treasury. The church and buildings were dismantled. Only ruins stand in the garden of the 17th century building there now.

Dallington

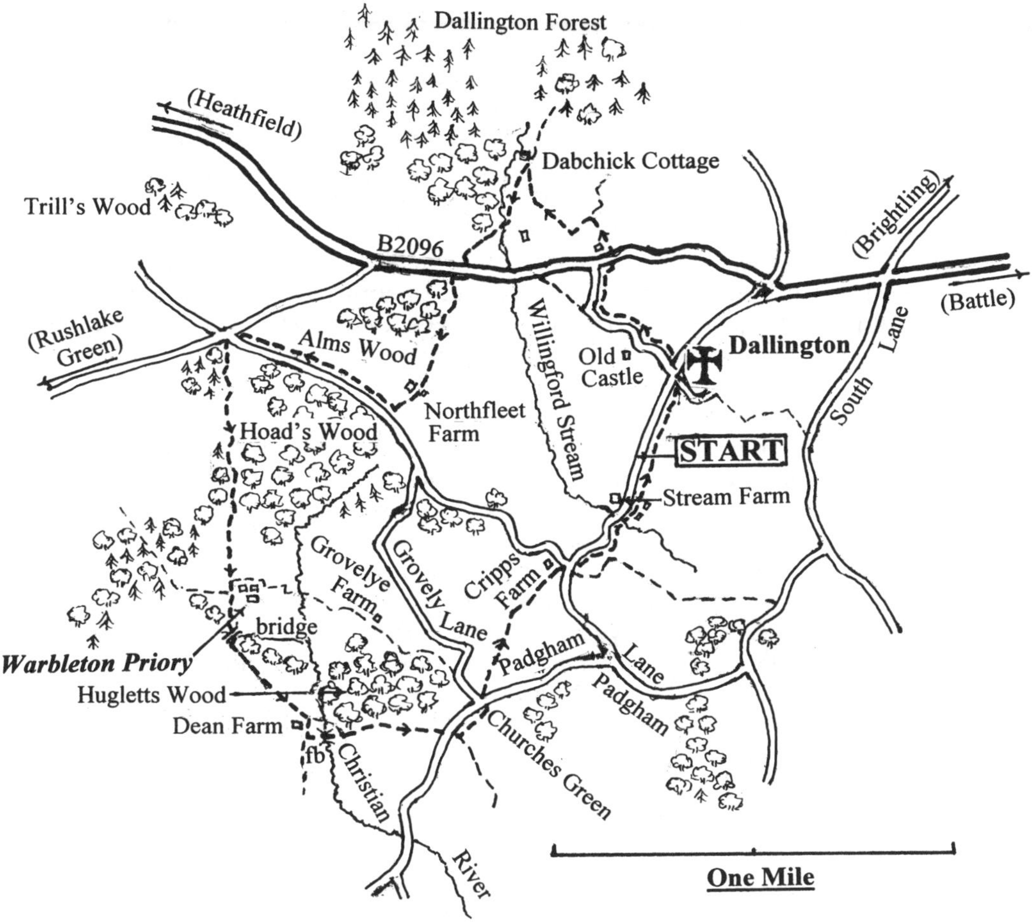
Dallington Forest
(Heathfield)
Dabchick Cottage
Trill's Wood
B2096
(Brightling)
(Battle)
(Rushlake Green)
Alms Wood
Willingford Stream
Old Castle
Dallington
South Lane
Northfleet Farm
Hoad's Wood
START
Stream Farm
Grovelye Farm
Grovely Lane
Cripps Farm
bridge
Warbleton Priory
Padgham
Lane
Padgham
Hugletts Wood
Dean Farm
fb
Christian
Churches Green
River
One Mile

The Walk

Walk up to Dallington Church. Turn left into the narrow lane opposite the church. Walk down towards Dallington Forest, seen on the hills ahead. In ½ a mile, after some bends, you reach the main road B2096.

Cross diagonally right to a narrow footpath beside a private nursing home. In 200 metres at a T-junction, turn left and follow the track for 100 metres. Turn right into a footpath across a field with Brooklands Farm on your left. In the next field go down towards a nearby cottage named 'Dabchicks'.

Here is another T-junction. Turn left onto a firm track beside Willingford Stream. You pass some small waterfalls and return to the main road B2096.

Cross diagonally right to another footpath heading south. You approach Alma Wood but do not enter. Instead, veer left and keep on course with the wood on your right. You can still admire the wood anemones under the trees in Spring.

When the wood ends, keep straight on up the sloping field and along the track through Northfleet Farm. Pass open barns and continue along the farm driveway where primroses thrive on the banks on either side.

At the tarmac lane, turn right and walk for ½ mile to Crossroads. On the corner on your left is the entrance to Warbleton Priory. Saunter downhill on the private tarmac drive and enjoy the rural views ahead. The driveway takes you southwards for 1 mile to a cluster of restored buildings on the site of the Priory.

For the best view of the main house and a glimpse of the ruins, turn left on the first footpath. It goes round the edge of the estate, a short detour.

Return to the driveway and continue south passing the gated entrance on the left. Keep on course over a small field to a wood. In the left corner a rough track slides down into the wood and takes you to a bridge.

Cross the bridge to come out of the wood and turn sharp left. You are on a slightly sunken overgrown path with the wood on your left.

In 100 metres you emerge to an open sloping field. Step boldly forward up through the centre. At the top you can see Dean Farm up ahead.

Go down to a slope on the left into a strip of woodland. Avoid the path to the left and climb out of the wood up to Dean Farm.

Take the next path on the left down in a corner of the sloping field. Cross a footbridge and climb the steep slope up to cross paths in the wood. Go straight on and leave the wood. Follow the field boundary on the left and head due east towards cottages at Churches Green.

You reach the byway opposite the entrance to Little Bucksteep Farm. Turn left and walk up the road past the cottages to a road junction. Turn left into Grovely lane and stop! There is a footpath in the hedge opposite.

This takes you northeast up over elevated fields. At the top make for a largish red house ahead. In the field next to the house you veer right to a stile and a drop to the road below.

Turn left and avoid the lane on the left. Keep along your lane which leads to Stream Farm. You cross Willingford Stream again and continue up the hill towards Dallington.

Walk 23: Warbleton to Vines Cross and Old Heathfield

Two churches, three pubs, four deciduous woods and five miles of open countryside with no main roads make this a popular walk. All is peaceful here now after the din of hammers and blasting of past centuries.

Starting point: Warbleton Church **GR**609182
Map: OS Explorer 123 **Terrain:** Gently undulating **Distance:** 5 Miles
Local Information: We have come to the upper reaches of the Cuckmere River. The main stream comes from Heathfield Park, just north of our walk. See the Introduction under 'Rivers' for more on the Cuckmere.

Iron was mined in this area in the 14th century. Old hammer ponds, furnaces and forges abound. The Heathfield foundry, started at the beginning of 17th century, made the fortune of the Fuller family, one of whose eccentric sons is mentioned in Walk 19. Guns were made for our army and navy.

The Churches

St Mary the Virgin, Warbleton stands on a ridge. It is partly inside a Neolithic earthwork. The 'tun' or farm of a Saxon lady, named Waerburh has given its name to the village, mentioned in Domesday as 'Warborgetone'. By 1351 it had acquired its present spelling, nearly. It is associated with iron working and iron masters. One iron master, Richard Woodman objected to the restoration of Catholic practices during the reign of Queen Mary (1553 – 1558). He was burnt at the stake at Lewes for his trouble. A memorial to him is set in the wall of the churchyard. The development of the church through the ages can be seen in the different styles of architecture. The chancel with lancet windows is Early English. It has a low Decorated side window and a Perpendicular east window. The windows in the north and south are Decorated. The tower and north arcade are Perpendicular. The squire has an elevated pew, set in1722 in the north aisle.

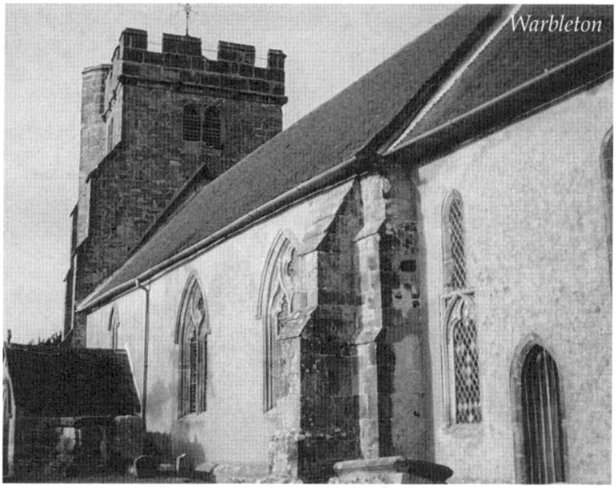
Warbleton

All Saints, Heathfield was built in 13th century in the little village with its old inn on a south facing slope. The parish was large then, stretching from the River Rother in the north to Horam in the south. The new town now has its own parish.

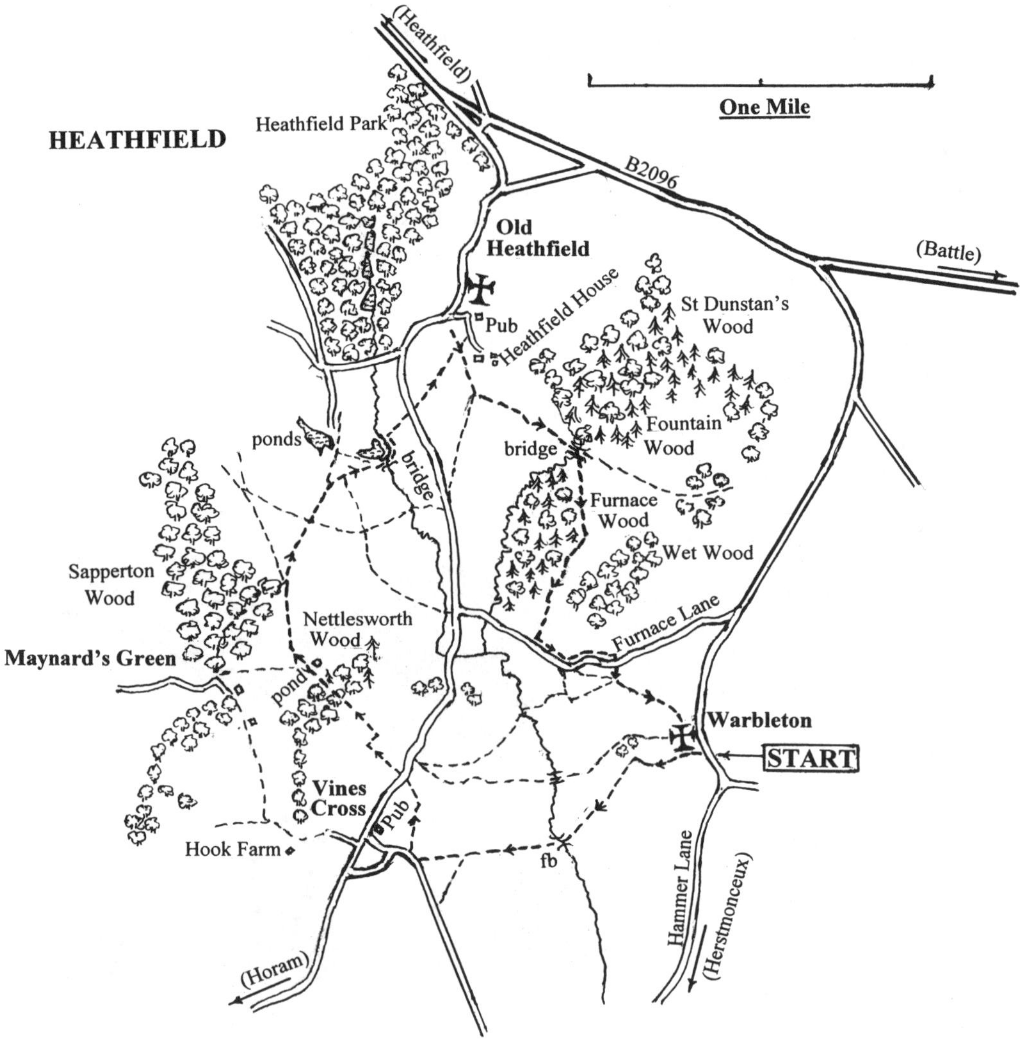
(Heathfield)
One Mile
HEATHFIELD
Heathfield Park
B2096
Old Heathfield
(Battle)
Pub
Heathfield House
St Dunstan's Wood
ponds
bridge
bridge
Fountain Wood
Furnace Wood
Wet Wood
Sapperton Wood
Nettlesworth Wood
Furnace Lane
Maynard's Green
pond
Warbleton
START
Vines Cross
Pub
Hook Farm
fb
Hammer Lane
(Herstmonceux)
(Horam)

Heathfield

The church is made of local sandstone. Despite thorough 19th century restoration, it retains some of the Decorated style in the four bays of the nave. The windows now hold Victorian glass. In the north aisle a window depicts Robert Hunt, a vicar of this church giving Holy Communion in the colony of America in 1607. Dame Margaret Rutherford unveiled the window in 1962. The tower has the date '1445', believed to be one of the earliest examples of Roman numerals. The spire was rebuilt in 19th century and re-shingled in Canadian cedar in 1950. There is a chapel in the north aisle. A charity school was held in the south aisle for 200 years from late 16th century to late 18th century.

The Walk

Go through the lychgate of Warbleton Church, pass the south porch on your right and enter an extra parcel of cemetery on your left. Here you will find a way through the hedge to a footpath heading southwest.

To your right on a distant hill you will see the spire of Old Heathfield Church. We shall get there eventually!

Meanwhile, follow the line of the footpath across a sloping field down to a dyke on the boundary. Turn left here and keep the dyke on your right for 250 metres. Then cross to the other side of the hedge so that it is now on your left. Keep on course. Go gently down to a generous new footbridge over the little river, our first sight of the Cuckmere.

After crossing the bridge with steps down to a meadow on the other side, keep straight on for 500 metres to a copse on the border. Go through to unmarked crosspaths and keep the hedge on your left. Veer slightly to the right to reach the lane that enters Vine Cross. Turn right for this hamlet.

***Either** continue along the village lane for 250 metres to a T-junction. The pub is on the right. At the junction, turn right and walk along the road for another 250 metres where a path crosses the road and turn left.*

Or stay on the edge of the hamlet. As soon as you reach the lane that enters Vine Cross, you will find a nearby footpath on the right. It cuts behind the village and heads north. In 350 metres turn left and follow the hedge on the left to the road. Cross to the footpath opposite. *(Vines Cross is to the left and topers have made their way from the pub along the road to join here).*

Both routes take the footpath northwest up to a farm. Pass the farm on your right then head towards Nettlesworth Wood. Keep on course through the wood. Pass a pond on the right when you leave the wood. Head for the top right corner of the field. Turn right here and head north over an elevated field with Sapperton Wood on your left.

Turn left and enter crosspaths at the edge of Sapperton Wood. Five paths meet here. Avoid two on the left and one on the right. Your clear course is under a little avenue where a wide track leads northwards. In ¼ mile you leave the avenue and can look across to Sapperton Manor on the right. Avoid turning right here. Instead, keep on the track as far as a single brick house on the left.

Stop here and look for the footpath on the right. You can see Old Heathfield Church on the hill ahead. Cross a small rough field diagonally left to a wooded slope. Here you reach unmarked crosspaths. Go slightly to the left and keep on course with the hedge on your right. Descend the slope to a large pond and turn right. A flat track takes you around the edge of the pond, over a bridge with a small cataract below and on to a cottage. The cottage has a driveway to the road. The overgrown footpath crosses the drive and also leads to the road.

Cross the road to the footpath opposite and climb gently up to the church. First you have to go through a metal gate and cross a handsome avenue. Heathfield House is on the right.

From Old Heathfield Church return to the avenue and go through the familiar metal gate. Turn sharp left now and head southeast hugging the boundary of Heathfield House on your left. In 250 metres the path opens to fields and a junction.

Fork left to continue beside the laurel boundary. In another 250 metres you have a fine view over open countryside watered by streams. Keep on course with a hedge on your right and walk gently down towards woodland. Leave your field at the bottom. Go through the gap between two woods in the valley. Fountain

Wood is on your left and Furnace Wood on your right. The track crosses a stream and goes up towards heathland and a parting of the ways.

Your way is to the right following the edge of Furnace Wood and keeping it at a distance. In ½ mile you reach a stony patch where hard core has been scattered to strengthen the surface. Go through a gate on your left and keep on course to a lone house. Pass the house on your left and take the track down to Furnace Lane at the bottom. As you descend, you can spy Warbleton Church on the hill ahead to the left.

Turn left to walk along Furnace Lane for ¼ mile. Shortly after passing a path on the right, you come to a bend and a farm sign. Turn right here, avoid the farm track and climb some steps to an open field with the church above. Turn left but veer away from the hedge on the left to cross to the next field.

In this field turn right to follow the boundary into a dip then climb the final path up to Warbleton Church.

Woodland near Heathfield

Walk 24: Penhurst to Ashburnham

A varied walk through ancient estates and deer parks. From a remote village church we have to make a long detour to see its grand neighbour.

Starting Point: Penhurst Church **GR**695166
Map: OS Explorer 124 **Terrain:** Undulating **Distance:** 10 Miles

The Churches

Penhurst Church, St Michael The Archangel 'stands on an eminence which falls gently to the south to the Ashburn brook with deer park and Ashburnham Place beyond', according to the church guide book. It also informs us that 'Penhurst' means the 'head of the wood'. Much more of interest is in this guidebook. I can only add my own satisfaction in finding this remote manorial hamlet that has changed so little over the centuries. 'Penehese' is mentioned in Domesday but the church building dates from 1340 to 1500. It consists of nave, chancel and tower. A small chapel was added in 17th century. William Ralph, who built the nearby

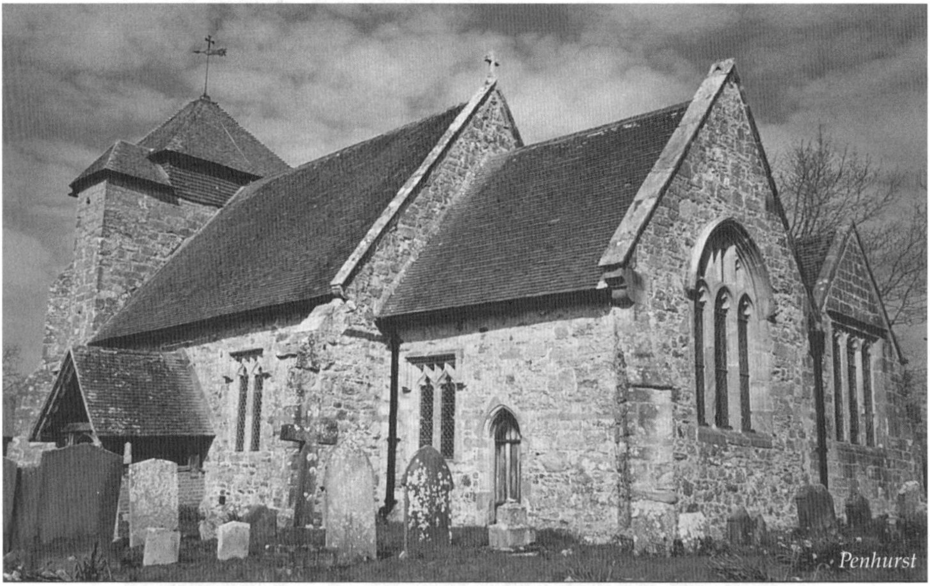

Penhurst

manor house may have added the chapel as a private pew. The tower has a pyramidal roof with reddish brown tiles. The tower arch inside is tall. The chancel has a barrel roof and the nave has kingpost. The 14th century oak screen divides the nave from the chancel. The oak box pews were made by carpenters on the Ashburnham estate in mid 19th century.

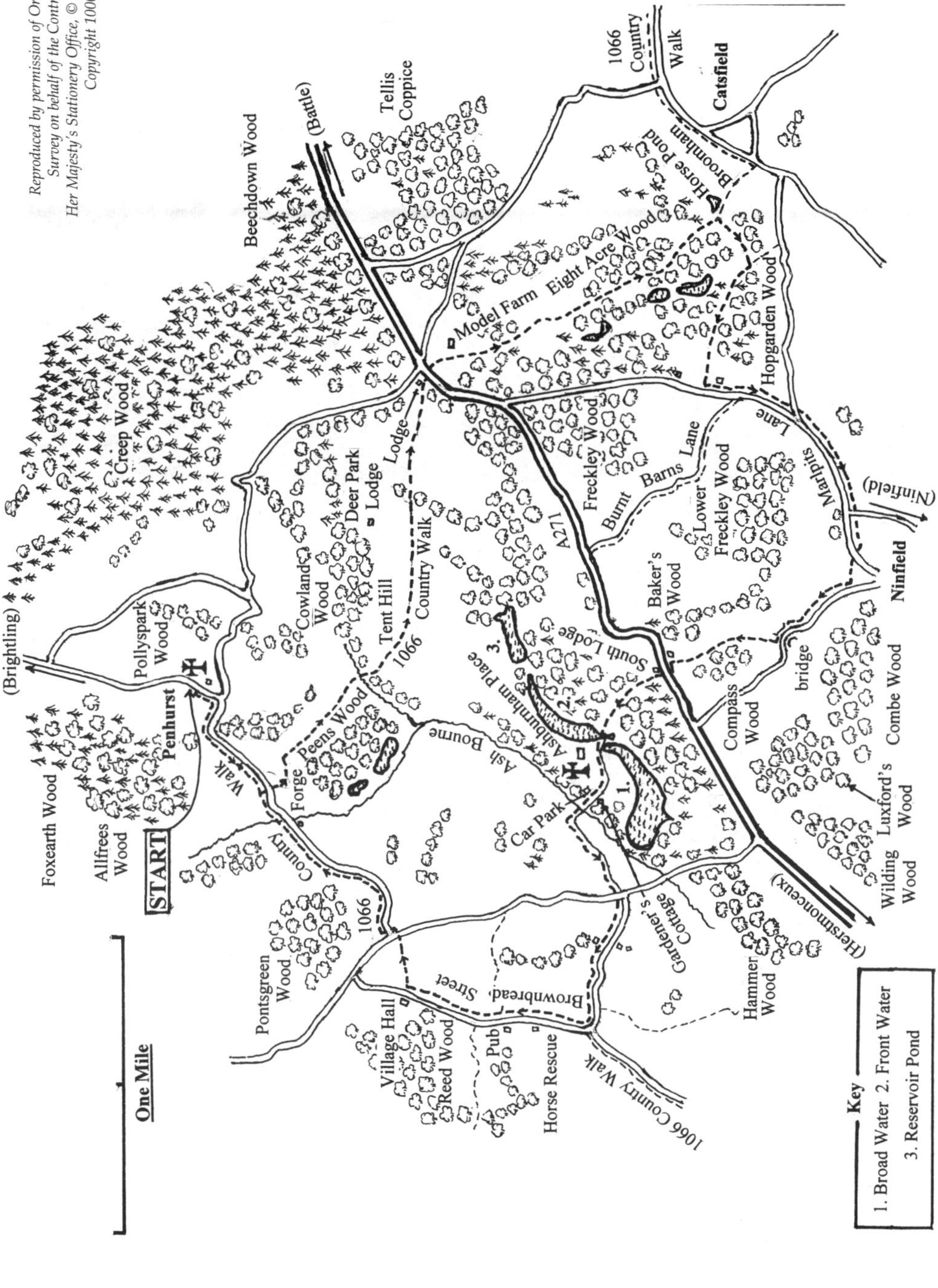

(Battle)
Tellis Coppice
1066 Country Walk
Catsfield
Beechdown Wood
Broomham
Horse Pond
Eight Acre Wood
Model Farm
Hopgarden Wood
Creep Wood
Lodge
Deer Park Lodge
Freckley Wood
Burnt Barns Lane
Lower Freckley Wood
Marlpits Lane
(Ninfield)
Ninfield
(Brightling)
Cowland Wood
Tent Hill
1066 Country Walk
A271
Baker's Wood
Pollyspark Wood
3.
South Lodge
Combe Wood
bridge
Compass Wood
Foxearth Wood
Penhurst
Peens Wood
Forge
Ashburnham Place
2.
Ash Bourne
1.
Allfrees Wood
START
1066 Country Walk
Car Park
Luxford's Wood
Wilding Wood
(Herstmonceux)
Pontsgreen Wood
Gardener's Cottage
Hammer Wood
Brownbread Street
Village Hall
Reed Wood
Pub
Horse Rescue
1066 Country Walk
One Mile
Key
1. Broad Water 2. Front Water
3. Reservoir Pond

Ashburnham Church, St Peter stands above the Ashbourne River and has seen many changes. In 1400 it was a village church dedicated to St Mary the Virgin. The Perpendicular tower and porch are of that period. The famous Pelham buckles are on the doorway of the tower. Cromwell`s men inflicted damage to the building. In 1665 John Ashburnham rebuilt the rest of the church in a style similar to the tower. This is a rare example of 17th century Gothic. In 1667 the church was re-consecrated and dedicated to St Peter. In 1995 the tower was repaired and church bells re-hung. There are some elaborate monuments to the Ashburnhams inside the church. They are descendants of Bertram de Ashburnham the Saxon Constable of Dover Castle who held out against William the Conqueror and was beheaded for this resistance. Another King, William 111 made John Ashburnham a peer. The family thrived and owned the whole parish. In 1959 the Revd. John Bickersteth, great grandson of the 5th Earl of Ashburnham gave Ashburnham Place to a Christian Trust and it has become a prayer and conference centre.

Local Information:

- Ashburnham Place. From its origins in 12th century the house has been rebuilt many times. Today`s brick face dates from 1850. The grounds bear the mark of Capability Brown.
- Ashburnham was a major centre of the iron industry. We pass forge cottage on our walk. Half a mile north of the forge was a large iron works. The river was dammed in the 16th century creating large ponds. Channels of water powered the drop hammers to make cannons for the Navy. It was the last Sussex iron works; closing in the early 19th century.

Warning: You have to brave a short walk on the verge beside the A271 in order to reach the entrance to the Ashburnham Estate. This is private land. The understanding is that you keep strictly to the driveways to and from the Church

and do not wander in the park.
Before embarking on this walk, inform the Ashburnham Christian Trust of your intention to visit St Peter`s Church, Phone (01424) 894239 or 892244.

The Walk

From Penhurst Church head south past the Manor and the duck pond. At the T-junction turn right to go down the wooded lane. It bends to the left and a single parapet shows that you are crossing a bridge. In under ½ mile you reach 1066 Country Walk.

Turn left here and make a short zigzag around a house then step out across fields on a clearly marked path, heading southeast. In ½ mile you come down to a wooded dell.

Climb out to the prospect of Tent Hill ahead. There is no alternative, you have to make the ascent. As you do so, there are landmarks to note. *To the northwest, beyond Penhurst Church and Manor, you will see the Obelisk and Observatory. To the south are the Downs and the Long Man of Wilmington.*

At the top of Tent Hill you come to elevated parkland. Turn left, heading east. Do not be tempted into any woodland until you come near Deer Park Lodge on the left.

Now you veer right to a wooded slope and go down then up to more open parkland. Go past a willow copse on your left and continue eastwards towards a lodge with tall thick chimneys. You are still on 1066 Country Walk. Pass the lodge on your left and you reach the A271 at Steven`s Crouch.

Cross diagonally left to the entrance to the erstwhile Normansworth estate.

Here the 1066 Country Walk follows the driveway, passing a Model Farm on the left and a caravan site on the right. Keep heading southeast on this drive for over one mile. It takes you through rhododendron groves, woodland and fields. When you reach a big pond and hamlet at Broomham, turn sharp right before the first house.

Walk along a flat track southwest to a small field, used for horse paddocks. The path forks here. You take the right fork to nearby woodland.

When you enter the wood, there is a confusing array of paths. You have to head west, so turn left immediately. Avoid being drawn back to the paddock on a path to the left. Instead, veer right into the depths of Hopgarden Wood and you will find a clear straight path west northwest. It may be muddy in places and people have found drier tracks parallel to the main path.

In 500 metres you come to cross tracks and turn left to leave the wood. Go west across a flat field towards a cottage ahead on the left. Pass this on your left by going through a newly planted beech hedge.

Come out at a lane, Freckley Hollow, and turn left. Pass Burnt Barns Lane on the right then Skinners Lane on your left. The next lane on your left is also to be avoided *unless you have time to visit Ninfield Church, a distance of 2 miles there and back.*

In ¼ mile a footpath on your right takes you across to Combe Hill. Turn right when you reach the lane and go downhill to a bridge over a tributary of the Ash Bourne.

Immediately after the bridge, turn sharp right into a sloping field and you see nearby Compass Wood. Bluebells flower here in the spring. Start climbing and keep close to the wood on your left until you are near the top. You will see a house up ahead. Go across the field towards the house which has an adjacent barn. You pass the barn on your right.

At the main A271, turn left to walk along the verge for 150 metres. Then cross with care to the entrance to Ashburnham Place opposite. You enter the estate at South Lodge and follow the smooth tarmac drive down through trees. It curves left to the magnificent sight of lakes in parkland below.

Cross the handsome bridge and continue to signposts. The church is marked to the left. Continue on the drive, past gardens and the fine stone buildings of the early 18th century stables. Keep on to the Car Park.

At the Car Park you will see the church up on the right.

From Ashburnham Church return to the Car Park. There is a walled garden in front of you. Turn right and follow the wall on your left. The drive here leads down to the River Ash Bourne. Cross the bridge over the river and turn left after the Gardener`s Cottage. You are now heading southwest on a track parallel to the river.

In ¼ mile you leave the estate and cross the road to a lane opposite. It is now a long haul uphill for 1 kilometre on this lane. Once past Lingham`s Farm, the slope seems even steeper! Near the top avoid a path on the left.

At the top you rejoin 1066 Country Walk and turn right for Brownbread Street. Pass a horse sanctuary on the left then a pub also on the left. Keep to the lane passing some white cottages on the right. Eventually you reach a large brick building on the left, this is Ashburnham Village Hall.

Turn right here and continue on 1066 Country Walk across elevated fields for 200 metres.

At the tarmac road, cross to the lane opposite. It leads for 1½ miles back to Penhurst. Half way, you pass Forge Cottages on the right and a footpath on the left up to the old iron works mentioned above under the heading, 'Local Information'.

Manor and Duck Pond, Penhurst

Walk 25: Guestling Church to Hastings Old Town and Country Park

This is a long, varied and rewarding walk. Do not under-estimate the hard trek back along the coast path with magnificent views. The tour of churches in Hastings Old Town could be extracted to make a short walk of its own.

Starting Point: Guestling Church **GR**856144
Starting Point *(Short town walk):* Hastings Station **GR**814096
Map: OS Explorer 124 **Distance:** 11 Miles or 1 Mile
Terrain: 1066 Country Walk to Hastings, rural and undulating.
Warning: The switchback coast path requires some stamina. There is a short cut to avoid this but it also leaves out Hastings.
Hastings can be explored using the instructions at the end of this walk.

Churches

Guestling

The Parish Church of St Laurence, Guestling stands alone commanding a fine rural view. The cosy name comes from the Saxon 'ing' or territory of Grystel, 'the gristly one'! In Domesday it is called 'Gestelings'. Even before the conquest, here was one of three courts in charge of the Cinque Ports. The first church was Saxon and probably had a timber tower. It now has a stone Norman tower of 1100 and a north aisle of the same date with some Norman windows. Further east in the Chapel of St John the Evangelist, there is a beautiful late Norman arch with

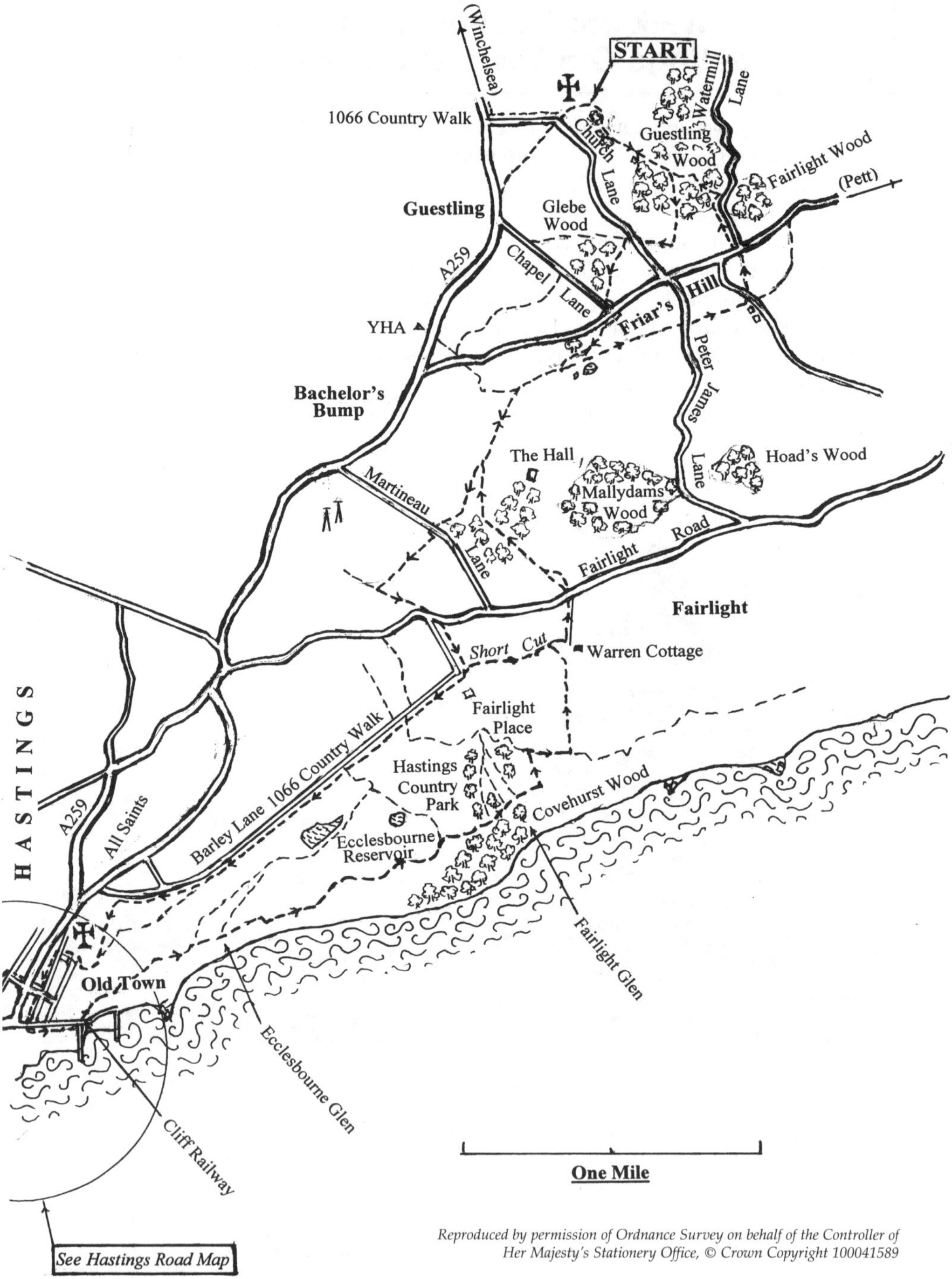
START
(Winchelsea)
1066 Country Walk
Watermill
Lane
Church
Lane
Guestling
Wood
Fairlight Wood
(Pett)
Guestling
Glebe
Wood
A259
Chapel
Lane
Friar's
Hill
YHA
Peter
James
Lane
Bachelor's
Bump
The Hall
Mallydams
Wood
Hoad's Wood
Martineau
Lane
Fairlight
Road
Fairlight
Short Cut
Warren Cottage
Fairlight
Place
Barley Lane 1066 Country Walk
Hastings
Country
Park
Covehurst Wood
HASTINGS
A259
All Saints
Ecclesbourne
Reservoir
Old Town
Fairlight Glen
Ecclesbourne Glen
Cliff Railway
One Mile
See Hastings Road Map

chevron and piers with foliated capitals. The chancel is 13th century with Decorated north and south windows. The east window is Victorian. The Ashburnham Chapel and the south aisle, both added in 14th century, have been restored. Bishop Ashburnham, who died 1798, is buried here. A mourner commented on the sad state of the church. Later, an aged member of the congregation said "Once she (the Church) was a country girl but now she has her town dress on". We are fortunate to see her at her best!

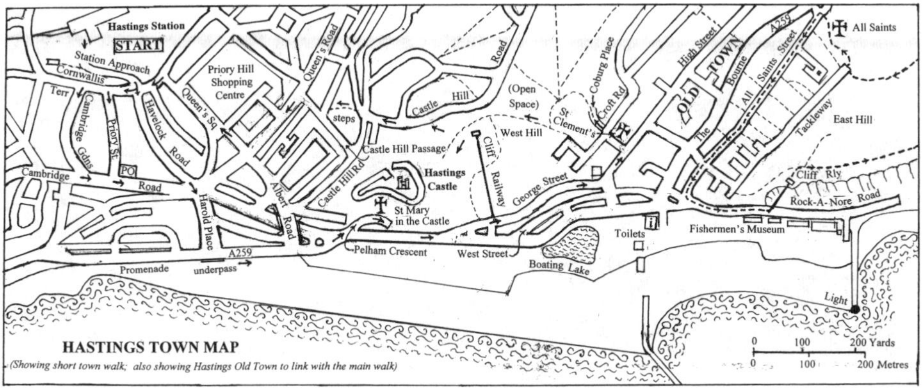

The Churches of Hastings

In medieval times there were seven churches in Hastings. Only two of them remain: All Saints and St Clements and they have moved a little inland away from the encroaching sea and the marauding French. In Saxon times they were both part of the Manor of Brede. King Knut presented this manor to the Abbey of Fécamp in Normandy in about 1020. The abbey supplied parish priests until 1413 when Henry V seized possessions of French monasteries in England. Both churches suffered damage in French raids into Hastings in 14th century. Both were rebuilt in Perpendicular style. From Norman times until 1939, the curfew bell was rung from St Clements at 8 o`clock every winter evening to tell people to extinguish all lights and fires. Originally this precaution was to prevent fire spreading to thatched roofs. After centuries in separate parishes, the two churches now form one parish working together to care for the sick and the poor.

All Saints was built in its present elevated position in 1400. The tower is part flint and part stone chequer. You enter the church through the west tower and find a spacious, well balanced interior. The most striking feature is the large painting of Doom above the chancel arch. Almost as old as the church, it shows Christ seated on two rainbows with the Virgin Mary on one side and St John on the other. Early worshippers must have been duly terrified at the unusual sight of the Devil hanging the damned on medieval gallows. Perhaps the towers of the New Jerusalem above gave them some hope. The fine arch from the nave into the tower has carved heads: a bat, a cat, a laughing dog and a man. More unusual carvings are on the ceiling of the tower. This is a lovely vaulted ceiling with fleur de lis in the ribs. In 1870 the church was restored and galleries removed.

All Saints

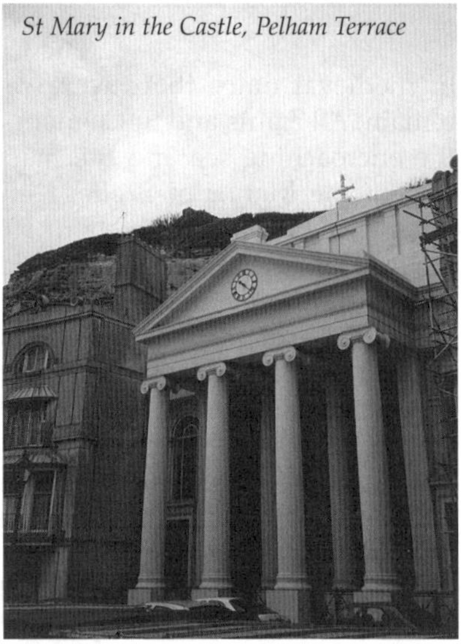
St Mary in the Castle, Pelham Terrace

St Clement is dedicated to the patron saint of mariners. Built in 1380 in the Perpendicular style of the period, it is quite different from All Saints. Part of the charm of this church is that it is not even and balanced. The southwest tower is set in the south aisle. The columns on the north and south of the nave are not exactly opposite each other. The 15th century font has sculptures of the instruments of the Passion. In the south aisle there are two piscinas. In the north aisle is a stained glass window to Viscount Chewton who was killed at Alma in 1854. There is no division between the chancel and the nave but plans are afoot to put in a division of wood and glass and to have part of the building as a community centre, open every day.

St Mary in the Castle is named after the church that once stood in the castle above. Today`s church is part of Pelham Crescent, one of the finest regency arcades in England. Joseph Cox designed it in 1820s to cater for fashionable society enjoying the seaside. The church has a classical façade and an immense auditorium behind. Today there are plans to restore the crescent.

The Fishermen`s Church of St Nicholas, Hastings was originally a chapel of Ease to the Parish Churches. In 1854 the chapel was licensed to hold Church of England services. Until 1884 the sea came right up to the south wall. In mid 20th century the church was closed to make way for a new road under the cliff. The road did not materialise but the church has become a Fisherman`s Museum with occasional services.

The Walk

Go past the porch of Guestling Church to find a footpath heading southeast downhill. This is '1066 Country Walk' and well signposted. Pass a copse sheltering a pond on the right. Continue down to enter Guestling Wood. Keep on course, passing sewage works on the right. In another 200 metres veer right, following the 1066 Country Walk. Head south and in another 250 metres you leave the wood. Keep going to cross paths.

Turn sharp right to walk along the edge of the field. In 50 metres come down to a private road. Keep on course to the byroad, Church Lane. Cross to the woodland path opposite. Keep to the edge of the wood with fields and gardens beyond its border on the left. This is Glebe Wood.

In 300 metres you come down to Chapel Lane. Turn left to a nearby main road. This is Pett Road. Turn right here and walk along the road verge. Pass roadside houses and start climbing the hill. In 100 metres after the last houses, turn left to a footpath up through a strip of woodland. Veer right uphill. If you reach a house you have gone too far. The path out of the wood is just below the house.

You soon emerge to open fields with views over the valley to the battlements of a tower. Immediately below you will see a pond and a lake. (There is a level path between your present position and this water. Remember this path for your return walk).

Meanwhile go down to a stile on the right and head southwest crossing the middle of the fields. A tall mast high on a hill makes a good guidepost.

Cross a narrow drive lined with newly planted trees. You soon enter woodland and fork left. Cross two small footbridges then walk beside a field boundary on the right, climbing steadily for ½ mile in a southwest direction, **'the long haul'**. Pass Fairlight Hall with its tower and battlements on the left. It is a private house in the style of Battle Abbey. Avoid turning left and you come up eventually to the heights of Martineau Lane.

Disregard Ordnance Survey Map at this point. *You cannot go straight across as shown on the map.* Instead, turn left at the boundary and walk parallel to the road for 200 metres. Pass the entrance to Fairlight Hall then cross with care to the footpath opposite. It is an enclosed path heading uphill southwest. The mast that acted as a guidepost is on the right. In 300 metres at a junction of ways, turn left.

Cross a field full of thistles at the time of writing. You reach Fairlight Road at a picnic site with toilets. Cross to the smooth lane opposite and head downhill at last! In 300 metres at a T-junction, turn right.

*If you wish to shorten the walk omitting Hastings and the demanding coast path, turn left here and head east on footpaths for ½ mile until you reach a cottage on the right, Warren Cottage then continue at * below, near bottom of page 135.*

For the full walk, continue on the lane taking a steady southwest course downhill for over a mile. This is still the 1066 Country Walk and also a cycle way. Halfway down you will see caravan sites and mobiles homes, drawn to nearby Ecclesbourne Reservoir. The useful shop on one site is open to passers-by and I was able to buy refreshments there.

The road becomes Barley Lane, an elevated route past the suburbs of Hastings. The 1066 Country Walk takes a left turn but we keep on down to Hastings. Avoid Gurth Road to the right. Keep straight on past houses until you come to a footpath sign on the left, just before a seat on the right.

Turn left into the dark footpath on the left, passing a cave-like rock. The path heads south and opens to bracken. Ignore paths to right and left. Your path curves to the right. Pass a notice board with the information that this is Hastings Country Park. Then you reach Tackleway Road.

Turn right for All Saints Church. Houses on the left overlook the churchyard. Follow their pavement down to the entrance to the church on the right and All Saints Street on the left. Turn left and walk on the elevated way along this delightful street, a scene from Dickens.

*To visit St Clements Church, turn right when you reach The Crown Inn, go along Court House Street, over the A259 to the High Street. Turn left and the church is up on the right.****

Rail travellers head for Hastings Station from here, see below, page 136.

All Saints Street ends in the tawdry 20th century. Cross the wide road diagonally right for Toilets beside the Tourist Information Centre. Yonder is the seaside.

At the end of All Saints Street, turn left to walk along Rock A Nore Road. towards unique dark wooden huts. Fishermen stored their tackle there. They had their own church, now a museum. Pass these on the right then take the east cliff railway on the left. For a small fee this funicular train lifts you out of Hastings and onto the open cliffs above.**

Rail travellers join here, see below, page 136.

At the top turn right, climb some steps and take the cliff path, heading east away from Hastings. Keep straight on along the coast path with the sea on your right. This is a delightful walk over soft turf with wide open spaces in sea, land and sky. You are in the nature reserve of Hastings Country Park. Many rare birds reside here on the heath or in the cliffs.

The coast path swings to the left and soon you have the steep descent into Ecclesbourne Glen and the inevitable climb out back to the cliff tops. The route is numbered and you follow the signs to Fairlight and Firehills.

The next descent is into the wooded Fairlight Glen, followed by another climb. At Warren Glen you come down to number 13. Turn left here onto a straight path skirting the wood on your left and heading inland. In ½ mile after a gentle climb you come to a T-junction of paths. Turn right to nearby Warren Cottage.

**Walkers on the short cut join here.*

Look for the driveway on the left leading from this cottage. Turn left and follow the driveway to Fairlight Road. Cross with care to the footpath opposite and a view of countryside to the north. An old sign directs you this way to Hastings Youth Hostel.

Start down the slippery descent on a neglected narrow path. It soon widens and takes you through woodland. In 500 metres you come to crosspaths at the driveway to Fairlight Hall. Veer right to emerge at a familiar field.

Cross the field to the path of **'the long haul'** above. Turn right on this path to retrace your steps. In 300 metres look out for the gap in the hedge on the left. Go through to the next little field and cross diagonally right.

Cliff path near Hastings

Enter the familiar woodland and re-cross the two footbridges. Return along the path in the middle of fields, this time heading northeast. Keep on the level path above lakes down on the right. (This is the path you remembered earlier). Avoid climbing back up to the woodland above on the left.

Instead, you have another small wood to traverse ahead. Emerge to gently rolling fields. Pett Church is in view in the distance. Keep on course northeast for ½ mile. You cross Peter James Lane to the footpath opposite. As you approach the next lane, you will notice a thatched cottage with speckled tiles on the right. This is on Rosemary Lane.

At Rosemary Lane discard your OS map for the moment – there is no footpath if you turn left. Instead, cross to the path opposite, go straight on for 50 metres then turn left to walk round the edge of paddocks uphill and look for a narrow way into Pett Road.

Turn right then left into Watermill Lane. Pass some bungalows. After the road curves to the right you will find a fingerpost on the left. Turn left here into Guestling Wood. Head northwest until you join the familiar 1066 Country Walk. Turn right onto this path and retrace your steps back up to Guestling Church.

Rail Travellers

To start the walk from Hastings Railway Station, *follow one of the roads south to the seafront. There is an underpass to the seafront near Harold Place. When you emerge, turn left, heading east. In ¼ mile you pass Pelham Terrace on the left where you will find the church of St Mary in the Castle. Resume your trek along the seafront past Old Town on the left, the Tourist Information Centre then fishermen`s huts on the right. Follow the above walk from the east cliff railway, marked **, page 135.*

*Complete your walk by reverting to the start from Guestling Church above. When you reach St Clement`s Church, marked *** above, you can either retrace your steps along the seafront back to the Station or you can go over West Hill.*

To reach West Hill, take the passageway, Coburg Place near St Clement`s Church. You have a steep climb past houses hanging on the hillside then turn left to a covered way up to the top. Cross the green and enjoy the views over the town. Pass Hastings Castle on your left, go down Castle Hill. Take Portland Steps down on the right. Return through Prior Meadow Shopping Centre to the Station.

The above instructions may be of use for a short walk in Hastings.

5 Walks
Near Rye

Walk 26: Rye to East Guldeford and Playden with a possible extension to Iden

From a busy church high on a hill town, cross the River Rother and pass a lone church on the marshes. Playden near Rye has a fine Norman church. Iden is a remote village church. Return through rolling countryside.

Starting Point 1: The Riverside Car Park on south side outside Rye, off A259, the Winchelsea Road **GR**918202
Starting Point 2: Rye Station **GR**919206
Map: OS Explorer 125
Distance: 6 Miles or 8 miles to include Iden **Terrain:** Mainly flat
Note: Early in this walk you cross 1 mile of marsh, aided by markers. Make sure visibility is good. I should also avoid a windy day!
Local Information: Three rivers meet at Rye. See the Introduction under 'Rivers' for more on the Rother, the Brede and the Tillingham.

The Churches

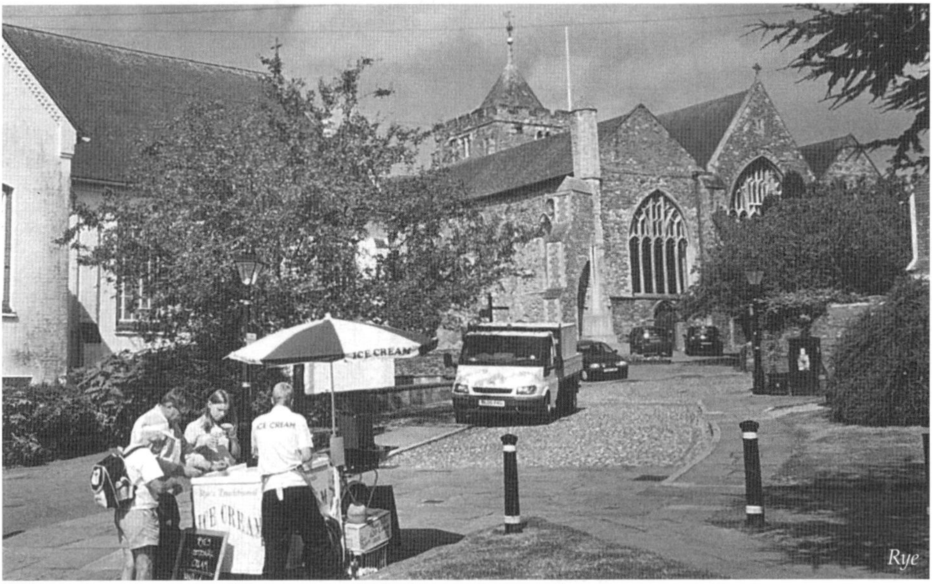

Rye

The Parish Church of Rye, St Mary the Virgin is basically Norman. The generous size of the church reflects the importance of Rye as a crucial 'cinque port'. It was built gradually under the guidance of the monks from the Abbey of Fécamp. They started on the long narrow oblong chancel decades before the Conquest of 1066. The church is cruciform with a low central tower. The transepts were added early in 12th century. The nave began around 1180 in the Transitional-Norman style of

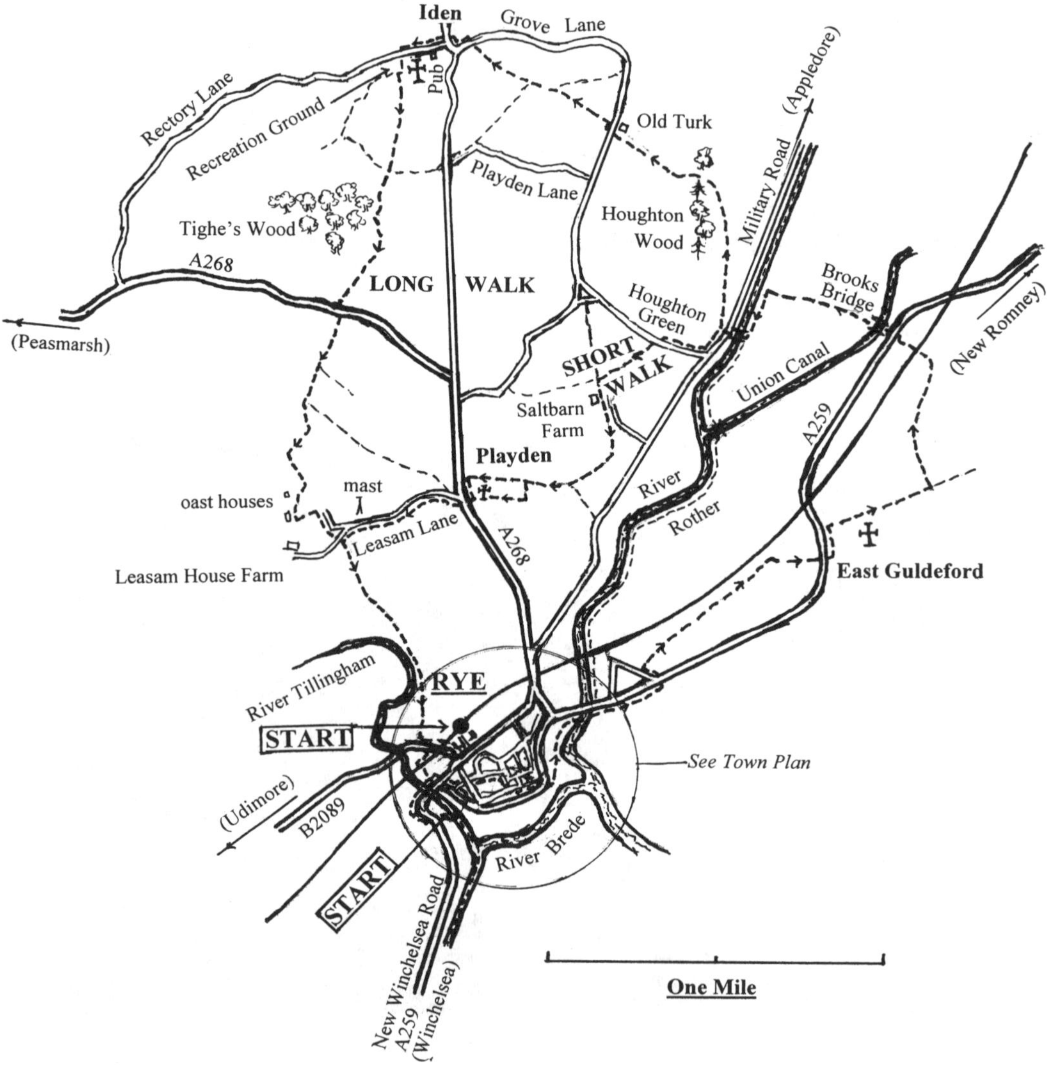
Iden
Grove Lane
Pub
Rectory Lane
Recreation Ground
Old Turk
(Appledore)
Military Road
Playden Lane
Houghton Wood
Tighe's Wood
A268
LONG WALK
Brooks Bridge
Houghton Green
(Peasmarsh)
SHORT WALK
(New Romney)
Union Canal
Saltbarn Farm
A259
Playden
mast
oast houses
River Rother
Leasam Lane
A268
East Guldeford
Leasam House Farm
River Tillingham
RYE
START
See Town Plan
(Udimore)
B2089
River Brede
START
New Winchelsea Road
A259 (Winchelsea)
One Mile

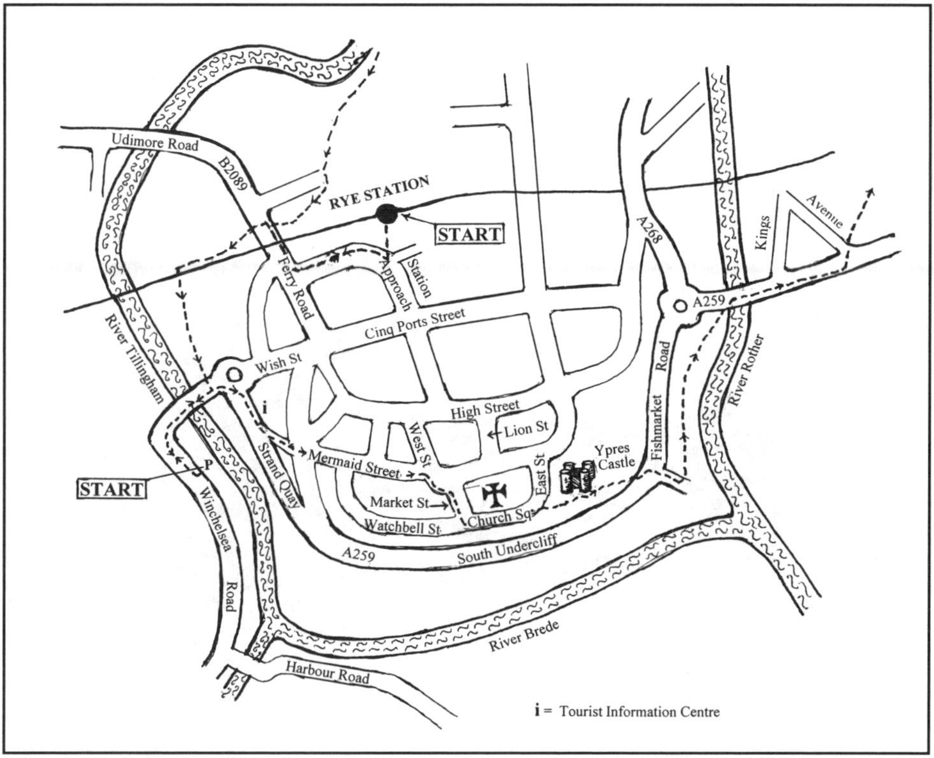

the period. The chapels on either side of the chancel are 13th century. After this favourable start, there came years of strife. In 1377 invaders from France set fire to Rye and looted both the town and the church. They stole the church bells and damaged the fabric of the building. In 1378 men from Rye and Winchelsea wrought revenge and retrieved the bells. Over a century later the people of Rye accepted many refugees in their midst. Huguenots fled from religious persecution in France in 16th century. Some held their own ceremonies in this church. We owe the oldest working tower clock in the country to a Huguenot. Lewys Billiard made it for Rye Church around 1560. The 18 foot long pendulum was added later. In 1760 the unusual 'Quarter Boys' were placed above the clock face. They strike the quarter hours. The tower has long served both as a landmark for sailors and a lookout point. You can still enjoy a view of the town from here. During Henry V111`s Reformation all ornamentation was removed and there was no investment in the church. It began to decay. The chancel was split into sections. Guns, a fire engine and reputedly smuggled items were in the north chancel. In a later century the graves of Allen Grebell and his murderer, John Breeds were found lying side by side in the north chancel. The south chancel was more respectable. An added upper floor later housed a school for the children of the poor. Vestiges of the fireplace are high in the chancel wall. In 1882 another restoration was needed. The

Victorians did a thorough job! For once I disagree with Simon Jenkins (England`s Thousand Best Churches). I admire the colourful stained glass. There is a sense of place in the Nativity scene in the Burne-Jones window in the north aisle. The brilliant blue of the west window glows. The novelist E.F. Benson donated this window in 1937. He and his dog are at the bottom. The east window was destroyed in the Second Word War. The glass in this replacement window was designed by Christopher Webb.

East Guldeford

East Guldeford, St Mary presents an unusual silhouette as you approach. It has two roofs with a bell turret in between them. It is one of the few Sussex churches built of brick. Sir Richard Guldeford, a knight of the garter is responsible for the building. It was consecrated in 1505. Sir Richard died a year later on a pilgrimage to Jerusalem. Panels show the Guldeford arms. There are corbels of angels. The pulpit and box pews are early 19th century.

Phone 01797 225386 for the vicar and 01797 222021 for the churchwarden.

Playden

Playden, St Michael is late 12th century with a Norman window in the north wall. The arches of the central tower are pointed. A 15th century screen is under the east arch and a screen of 1310 is under the north arch.

The arches of the arcade are rounded. The columns are alternately round and octagonal. The chancel was rebuilt in 16th century.

The Parish Church of All Saints, Iden stands at the edge of the village where once a 'denn' or Saxon swine pasture gave the place its name. Little remains of the early 12th century church. Most is now Perpendicular including the castellated tower with beacon turret. There is a fine view from the top of the tower and the Saxon world does not seem so far away. Inside the tower, a room is fitted with a 15th or 16th century fireplace. Did the priest stay here? The north chapel and chancel were also rebuilt in 15th century. The altar in the chancel was rescued and reconstituted in 1959. There is a striking 16th century Flemish wooden statue of St Christopher with Christ Child in the nave. Most windows in this church have plain glass and give light to a pleasant uncluttered interior.

The Walk

Make for the Tourist Information Centre on Strand Quay. It is on the opposite side of the river to the car park. From this car park you have to cross the road bridge and turn right into the Quay.

From the station*, go along StationRoad to the T-junction, turn right and walk along the main road as far as The Quay. Turn left. The Tourist Information Centre is on the left.*

The Church of St Mary`s is at the highest point in Rye. Go up Mermaid Street and West Street to reach Church Square.

Go behind St Mary`s Church to Ypres Castle. Pass the entrance to the castle and make for an arch and view point. Turn left before the arch and go down steps passing Castle Pub. Cross a busy road to the little lane opposite, Rock Channel East with workshops. Do not enter the lane but turn left to follow the path around the edge of a park. The river is hidden behind the fish market on the right. At a roundabout turn right onto A259 as it heads for New Romney. First, cross the road bridge over the river then walk along the pavement beside the main road with a housing estate on the left. Take the second turning left into Kings Avenue. Almost immediately turn right into a footpath signposted to East Guldeford.

Go through to a wide flat plain. Trees on your left hide the railway line. Keep these trees at a good distance and strike out across the plain. You are heading northeast. Go through a gate in a fence and continue on course, heading for a distant telegraph post. Go through another gate and you can switch your gaze from the post to East Guldeford Church, now seen in the distance. The footpath divides as you approach the church and there is no definitive route. The residents of a black and white cottage welcomed us through their driveway and we reached the A259 at East Guldeford.

Turn left then right to join the enclosed path to the church. At the end of this path with the church looming ahead, you will find a way to a footbridge on the left.

Cross this bridge to dry flat marshland and turn immediately right. The landscape is almost featureless. Hug the watercourse on your right. There are reed birds here. In 500 metres you come to cross paths. Turn left and head for a marker post in the middle of nowhere. When you reach this marker, cross a long stile. Look ahead slightly to the right and make for another marker. Here you cross a footbridge and keep straight on towards a finger post. Now you have reached the railway.

Climb steep stiles on either side of the railway line. Take care no train is coming! Veer left across a narrow field and up to the main road – A259 again. Cross with care diagonally right to a cottage where a track crosses the Union Canal at Brooks Bridge.

After crossing the canal, keep along the track to the River Rother. Turn left at the lock cottage and walk through a concrete yard to a sturdy bridge. *The footpath back to Rye continues southwest on this side of the river.*

The Short Walk to Playden (omitting Iden). Cross the sturdy bridge over the River Rother and turn left into Military Road. In 150 metres, turn right into Houghton Green Road. In another 150 metres at a bend in the road, turn left and go through a farm gate into a field.

Follow a stream in a dip on the left. Cross a flat bridge over a branch of the stream. You soon come to a little gate in the hedge. Go through to a wide field and head west with the stream on your right. In 300 metres just before the field boundary, turn left heading south up to Saltbarn Farm.

Go through farm buildings and down the access drive as far as cross tracks. (Saltbarn is indicated here). Turn right. Do not enter the private driveway. Instead, seek out a hidden stile beside it. Go down into a narrow sloping field. This opens to a little valley with a house on the left. Head towards trees on the elevated boundary opposite. Avoid gates and stay in the field. Turn right at the boundary keeping the trees on your left and it soon becomes apparent that this really is a footpath. The path goes through the field corner.

Enter another field and cross diagonally right uphill. At the top avoid the footpath on the left. Instead, turn right and go through a farm gate to a track behind houses. Follow this enclosed track. It is soon joined by another track from the left. In 250 metres turn left at a way marker and enter a little paddock. Cross to the opposite boundary and turn right to find a narrow way to Playden Church.

To walk from Playden to Rye, go past Playden Church on your right and continue to the main road, A268. There is a bus shelter on the right and a modern care centre opposite. Turn right, walk past the care centre then cross to Leasam Lane opposite.

Avoid a footpath on the right. Go down Leasam Lane behind the care centre and head west. In ¼ mile pass a large mast on your right and you soon come to a junction. Turn left, then in 50 metres left again into open fields. **The Iden Walk joins here.**

To continue the walk to Rye, see below*, page 145.

***The Long Walk** (to include Iden). After crossing the sturdy bridge over the River Rother, look for a footpath opposite, on the other side of Military Road. Climb the cliff here with care.*

This is a steep footpath, neglected at the time of writing.

Emerge with relief to a plateau and follow the path north towards woodland. Turn to look back to the view to Rye. Skirt a limb of Houghton Wood on your left. Cross a small field to enter the wood on the north. There are plank footbridges at either end of the short walk through the wood.

Keep on course northwest across fields. The field boundary is at first on your left, then in 200 metres, cross through the hedge. Now the boundary is on your right. You come to Houghton Lane and turn right.

Opposite 'Old Turk', a nearby cottage on the right, a footpath enables you to continue on your field way. In 350 metres you reach cross paths and turn half right to continue northwest. In another 350 metres you reach houses at Grove Lane in Iden.

Turn left and at cross roads keep straight on, passing the pub on your left. The church is another 150 metres, also on the left.

From Iden Church go to the neighbouring recreation ground and turn sharp left. The children`s play area is on your right. Half turn your back to the play area to search for the unmarked footpath in a gap in the hedge.

The path heads south across fields. In 500 metres you come to a rough track, known as Randolph`s Lane and serving a few houses. Cross this track to the path opposite and open fields ahead.

Continue south to the boundary on the other side of the field where you will find a unique makeshift metal stile. Cross to the sloping field and go down to woodland on the right. Follow the wood on your right and you will find a twin metal stile.

Keep heading south for 450 metres to the A268. Just before you reach this main road, you

pass a small holding and shop on your right. We bought some local strawberries.

At the main road turn left then immediately right onto a bridleway. Ahead you can see a mast on the ridge. After the first field, the bridleway enters an enclosed track on the right and climbs its cheerless way uphill. Some riders have preferred to stay in the field and go parallel to the track.

At the top pass some attractive cottages, once oast houses of Leasam House Farm. The track turns left (follow it to Playden to visit the church). Otherwise cut through the wood on the right to join another track and a footpath opposite.*

Both walks return to Rye.

Hug the hedge on the left and enjoy the view over the River Tillingham and Rye beyond as you walk downhill.

At the bottom, pass a largish house on the left then veer right to the river bank. Walk along beside the river on your right. Enter a tarmac path. Pass allotments and playing fields on the left then a row of houses on the right. Go through an alleyway leading to Ferry Road. *Turn left for the Station then left again.*

Keep straight on towards a windmill. There is another alley past this mill that brings you out near the road bridge over the River Tillingham. Follow A259 back to the car park.

Walk 27: Icklesham to Winchelsea

So much of this walk is through Medieval history and yet it may be just a country stroll to a picturesque hill town. The River Brede is part of that history. See the Introduction under 'Rivers' for more on the River Brede.

Starting Point 1: Icklesham Church off A259 **GR**881164
Starting Point 2: Winchelsea Station (northwest of the town) **GR**899184
Note: Look for the heading: 'Rail travellers join us here', page 149.
The train service has been curtailed. Phone 0845 748 4950 for details.
Map: OS Explorer 125
Distance: 5 ½ Miles **Terrain:** Flat riverside and some hills

The Churches

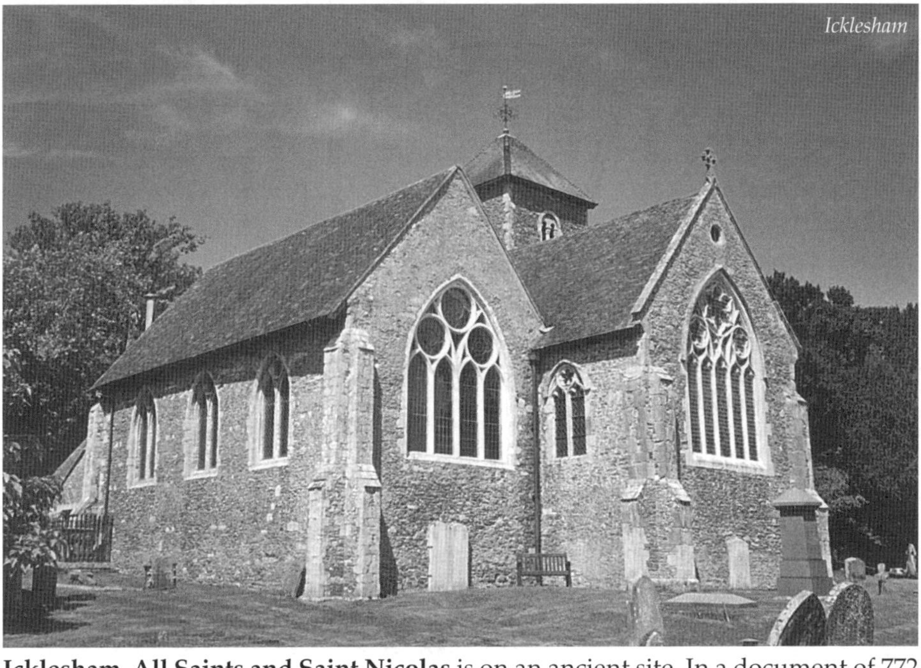

Icklesham, All Saints and Saint Nicolas is on an ancient site. In a document of 772 A.D. King Offa of Mercia gives land in 'Ikelesham' to the See of Selsey. The hill of Iham was part of the parish. (This was before the people of Winchelsea fled to the hill and established the town there). The present large church of Icklesham is basically early Norman. Remnants of stonework of the first church can be seen in the west wall outside the porch. The tower and arcades in the nave are Norman. Each pillar has a different carving at the top. There are small Norman windows in

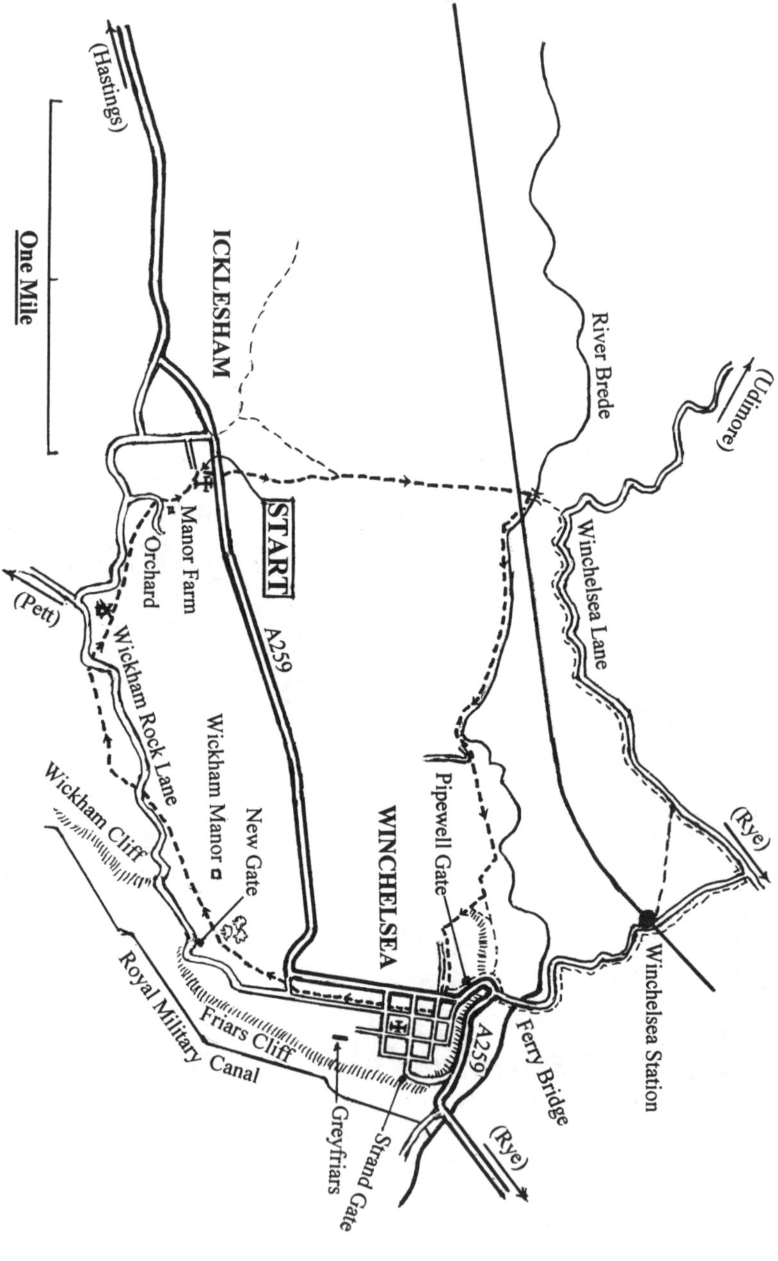
(Hastings)
One Mile
ICKLESHAM
START
Manor Farm
Orchard
(Pett)
Wickham Rock Lane
A259
Wickham Manor
New Gate
Wickham Cliff
Royal Military Canal
Friars Cliff
Greyfriars
Strand Gate
WINCHELSEA
Pipewell Gate
A259
Ferry Bridge
(Rye)
Winchelsea Station
(Rye)
Winchelsea Lane
River Brede
(Udimore)

the south aisle. A single roof covers the nave and both aisles. The north aisle ends in a Norman arch to the tower. There are carved heads in the western corner of the tower. The chancel was extended in 14th century. The chancel arch is Early English. It has carved stone corbels. The chapel of St Nicolas was added at the same time. During the church restoration by Teulon (1848 – 49), a hexagonal porch was added.

Winchelsea, St Thomas of Canterbury is unique. The old town on the sea plain was flooded and the people moved up to this hill of Iham (1288). They built a fortress here and held a port below. King Edward 1 planned the new town on the gridiron system of Aquitaine where he had a domain. On their way to and from France, he and Queen Eleanor inspected the building of this beautiful church. Skilled masons worked in stone from Caen, marble from West Sussex and rubble salvaged from the wrecked church of Old Winchelsea. The plans were ambitious: a huge nave, a grand central tower, transepts and lofty chancel. Repeated French invasions in 14th century wrought havoc on the town and finally the nave and tower were demolished. The harbour silted up in 15th century, Winchelsea lost its trade and the poor people were left to patch up their church. The chancel and chapels remained from the original building and they are magnificent. Here is the best example of Decorated work in Sussex. The choir is separated from the aisles by three high arches with pillars of fluted shafts in alternate Caen stone and Sussex marble. The recesses have fine diaper work. The south aisle contains the canopied tombs of the Alards. Gervase Alard was England`s first admiral around 1300. Stephen Alard was admiral of the Cinque ports in Edward 11`s reign. In the north aisle are three canopied tombs and effigies in Sussex marble. It is believed that three effigies have been rescued from the old church that was flooded. Three windows are breath-taking in their beauty. The stained glass is by Dr Douglas Strachan (1875-1950). His themes are Land, Air and Fire, and lastly Sea. They are inspired and passionate works of art. There is some medieval glass in the chancel north window.

Winchelsea

The Walk

From Icklesham Church walk down to the main road, A259 and cross with care diagonally right. Go through large wrought iron gates and onto the driveway of Old Place. Pass the house on the right and follow the enclosed track on the left. It leads downhill, due north and gets rougher. This elevated track emerges to give a wide view over a flat plain crisscrossed with dykes. Pass above a pond on the right then come down to open ground. You may not realise that a path joins from the left. We have to go straight on, keeping the dyke on our left. Go through a succession of farm gates. An oast house can be seen ahead beyond the railway line and the River Brede.

Cross the railway line using steep stiles. Head towards but not across the footbridge over the river *unless you are a rail traveller with separate instructions at the end of this walk*. If you started from Icklesham, you have to turn right and cut back to the railway. Re-cross here and go down the slope to join the path above the river. Keep the narrow river down on your left and admire the yellow water lilies in summer and a possible sight of swans. In 1 kilometre, after an electricity sub-station, you come to a tempting hard-core track. Avoid this. Your way is on the left along a path parallel to this track. You have to make a bee-line east through overgrown fields until you rejoin the river in 500 metres.

You do not stay with the river but have to veer right over rough ground. Head for the trees on the hill ahead. Here is the old hill of Iham. When you reach the trees turn right and climb on a grassy path through earthworks up to Winchelsea. Pass a beacon, then Mill Farm. Go along Mill Lane to the main road. Pipewell Gate, one of the medieval entrances to the fortified town is down on your left. Cross with care to Mill Road opposite.

Rail travellers join us here. *They have walked up station road and through Pipewell Gate and turned left into Mill Road.*

You are in Winchelsea now. The names of the roads are not marked. If in doubt you may have to ask a townsman. Take the first turning to the right. Pass the museum on your left and cross the road (the shop and tea rooms can be found down this road, High Street). Pass the Inn on your right. St Thomas`s Church is on your left. Keep on course past these impressive remains and keep heading south. The road is called Monks Walk and passes the site of a priory away to the left. *Grey Friars moved to Iham even before the new town came up onto the hill. Their home was destroyed in the Reformation.*

When you reach Wickham Rock Lane leading out of Winchelsea, turn right and find a footpath marked to 'Icklesham, 3 miles' on the left. Turn left here into an open field and veer right. Cross a track to enter another field and veer further right to Town Ditch. *Over on the left is the deserted New Gate, well outside the Winchelsea of today. There were rumours that a traitor let in the French enemy through this gate in 1359.* All is peaceful here now. Turn away from the gate to keep on course, crossing the next field diagonally left.

Pass Wickham Manor on the right and continue through another field. We come to Wickham Rock Lane again and cross diagonally right. Here are more small fields, hedged by trees on the right. There are views to the left over Pett Level to the sea. A National Trust permissive path offers a tempting diversion down to the

sea. Resist This! Keep on course heading west and you meet Wickham Rock Lane yet again. Turn left. Pass a house on the left. Then turn right on a footpath to a nearby windmill on a little hill.

Pass the windmill on your left and enjoy the views from the top of the hill. Rejoin Wickham Rock Lane for the last time. Keep on course along the lane and take the second footpath on the right to enter an apple orchard. Walk between the row of trees facing you. In 40 metres look for an arrow low down at boot level on the left. Turn left here and go through trees to the lane. Turn right here to a neat oast house, now a hotel. Pass this on your right as you head north along this private lane. It becomes a grassy path leading to Icklesham Church.

Rail Travellers *go to the middle section of this walk and follow instructions to the end. Then revert to the start of the walk and go as far as the footbridge over the River Brede. Cross this footbridge. Head for the oast house, then turn right before you reach it. This is Winchelsea Lane. In just over 1 mile, turn right for the station.*

Walk 28: Doleham Station to Westfield and Brede

Most of this walk through fields and woods is gently undulating. Brede is on a fairly steep hill with extensive views over the river. See the Introduction under 'Rivers' for more on the River Brede.

Starting Point 1: Doleham Station **GR**836165
Starting Point 2: Fourteen Acre Lane, a lay-by and 3 gates at a bend in the road at Ashenden **GR**838162
Map: OS explorer 124 **Distance:** 6 Miles **Terrain:** Undulating
Warning: After visiting Brede Church, you have to walk on the pavement for ½ mile then a few yards on the verge beside the A28 to reach the river.

The Churches

St John The Baptist, Westfield is a venerable stone church, a contrast to the nearby suburbia. The lower part of the tower may be Saxon. The Normans made it higher and thick buttresses were added in 13th century. Does this church have the most buttresses in Sussex? The church walls are 12th century with some round windows of the period. The outstanding focus of this church is the Norman chancel arch. It is typically narrow with a round arch. It has shaft columns with decorated capitals. Once there were tiles and a text around the arch. On either side of the chancel arch are Squints, cut 32 inches through the walls to allow worshippers a view of the priest. The chancel itself was lengthened in 13th century. The south door has a pointed arch with a fitting oak door dated 1542. There is another more ornate pointed 14th century doorway in the west wall.

Westfield

St George`s Church, Brede overlooks the wide valley of the River Brede. The river was navigable to Norman vessels in 12th century. In 1017 King Cnut granted land, including Brede, to the Benedictine Abbey of Fécamp in Normandy. Monks came to build the church around 1180. The round pillars and arches of the south aisle are 12th century. The north aisle was added in 13th century. It has octagonal pillars. The chancel arch is 14th century. Otherwise, most of the church is now

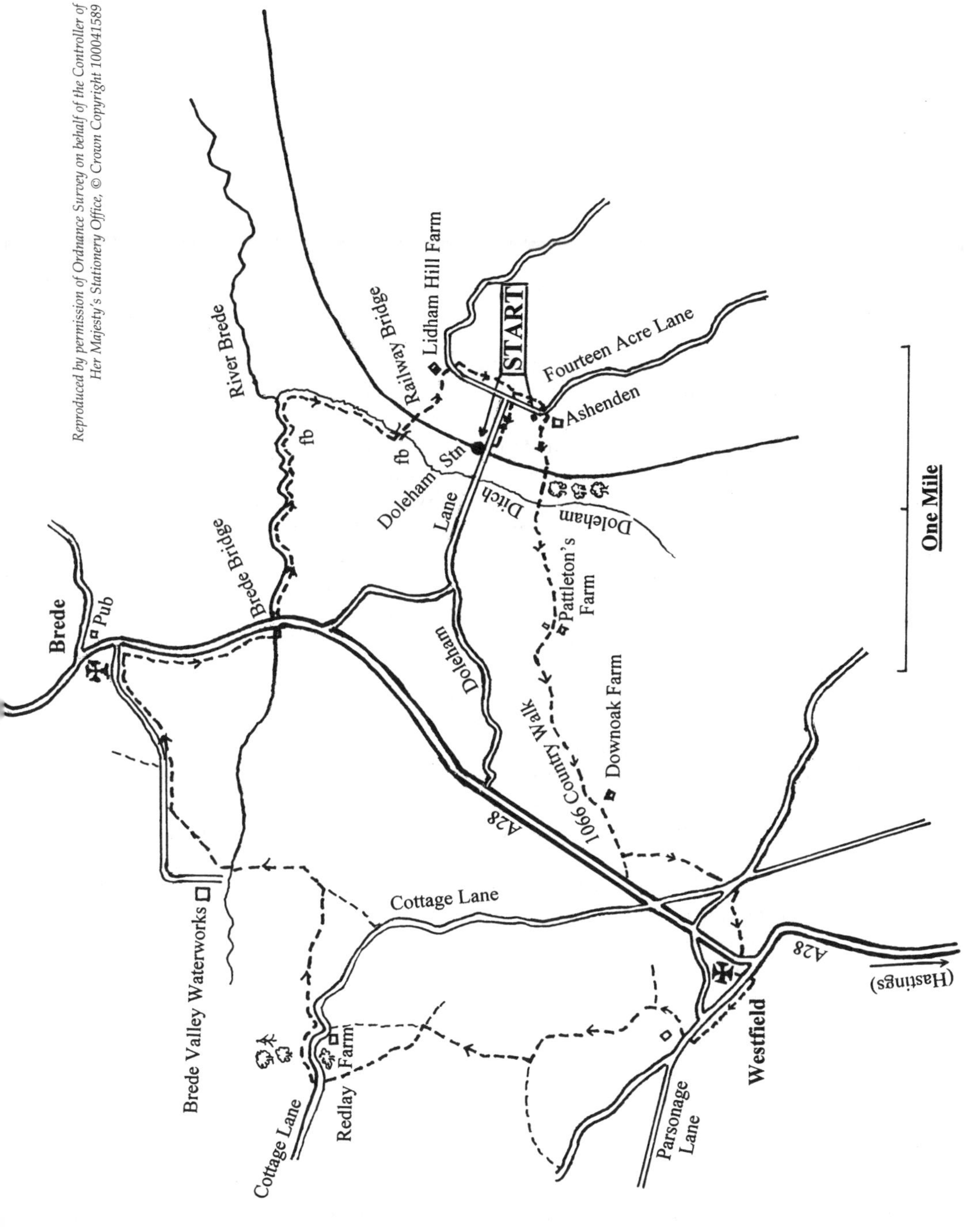
START
Lidham Hill Farm
Railway Bridge
River Brede
Fourteen Acre Lane
Ashenden
fb
fb
Doleham Stn
Lane
Ditch
Doleham
Brede Bridge
Brede
Pub
Doleham
Pattleton's Farm
Downoak Farm
1066 Country Walk
A28
Cottage Lane
Brede Valley Waterworks
Redlay Farm
Cottage Lane
Parsonage Lane
Westfield
A28
(Hastings)
One Mile

Perpendicular, including the fine windows of the south aisle and the tower. The 16th century Oxenbridge Chapel is at the chancel end of the south aisle. The east window of this chapel, built around 1537 has unusual tracery and may be the work in Caen stone of French masons. It has an open arch to the chancel. Sir Goddard Oxenbridge (died 1531) is depicted as a recumbent knight in armour on a tomb. A large man, he was known as the 'Brede Giant'. 20th century additions include a fine statue of Our Lady and Child made by writer and sculptor Clare Sheridan. It stands in this chapel in memory of her son. She herself is now buried in the churchyard. Starting in this chapel on the north side are the 'Stations of the Cross' by Sir Thomas Monnington, former president of the Royal Academy. They were installed in 1960.

The Walk

Starting Point 2: From Doleham Station, head east uphill along Doleham Lane, passing houses on the right. In 250 metres you reach a T-junction with Fourteen Acres Lane and turn right. In another 250 metres at a bend in the lane there is a lay-by with three gates on the right. This is the car park for

Starting Point 1. Look for the '1066 Country Walk' on the right and head west through trees. You come to a small field and cross to woodland hiding the railway line. Cross the line with care and continue westwards. Avoid turning left on the link to Hastings. Instead keep straight on towards Pattleton`s Farm.

Pass the converted oast house and pond on the left. Follow the drive to the right for 75 metres then turn left into a footpath hidden in the hedge. Head southwest across more fields. Pass a cottage on the right, go through a kissing gate at Downoak Farm and keep on course, passing another oast house on the left.

At a cricket pitch, you are on the edge of Westfield. Veer left into woodland. You emerge from the trees to cross paths. You leave the '1066 Country Walk' here. Turn left into a little path heading south through more woodland. Keep on course through a small field and join a rough track, Fishponds Lane. A bungalow of the same name is on your left.

The track brings you to a wide road junction in residential Westfield. Cross with care to the pavement opposite and turn right. Avoid the fork to the right. Pass a side street on the left then turn left into the next road, Heathlands. Go through houses to tennis courts at the end of the road. Take the path around the edge of the tennis courts and cross the main road to the church opposite.

From Westfield Church, leave by the main path through the lych gate into Vicarage Lane. (Not to be confused with Parsonage Lane further west). Turn right to walk downhill. In 400 metres Wheel Lane joins from the right. Cross to Wheel Farm Industrial Estate where notices advertise everything apart from the footpath. Undeterred, turn right at the first building and pass large work sheds on the left. Hug the boundary on the right and take the track leading away from the sheds. In 150 metres you rejoin '1066 Country Walk'. (There are markers on the gate on your right).

Turn left following the trail as it curves by the edge of the field and enters woodland. The trail then heads north at the base of a hill on the left. Next, go through a tree covered track. (Someone has ripped markers off the gates here). At

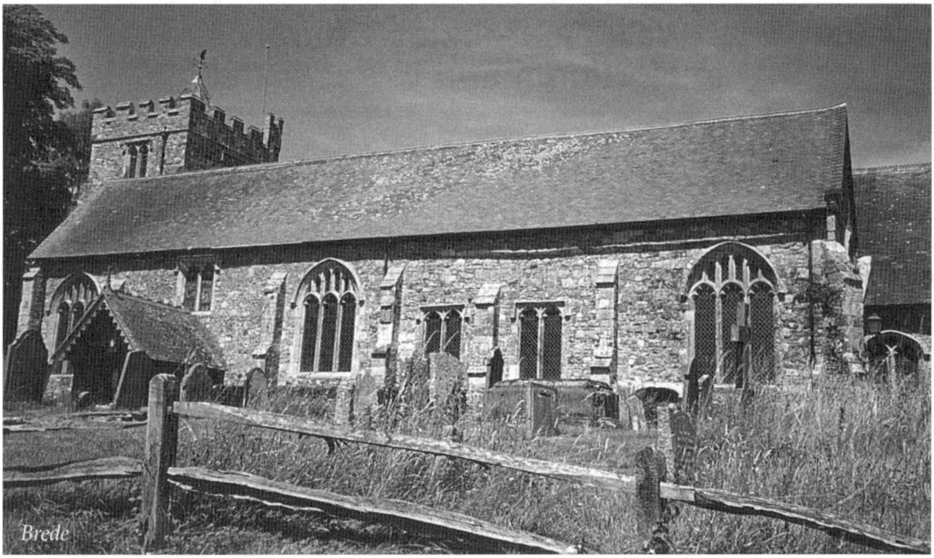

the end of this short track '1066 Country Walk' turns left. You go straight on heading north across a meadow. At cross tracks turn left and climb 400 metres towards power cables. Go under the cables and up to the byroad, Cottage Lane.

Turn right and walk along Cottage Lane. Pass the dairy of Redlay Farm on the right and cottages. As the lane bends to the right, turn left past a house on the left. Then, immediately turn right heading east with rickety stiles to hinder the way. Go under more power cables then cross the field diagonally left to descend to a stream.

Cross the footbridge and turn left, following the dyke on the left. 'Pond Bay' is to the left and Crowham Marsh is on your right. Keep heading north to cross the tiny River Brede. Pass the impressive buildings of Brede Valley Waterworks on the left and climb the sloping field towards woodland. Turn right on the waterwork`s own road. It follows the edge of the wood on the left. In 450 metres pass a path on the left. Continue on the road as it climbs a steep slope up to Brede Church. Go behind the church for the pub opposite.

From Brede Church go to the nearby A28 and turn right. Follow the pavement on the right down Brede Hill. When the pavement runs out, cross with care to the grass verge opposite and continue down to the river.

Cross Brede Bridge and turn left to walk along the river bank for nearly 1 mile. The river departs to the left and you turn right, still on a bank beside a dyke, Doleham Ditch. When you come to a footbridge, turn left and climb up towards trees. Go under the railway bridge and cross the field diagonally left towards Lidham Hill Farm. Pass this on the left and you reach a lane. Turn right. In 250 metres you come to Doleham Lane on the right.

Rail travellers turn right here for the station.

Road users keep straight on for another 250 metres to reach the lay-by on Fourteen Acres Lane.

Walk 29: Beckley Church to Northiam and Great Dixter

Follow the Sussex Border Path to ancient villages and a famous garden. After a tour of Northiam, retrace your steps to Beckley.

Starting Point: lay-by, just north of the church off B2088, Church Lane **GR**843237 **Map:** OS Explorer 125 **Terrain:** Mainly flat, two gentle uphill slopes on the outward walk **Distance:** 5 ½ Miles

The Churches

Beckley, All Saints is an ancient church, mentioned by King Alfred (845 –900). The brother of William the Conqueror, Robert of Eu gave this church, together with Northiam and Peasmarsh to the priests of St Mary-in-the–Castle, Hastings. Some of the original fabric has survived in Beckley. The tower is Saxon with some Norman windows. It has a broached spire. The chancel and north chapel are Decorated. The east window has the typical ornate tracery of that period. The glass by George Ostreham is dedicated to All Saints. There are three medieval carvings of the Green Man, a pagan symbol of fertility in the north and south aisles. One is known locally as 'Jack in the Green'. Dormer windows were installed in the nave 1773 - 1806. Galleries were added at the same time and removed during the 1885 Victorian restoration. Note the magnificent roof timbers in this church.

The Parish Church of St Mary Northiam has a tall tower; the lower part is Norman. A rare octagonal stone spire dates from 1500. An early history describes the nave as 'gloomy' and 'empty with open timbered roof thatched with reeds, the floor of earth covered with rushes'. Today by contrast the nave is Early English with north and south aisles added in the early 14th century making this quite a grand church. The windows are Decorated apart from a small lancet in the south aisle. Most of the glass is Victorian and allows in plenty of light. The chancel was rebuilt in 1835 – 8. The unusually large Frewen Mausoleum was added in 1846 and contains monuments and heraldic memorials.

The Walk

Head north along Church Lane. In ¼ mile just before a large house, turn left into a field. The garden of the house is on your right. You are on the Sussex Border Path going west. At first walk under a low canopy of trees on the edge of the field. Then turn right into a small muddy field. Go down to the left corner and cross to a third field.

Here you keep on course, cutting across the right hand corner of the field and entering Gilly Wood at a gap. Go down into the dark wood, cross a footbridge and veer to the left. When you leave the wood, continue on the path to the field boundary. *At the time of writing, preparations for a footbridge are under way, a bit to the right of the present crossing.* Meanwhile, markers on the telegraph posts point the way up to Hilly Wood.

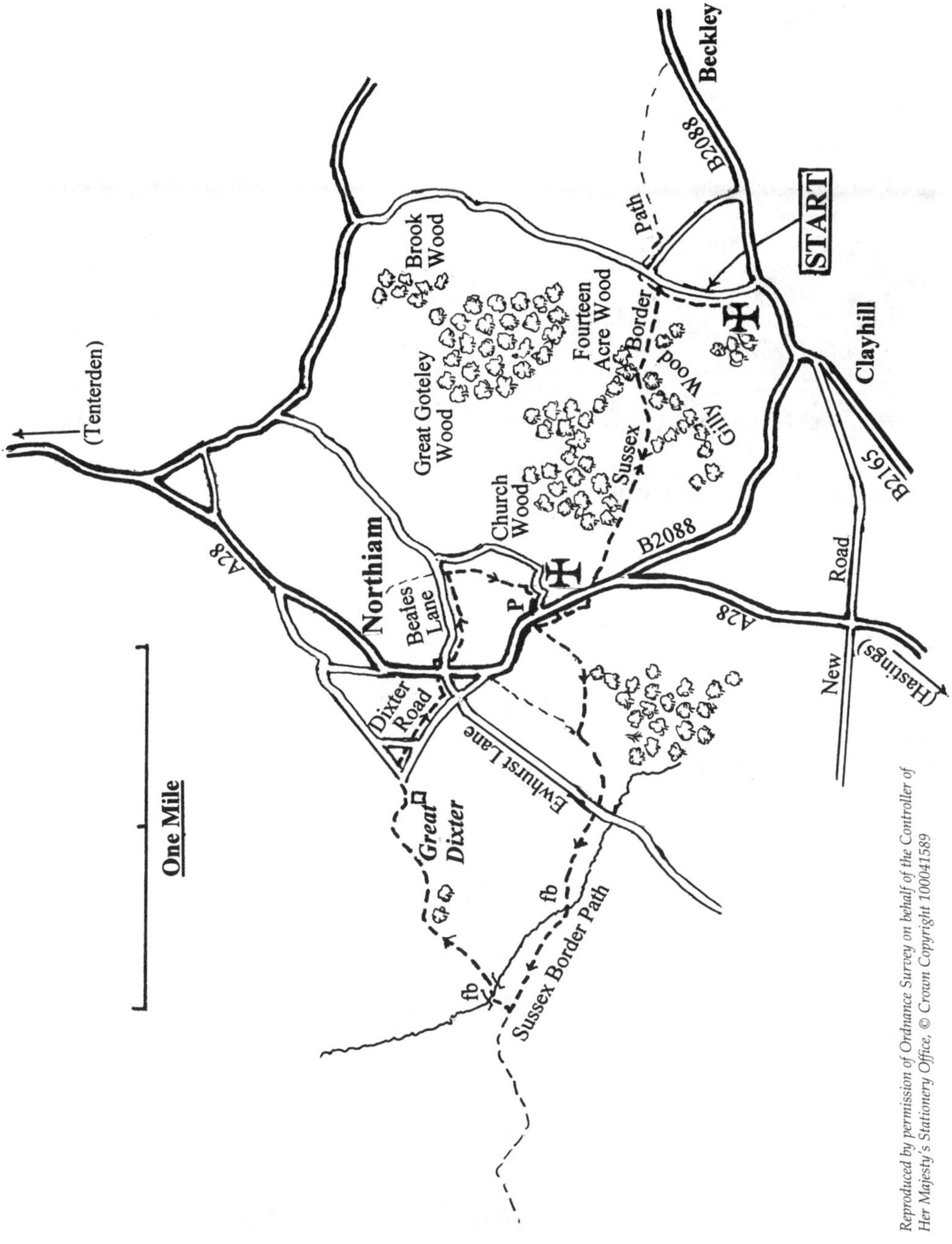
Beckley
B2088
START
Clayhill
B2165
New Road
A28
(Hastings)
B2088
Path
Sussex Border
Fourteen Acre Wood
Gilly Wood
Brook Wood
Great Goteley Wood
Church Wood
Northiam
Beales Lane
P
A28
(Tenterden)
Dixter Road
Ewhurst Lane
Great Dixter
fb
fb
Sussex Border Path
One Mile

Beckley

The path goes through a corner of the wood and turns right. Follow the boundary on your right and climb up to the first houses of Northiam at the top of the slope, on the left.

Join the road on the edge of Northiam and you come to the village green. Walk along the right hand edge of the green with the main road, A28 on the left. At the tarmac lane turn right to the nearby church.

From Northiam Church go back down the lane and continue to the A28 where there are some shops. Cross the main road with care and turn right. In about 50 metres, opposite a car park on the right turn left into a shingle driveway. This is still the Sussex Border Path and emerges to open fields.

Keep straight on heading west for ¼ mile to a T-junction of paths. Turn left and avoid a path off to the left. You follow the Sussex Border Path down to a nearby stile. In the next

Northiam

Northiam

field hug woodland on the right and you come to Strawberry Hole Cottage on the Ewhurst Lane.

Cross the lane to the footpath opposite. Here the Sussex Border Path follows the valley of a little stream on the left. You have a good vista along the valley and up the open slopes on the right. Keep to the field boundary on the left for 450 metres then cross to the other side of the hedge. Turn sharp right so that the hedge is now on your right. In 400 metres a footbridge on your right takes you away from the Sussex Border Path.

After crossing this bridge, go uphill and northeast towards a small wood. Skirt this on your right. The path curves left and right up to Dixter. First you pass the car park for visitors to Great Dixter House and gardens then the entrance booth. Keep straight on along the lane for the return walk.

From Great Dixter House, head southeast along Dixter Road, avoiding all turnings to the left until you come down nearly to the main road, A28. Turn left just before this road and cross with care to Beales Lane opposite.

You are now heading east along this quiet lane. In 500 metres a footpath crosses the lane. Turn right into the enclosed path past private gardens. You come out to a field with a delightful view of half-timber houses and an oast house down on the left.

Keep on course to Church Lane. Pass Northiam Church again and continue to the village green. Retrace your step along the edge of the green to rejoin the Sussex Border Path and return to Beckley along the same route as before except that now you are heading east, mainly downhill with wider views. In fact the church spire beckons you.

Walk 30: Ewhurst Green to Bodiam

This walk starts on a ridge above the valley of the River Rother, goes down into the valley and up to the ridge on the other side. The two churches stand on either ridge. We visit Bodiam Castle and National Trust tea rooms.

Starting Point: Verge next to the pub car park, Ewhurst Green
GR796246 **Map:** OS Explorer 136
Terrain: Quite Hilly **Distance:** 5 Miles
Local Information:
1. Bodiam Castle (1385), in the care of the National Trust is open at 10.30 all year. It is a square castle with round turrets and moat, all in excellent condition thanks to Lord Curzon who bought it in 1917.
2. The River Rother was navigable as far as Bodiam Bridge in Middle Ages. See the Introduction under 'Rivers' for more on the Rother.

Note: At the time of writing, some paths, even the Sussex Border Path lack signposts in places. A compass might be useful.

The Churches

St James the Great, Ewhurst is built of fine sandstone. It is on a sandstone ridge. A minster church may have been here before the Norman Conquest. Then St Mary in Castro, Hastings was responsible for Bodiam and Ewhurst. In the 12th century a stone church was built here. The lower part of the tower and the handsome west doorway are part of this building. The west door has a semi-circular inner arch and a more pointed outer arch. The upper part of the tower is 14th century with windows inserted later. In 18th century the spire was struck by lightning and its unusual shape seems to be the result of its repair. The nave is 14th century and the north arcade has the pointed arches of that period. A plump face has been carved at the west end of the north aisle. The south aisle is late 12th century with round headed arches.

Ewhurst Green

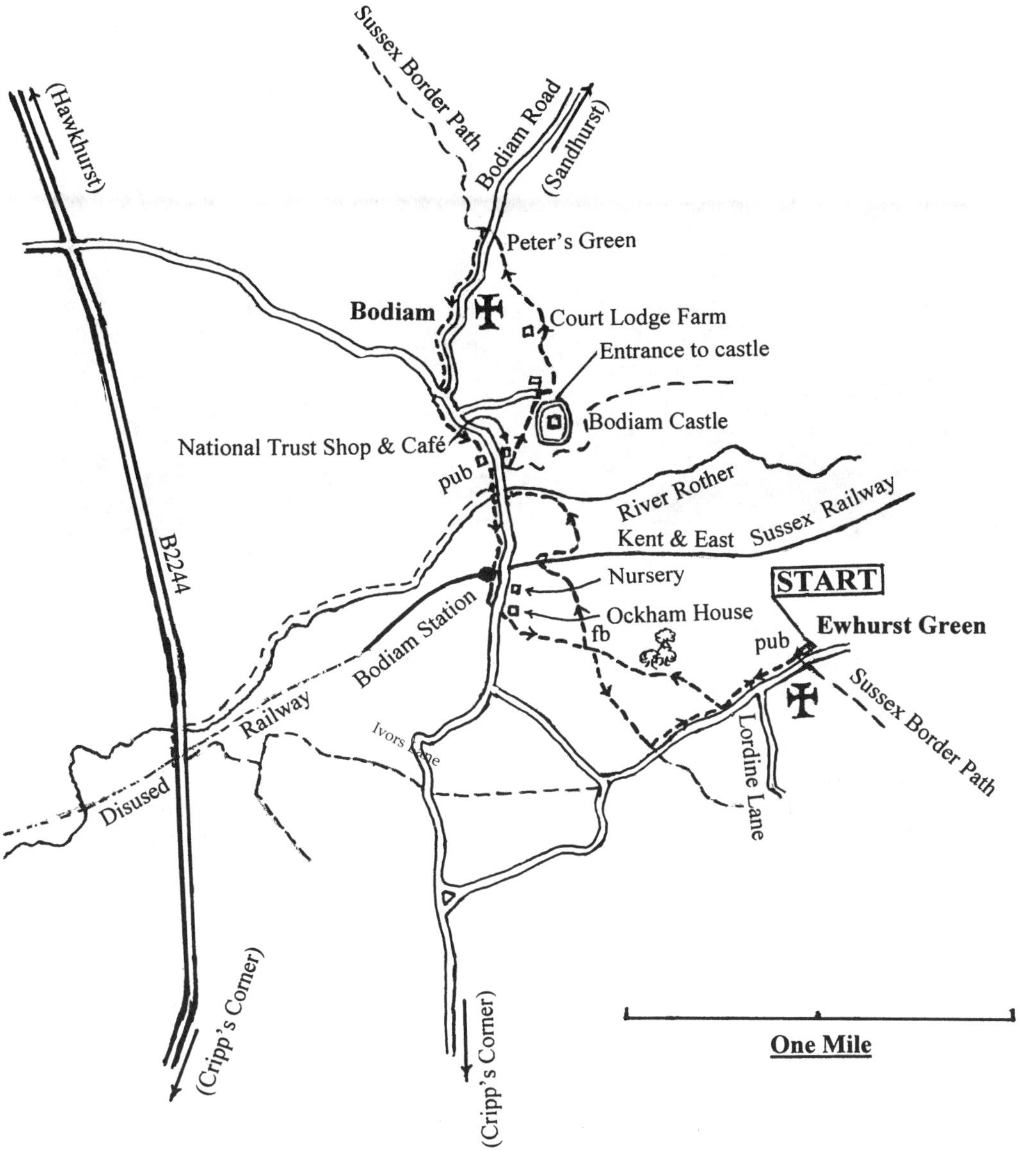
Sussex Border Path
(Hawkhurst)
Bodiam Road
(Sandhurst)
Peter's Green
Bodiam
Court Lodge Farm
Entrance to castle
Bodiam Castle
National Trust Shop & Café
pub
River Rother
Kent & East Sussex Railway
START
Nursery
Ockham House
fb
Ewhurst Green
pub
Sussex Border Path
Bodiam Station
B2244
Railway
Disused
Ivors Lane
Lordine Lane
(Cripp's Corner)
(Cripp's Corner)
One Mile

Above, the sparkling glass in the clerestory windows is by Margery May (1971). The frame of the east window is a good example of early Perpendicular. The glass of 1860 is from the O`Connor studio. The chancel arch is 14th century. The font of Petworth marble is 12th or 13th century.

St Giles Church, Bodiam stands among trees outside the village. Osbert de Bodeham was thane here in 1086 according to Domesday. In 1250 de Wardeux held the manor. It then passed through marriage to Sir Edward Dalyngrigge who built Bodiam Castle in 1385. The fabric of the church is 14th century. Large blocks of sandstone, similar to masonry in Bodiam Castle are in the chancel. The chancel arch and windows in the south wall of the chancel are Early English. The oblong tower is Perpendicular. The church was much restored by R.C. Carpenter in 1845 – 1856.

The Walk

Step across the road from the pub to the church in Ewhurst Green. Continue southwest through the village, passing Lordine Lane on the left and a magnificent cluster of oast houses on the right. You are in fact on the Sussex Border Path. In another 100 metres you come to a farm gate and a kissing gate on the right. There is a view across the wide valley to Bodiam Castle. Turn right here. You are still on the Sussex Border Path even though the signpost is overgrown and hidden.

Follow the field hedge on the left and head northwest down towards a small wood. Veer left and pass the southern tip of the wood to enter the next field. Follow the boundary on the right and come down to a finger post at a T-junction of paths. Turn right to a little footbridge at the bottom of the slope.

Cross the footbridge and avoid the path to the left. Keep heading north to the

Bodiam

Bodiam

railway line, Kent and East Sussex Railway. Here there is a stile on the left. Once across, turn sharp right. Follow the railway line on your right as far as the field boundary. Turn left and head north again to the raised banks of the River Rother. Turn left and walk beside the river to the nearby Bodiam Bridge. Just before the bridge you have to veer left to reach the road.

Turn right at the road and head north to cross over Bodiam Bridge. Pause to view the wide flat valley of the River Rother. You soon enter the lower edge of Bodiam. There is a pub on the left. On the right you pass the National Trust Car Park then the shop and tearooms.

Take the gravel path on the north side of the National Trust complex. It heads northeast uphill and curves to the left, passing close to Bodiam Castle on the right. You soon find you can see the entrance to the castle, a bridge across the moat to the gatehouse down on the right. This is not our route.

Head for the long low building up on the left. This is the ticket and information centre catering for disabled visitors and others. Pass this on your left and in 75 metres look for the Sussex Border Path hidden in the hedge on the northern boundary of the castle grounds.

Follow the Sussex Border Path uphill and northwest. Vines growing here take advantage of the sunny slope. The enclosed path leads past horse paddocks and up to Court Lodge Farm on the left. You have a tantalizing glimpse of Bodiam Church beyond the farm but the way is private. You have to stick with the Sussex Border Path still.

Cross the farm drive and go down a little sloping field to the corner among trees. You have to go round the edge of more paddocks before escaping to a wide field on the right with a view north towards Sandhurst.

Cross the field diagonally left and you come down to Bodiam Road at Peter`s Green. Here you leave the Sussex Border Path as it departs across the road. You stay on this side of the road and turn left. Fortunately there is a path on the slope above the road. It leads up to St Giles Church, Bodiam.

From Bodiam Church go through the lychgate to the top of the road and turn left. On the right you pass first the entrance to a housing estate, next the village school and then the old building of the former school. You come down to a forked road junction. Cross with care and continue downhill.

Bodiam Castle

There is an elevated enclosed path on the right leading down behind the village houses. Go down the steep slope to emerge at the familiar pub near Bodiam Bridge. The National Trust tearoom is opposite.

Cross the river and continue south on the road to Bodiam Station. After the level crossing you pass a plant nursery on the left. You also continue up past Ockham House on the left. (Ignore the Ordnance Survey Map here). The path is on the south side of Ockham House. There is a concrete footpath sign on the ground just past the house.

Turn left here into a track. Then take the footpath on the right into a small elevated field. Cross the left corner of the field and avoid turning right on a track. Follow the grassy way ahead southeast. It passes the back garden of Ockham House on the left then keeps on course down to a field entrance.

Go through and turn right to cross the footbridge of the outward walk. Veer left to the familiar finger post. Instead of taking the path straight ahead that brought you here, turn right. Follow the field boundary on the left uphill all the way to Ewhurst Green Road at the top. Turn left for the church and pub.

Long Distance Paths or Ways encountered on these walks:

South Downs Way 100 Miles, Eastbourne to Winchester, east – west over downland. Possibly the oldest way in our book, it was the high route of ancient nomads above swamps and thick forests (Walks 2, 3, 5 and 6).

Sussex Border Path 150 Miles, keeps close to the county boundary. It extends from Emsworth in West Sussex to Rye in East Sussex. In places it shares the route with other ways (Walks 14, 16, 26, 29 and 30).

Sussex Ouse Valley Way 42 Miles, a young route from Lower Beeding through Lewes to Seaford. For more information on the River Ouse, see the Introduction under 'Rivers' (Walks 1, 13).

High Weald and Landscape Trail 89 Miles, takes a picturesque route from Horsham Station through East Sussex with a little diversion into Kent before arriving in Rye (Walks 14 and 20).

1066 Country Walk 31 Miles This walk through history follow the route of William the conqueror from Pevensey to Battle then continues to Rye. There are two extra links. They are Battle to Bexhill 6 miles and Doleham to Hastings 7 ½ miles. (Walks 9, 21, 25 and 28).

The Wealdway 80 Miles from Gravesend to Beachy Head, north – south. It crosses the Weald including Ashdown Forest and heads southeast over the Downs past Jevington and Eastbourne (Walks 6, 7, 8, 11, 12 and 14).

Vanguard Way is a sister route to the Wealdway heading north – south. It crosses the Wealdway in Ashdown Forest. The two ways nearly meet again at Arlington Reservoir. Vanguard Way sets off from Croydon, taking Londoners to the countryside through Surrey, the Weald, the Downs, along the Cuckmere then on more downland to Seaford. (Walks 1, 4, 5 and 7).

Bibliography

The Buildings of England – Sussex – By Ian Nairn and Nikolaus Pevsner (1996)
Penguin Books

Notes on Sussex Churches (1920) By Frederick Harrison
Cambridges, Hove

Sussex By Esther Meynell (1950) *The County Books Series, Robert Hale Bedford Square, London W.C. 1*

Sussex By John Godfrey (1990) *Penguin Books*

Limen – A Biography of the East Sussex Rother By Tony Cardwell
The Wealden Advertiser Ltd, Cowden Close, Horns Road, Hawkhurst, Kent, TN18 4QT

The Sussex Ouse Valley Way By Terry Owen and Peter Anderson
Per-Ambulations, Larkshill, Cranston Road, East Grinstead, West Sussex, RH19 3HL

Sussex River, Journeys along the Banks of the River Ouse
By Edna and Mac McCarthy

The Cuckmere, Another River
By Edna and Mac McCarthy

The Cuckmere, A Sussex River By Ann Botha
SB Publications, 19, Grove Road, Seaford, East Sussex, BN25 1TP

Portrait of the River Medway By Roger Pear
Robert Hale, London